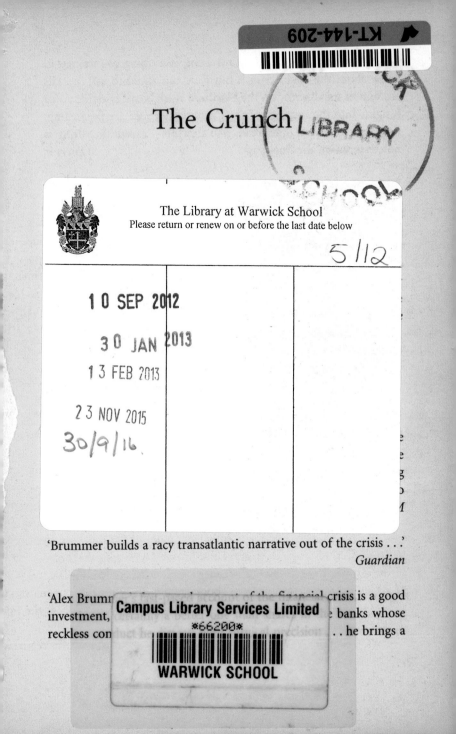

The Crunch

'Brummer builds a racy transatlantic narrative out of the crisis . . .'
Guardian

'Alex Brumm... ... ...st of the financial crisis is a good
investment, ... e banks whose
reckless con... ... .. he brings a

journalist's relish to his task of revealing everything you wanted to know about the credit crunch but were too afraid to ask . . . His account of the disarray on the Northern Rock board is vivid . . . his insights into the routines of the City's master race are fascinating. Brummer's account often reads like a thriller – except that order is not restored on the final page.'   *Observer*

'This is the roller-coster version of events – and a surprisingly entertaining book about an otherwise dreary subject . . . timely and interesting . . .'   *New Statesman*

'. . . a handy first draft of history.'   *Bloomberg*

ALEX BRUMMER

The Crunch

How Greed and Incompetence
Sparked the Credit Crisis

BUSINESS
BOOKS

Published by Random House Business Books 2009

8 10 9

First published in Great Britain in 2008 as *The Crunch: The Scandal
of Northern Rock and the Escalating Credit Crisis* by
Random House Business Books

This updated edition first published in 2009 by Random House Business Books
Random House, 20 Vauxhall Bridge Road,
London SW1V 2SA

www.rbooks.co.uk

Addresses for companies within The Random House Group Limited can be found at:
www.randomhouse.co.uk/offices.htm

The Random House Group Limited Reg. No. 954009

A CIP catalogue record for this book is available from the British Library

ISBN 9781847940094

The Random House Group Limited supports The Forest Stewardship
Council (FSC), the leading international forest certification organisation. All our
titles that are printed on Greenpeace approved FSC certified paper carry the FSC logo.
Our paper procurement policy can be found at www.rbooks.co.uk/environment

Typeset by Palimpsest Book Production Limited,
Grangemouth, Stirlingshire

Printed in the UK by CPI Bookmarque, Croydon, CR0 4TD

Contents

To our grandson Rafi Rosenfield,
who has brought us so much joy

Preface

In the autumn of 2002 my editor at the *Daily Mail* Paul Dacre suggested I spend some time in Washington. Since I had formerly been a Washington Bureau Chief for the *Guardian* he wanted me to use my experience and contacts to comment on the build up of President George W. Bush's war against terror and the increasing likelihood that the United States and Britain would go to war with Iraq. The visit provided me with an opportunity to meet with my old Washington acquaintances and friends dating from my period in the United States from 1979 to 1989, embracing the last days of Jimmy Carter, and the arrival on the scene of Ronald Reagan and George Bush Snr.

I was quickly back on the very active Washington dinner party circuit. One evening I found myself at the table of an old acquaintance the British economist Charles Taylor and his American wife Mary Ellen, a former banker and now an American financial regulator. The company at the table was made up almost exclusively of senior Senate and Congressional aides and bank regulators. The assembled group had two issues on their minds. The first was the shortcomings in the behaviour of Citigroup, America's largest international financial group. Amid a series of scandals its chairman Sandy Weill had been summoned to appear before the Senate Banking Committee. The feebleness of Citi's internal controls would become evident in the credit crunch post-9 August 2007.

The second topic under discussion was the poor health of America's mortgage intermediaries Fannie Mae and Freddie Mac.

Mary Ellen subsequently sent me an unpublished report on the causes of their difficulties. During the low interest rate, fast growth years which followed the terror attacks of 9/11 these mortgage lenders, intended to help lower-income Americans seeking home ownership, had embarked on an unprecedented expansion.

They were able to fund their lending to less well off borrowers across America through a process known as 'securitisation'. The mortgage loans that they made were packaged up, sliced and diced and sold off to enthusiastic investors in the money markets. Investors believed these loans to be absolutely safe as the lenders Fannie Mae and Freddie Mac had the notional backing of the federal government in Washington. The regulators present were concerned that the lenders had embarked on a business they didn't really understand and that was not fully supported by their capital. Worse, should Fannie Mae and Freddie Mac become over-extended in their securitisation activities, the liability would fall back on the American taxpayer.

Until that evening in October 2002 I had only been vaguely aware of securitisation and its potential dangers. I was struck about how little anyone knew about the process, its implications and who would pick up the tab if the market went badly wrong. Then my mind tracked back to Britain and time I had spent in the past with the mortgage lender Northern Rock.

I vaguely remembered the enthusiasm of its chief executive Adam Applegarth for securitisation, but I had never heard him or for that matter anyone else speak of the risk. But if these American bank regulators and monitors were so concerned about the dangers of this marketplace, maybe we in Britain should be, too. A few days later I wrote my first column for the City pages of the *Mail* on the risks of securitisation and in passing made reference to Northern Rock. There would be several more references in the coming months and years, some of which would draw protests from Newcastle, the home of the Rock. Yet little did I know that the collapse and exposure of the securitisation market would provoke the worst financial crisis since the Great Depression – not my view but that of the International Monetary Fund in Washington.

When the credit crunch hit in August 2007 it came as a terrible shock to many people in the financial world, who had only lived through the good times. For me the events had a familiar ring. The warnings I had heard about securitisation were still fresh in my mind.

Banking crises have been part of my life since I was a young reporter. In 1973–4, my first years as a City reporter on the *Guardian*, I was involved in uncovering the misdeeds of a bank, London & County Securities, which eventually collapsed. It was the first of 25 or so secondary banks to run into trouble. The crisis was considered serious enough for then governor of the Bank of England, Sir Gordon Richardson, to launch a £1.5 billion 'lifeboat' to shore up the whole financial system. At one point in the crisis the stability of one of the nation's largest banks, National Westminster – since 2000 part of the Royal Bank of Scotland – came into question. The parallels were very vivid in my mind and helped to shape my reporting of the unfolding events of the credit crunch, including the run on Northern Rock.

When I suggested a book on the credit crunch to Jonathan Pegg of Curtis Brown, who had been working with me on book projects over several years, he was immediately enthused by the idea and very encouraging. He identified Nigel Wilcockson at Random House as a possible publisher and Nigel quickly embraced the idea. He has been a terrific editor, providing invaluable guidance and insight throughout the process of producing a book against a tight schedule and an ever changing landscape.

As a City Editor on a daily newspaper, writing and commenting on events almost every day, I could never have completed this project without considerable help from others. Huge thanks must go to former *Guardian* journalist Norman Hayden, the main collaborator on the book, who worked tirelessly on identifying case studies and on the shape of the manuscript. Norman, a friend from university days, who had many moons earlier worked on *The Journal*

(Newcastle) was able to bring his local knowledge to bear and has been there to advise and counsel throughout the project.

I have also received considerable help from my colleagues in the *Daily Mail* City Office – most notably, my deputy Lucy Farndon, an excellent journalist whose day-to-day reporting of Northern Rock and the broadening crisis in UK banking always kept me fully informed and alert to new developments. She also patiently stood in for me when I was away on writing days. Credit must also go to my personal assistant Edwina O'Reilly who juggled my diary and made many of the appointments with sources. Thanks must also go to Editor Paul Dacre of the *Mail* and Features Editor Leaf Kalfayan who have given me the freedom to write about events as they took place right across the paper and not just on the City pages.

As a working journalist, covering events as they have unfolded, I have enjoyed excellent direct access to the main players who shaped events during the credit crunch. These have included bankers, their advisers and politicians as well as policymakers at the Treasury, the Bank of England and the Financial Services Authority. All have been enormously helpful to me in my shaping of a complex narrative. I have also drawn heavily on my colleagues in financial journalism from across the media. Among the most useful sources have been the BBC website, the BBC *Money Programme*, the *Wall Street Journal*, the *Financial Times*, the *Economist*, *Moneyweek*, the *Spectator* and Bloomberg.

All of these sources helped to inform me of events and fill in the blanks in the story of the credit crunch. Obviously, though, I take full responsibility for any errors that may have crept into the manuscript.

Finally, I would like to thank my family, especially my wife, Tricia, who has been fantastically supportive throughout this process, despite the disruption to our social lives. Without her tolerance and the keen interest of the rest of the family including my sons Justin and Gabriel, my daughter Jessica and son-in-law Dan, this book would never have happened.

We Want Our Money

When Northern Rock's savers panicked

The alarm clock thudded into life in Graham Hallworth's home in Macclesfield, Cheshire. It was 6 a.m. on Friday, 14 September 2007. He had a busy day ahead and decided to make an early start before his wife and children were up and about. Graham had things to do, and top of his list was paying his builders, so he needed to switch money from his Northern Rock internet deposit account into his current account. He had carried out similar transactions many times before, but this would prove to be no ordinary transaction on what was to be a far from ordinary day for him and thousands like him.

As he switched on his computer and logged on, the website froze. After it failed several times more, Graham decided to leave it for a while. It was only when the morning newspaper arrived that he realised what was wrong. 'Having been out to dinner the night before, I hadn't seen the TV reports about Northern Rock's financial problems,' Graham explained. 'When I saw the press headlines, I put two and two together and realised that this could be connected with the internet problem. I made a concerted effort to get on to the website and transfer the money. I tried for an hour or so without success.'

With significant sums in the individual accounts that he and his wife had, Graham became alarmed. Fearing that their money was in jeopardy, he quickly woke his wife and gave her the bad news. 'We've got major problems,' he told her. 'We need to get to Stockport as soon as we can.' They immediately drove the 10 miles to their nearest branch. When he arrived in the high street, the queues told him all he needed to know. Branch staff tried to reassure him, but Graham insisted on withdrawing all but £1 from both accounts, and later that day an electronic transfer allowed him to breathe a sigh of relief.

'What really angered me,' he said, 'was the credibility gap between what the bank was saying and the reality of the situation. They claimed their assets were intact. But if you don't have the money to trade because funds have dried up, then technically you are bankrupt. And if I can't access my money online when I want to, then, as far as I'm concerned, the bank isn't trading.'

The scenes at Stockport were being reproduced along high streets the length and breadth of the country that Friday morning, as anxious savers reacted to media reports of Northern Rock's problems by trying to rescue their money. They thought they might lose their savings, and they wanted to get their hands on their money fast. In one day alone an estimated £1 billion was withdrawn. Faced with such panic outside its branches, Northern Rock called for calm. However, calmness was in short supply among the company's bosses that Friday evening as they despatched a team to two of its major centres in Dublin and Guernsey, where they were paid triple time over the weekend to stuff envelopes with cheques to cope with the torrent of irate customers who wanted to withdraw their money. All this had failed to stem the tide on the Friday, and, as word spread, the queues were even longer on the Saturday morning. Just as they had done the day before, branch staff literally shovelled money out to queuing savers. 'It achieved nothing,' said a company insider. 'It didn't stop the rot. It actually made things worse.'

Meanwhile, in Kew, west London, 66-year-old Pam Hilleard was beginning to realise that she was having yet another bad experience in what had already been a dreadful year. Her husband had died after a long illness, and although she had the support of her daughters, Charmaine and Sharon, she was still grieving and was also left with the responsibility of sorting out the estate and managing the family's business affairs. She was certainly comfortably off – particularly after selling a farmhouse in Bedfordshire for over three-quarters of a million pounds. With a lot of paperwork still to deal with she decided, for convenience, to put the proceeds of the sale into a short-notice account with Northern Rock. 'I saw no reason not to,' Pam explained. 'I had placed deposits with them before. In fact, I had a soft spot for them – believing them to be solid and dependable.'

But something was different this time. Soon after she deposited the £780,000 in a revolving 30-day account during the balmy days of last July, she suddenly felt a nagging feeling that things were not quite right with the former building society. A voracious reader of the financial pages of the national newspapers, she had spotted a profits warning from the bank, but felt there was more to it than just a temporary blip. So, seeking reassurance, she went to her nearest branch in Kingston, Surrey, to voice her concerns. An assistant manager tried to calm her fears. 'Look,' he insisted. 'If there was anything wrong, we would know about it. After all, we've got careers and mortgages resting on it. If you're that concerned, take your money out.'

The reassurance seemed plausible, but Pam's discomfort would not go away. It was only because she didn't want to lose £2,000 of interest that she kept her money where it was – with withdrawal day set for Monday, 17 September. Looking forward to this, she then sat down four days before the due date to watch the BBC ten o'clock news – only to discover what the whole nation was finding out about the plight of Northern Rock. What she heard was shocking: Northern Rock was in danger of running out of ready cash and had been granted an emergency lender of last resort loan from the Bank of England. Since her husband's death she had become an increasingly experienced saver and investor, and she didn't panic then or the following morning when the newspapers were full of it. If the assets are sound as was reported, she reasoned, my money must be safe.

By the Saturday, however, calm had been replaced by a sick feeling as she read about the £2 billion run on the bank. 'I couldn't eat or sleep. I was feeling desperate about the money. I thought, "What if they don't open?" Although I was beginning to panic like the other savers, I just had this feeling that I didn't want to be the last person on a sinking ship. So, I determined to grab a lifeline and go to the bank.'

After spending all Sunday fretting, Pam couldn't get to her local branch in Kingston, Surrey, soon enough on the Monday morning. She left home in the dark at 5 a.m. and, as she didn't drive, caught a bus for the 30-minute journey to the town, only to find 20 people already in the queue in front of her. Faced with queues, such as the one in Kingston, re-forming at dawn, Northern Rock's chief executive had ordered branches to open an hour earlier and issued an apology. 'I feel very sorry for our customers having to wait,' insisted Adam Applegarth. 'I'm grateful to the staff who have kept the branches open until 10 o'clock at night to ensure everybody in the queue gets served.'

In the queue in Kingston Pam Hilleard was determined to get her money out. 'This was my security and that of my daughters – my family's security was about to be blown away,' she said. Four hours later she was given her cheque for the full amount, but her faith in the banking system had been destroyed. 'We're not a "banana republic," for goodness sake,' she said. 'How can you trust the system? Adam Applegarth was playing Russian roulette with my money. If it can happen to a bank like Northern Rock, it can happen to any of them.'

Hilleard had been caught in the first fully fledged run on a British bank for a long time. In fact, it had been over 100 years since the last full-scale crisis. Back in the late 19th century there had been a spate of runs involving dodgy bankers and highly questionable investments, the three most spectacular being Overend, Gurney & Co. in 1866, City of Glasgow in 1878 and Baring Brothers in 1890. Overend was not a retail bank, like Northern Rock, but a London wholesale discount house that borrowed from other banks and placed its money into riskier, longer term investments such as shipping lines and railways. It eventually collapsed with the loss of £11 million (around £900 million in today's prices). Its directors later stood trial at the Old Bailey charged with fraud arising from a false prospectus to investors. The Victorian economist and writer Walter Bagehot famously observed that the bank made losses 'in a manner so reckless and foolish, that one would think that a child who had lent money in the City of London would have lent it better'.

Twelve years later the City of Glasgow, another very reputable bank that had 133 branches and that issued its own banknotes, also got involved in funding risky ventures, and although it had assets of £7 million, it developed £12 million in liabilities and was brought down by the liquidity crisis that gripped Britain's financial sector. A further 12 years on Baring Brothers, which had been started by a Lutheran family from northern Germany that built a fortune on financing international deals – particularly funding armaments for nations in overseas wars – came unstuck with a South American drainage project that went badly wrong, and the Bank of England, fearing that its failure would harm Britain's reputation for financial probity, was forced to ride to its rescue with £17 million.

When Barings, the nation's oldest investment bank, hit trouble for a second time in 1995, after 27-year-old trader Nick Leeson recklessly made an £850 million bet on the Singapore bourse, it was not so lucky. The Governor of the Bank of England, (Lord) Eddie George, sounded out other City financiers and pronounced that this time Barings was on its own and would be allowed to collapse.

In 1973–4 the Bank of England, supported by the high street banks, launched a £1 billion lifeboat to help a number of fringe banks brought to the edge by a collapse in commercial property values. The retail banks felt they had no choice because this time confidence in one of their own number, NatWest, appeared to be threatened. There were even newspaper pictures of savers queuing outside the in-store branches of London & County Securities, a dodgy bank, of which former Liberal leader Jeremy Thorpe was once a director, that had become overextended.

But for most savers like Graham Hallworth and Pam Hilleard the crisis at Northern Rock was something they had never witnessed before, which made it all the more dramatic and beyond comprehension. Britain, after all, was not a South American 'banana republic' where such things had been common. Nor was it a country in crisis like the Weimar Republic in Germany in the 1920s before Adolf Hitler rose to power. It was a prosperous country that had experienced more than a decade of low inflation, economic expansion, rising living standards and increasing prosperity.

The public had been constantly reassured by the former Chancellor, now Prime Minister, Gordon Brown that the steps he had taken to ensure economic stability, including giving the Bank of England its independence from government, had brought to an end the era of 'boom and bust'. Britain had escaped its past history of high inflation, strikes, violent swings in the economy and nationalisations. The City of London now had a reputation as one of the world's top business centres, and financial services had become one of the nation's richest and fastest growing industries. What was happening was reminiscent of the dark days of the past when financiers were regarded with suspicion and contempt and banks were so fragile that they could not be trusted. How was it possible that, amid all the financial sophistication and strength, there could be such shocking scenes at Northern Rock? Who was to blame for the disaster? And who would step in to sort things out?

CHAPTER 1

The Rise and Fall of a
Northern Legend

The Rock's rocky history

If at the start of 2007 few people could have imagined the turn of events that would bring down Northern Rock, there surely would have been even greater incredulity on the part of its 19th-century founding fathers about the sort of rash company it would become. The modern, competitive 21st-century Northern Rock was a far cry from its origins as a friendly society amid the grinding poverty of the industrialised northeast of England.

Northern Rock traces its history back to the self-help groups started by what were described as the 'respectable' working classes. These groups were known as the friendly societies, and for 100 years or more they helped people to save first and then to buy their homes. In 1965 two of these institutions – the Northern Counties Permanent Building Society, established in 1850, and the Rock Building Society, founded in 1865 – merged to form the Northern Rock Building Society. As Martin Vander Weyer, a scion of one of the founding families of Barclays noted in the *Spectator*, it was a marriage that was bound to hit problems. The Rock, the more spirited, aggressive entity, was always likely to get the more staid, prudent Northern into trouble one day.

For the time being, however, the union appeared to bring harmony, and the society's *raison d'être* remained the assistance of home owner-ship. That said, the new organisation displayed a distinctly 'amateur' element in the way it was run: the chairmanship of the board was assumed by the local aristocracy – principally the Ridley family based at Blagdon Hall, Northumberland – and other well-heeled families on Tyneside. Indeed, this was an aspect of its management that would come back to haunt it in 2007. As Professor John Tomaney of the University of Newcastle told BBC television's *The Money Programme*: 'On the one hand, you had the institution growing out of a working-class self-help ethic. On the other hand, it melded with this kind of "old money", paternalistic, landed gentry type of interest.'

In the late 1980s the Thatcher government's 'Big Bang' revolution set free financial markets from the rules and regulations that restricted their operations. At the same time many building societies decided to change their status and become banks, obtaining stock market quotations. Historically, building societies had been run for the good of their members, providing savings services locally and helping young people take their first steps on the housing ladder. In fact, the nation's second largest mortgage lender, the Nationwide, has remained loyal to the mutual model. However, as banks, the former building societies could be run to earn profits and dividends for their shareholders, and directors had the opportunity to become rich through the rewards of bonuses and share options tied to performance. Northern Rock waited a while before changing, but it finally succumbed to temptation and, following the lead of a number of other societies, such as the Abbey National and the Halifax, converted into a bank in 1997 with the intention of expanding its business.

But there were dissenting voices. In common with many other UK building societies, Northern Rock faced opposition to making this switch – 'demutualisation' as it was known. Fears were voiced that assets built up over many decades would no longer be run for the benefit of present members – the existing savers and borrowers – and it was also said that demutualisation was a betrayal of the community that the societies had been created to serve. Northern Rock chose to address these concerns by establishing the Northern Rock Foundation, which was intended to assist charitable and community organisations in the region. The Foundation, in receiving an annual commitment from Northern Rock of a percentage of the bank's profits to fund its work, also proved a useful buffer to any takeover attempt by a rival.

A further question mark arose in 1998 when, without warning, the company switched 200,000 savers into new accounts, some paying interest rates 2 per cent lower than before. The outcry was enormous, and once-loyal customers deserted in droves. The episode landed Northern Rock with an image of being something of a sharp operator that it has never quite been able to shake off in some quarters. Despite these misgivings, Northern Rock started to motor. Within three years of becoming a bank, it had slipped into overdrive and sped into the FTSE-100 Index, which meant that it was a permanent presence in many of the insurance, investment and pension funds in which we all have a stake. The force behind this move into the financial 'big league' was its newly appointed chief executive Adam Applegarth.

Proud of his local roots, Applegarth had joined the company straight from Durham University and had risen through the ranks. At only 38 and without any banking qualifications, he had shot to the top of Northern Rock and was the second youngest FTSE-100 boss. As the veteran City pundit David Buik observed wryly: 'He was good company, yet brazen and massively confident. He was a sports freak and to be found on everybody's committee. You can't say anything other than he was very charismatic.'

At the turn of the century, as a mark of its new status, Northern Rock introduced a new corporate identity consisting of a magenta square containing the company name, largely replacing the NR 'blocks' logo. In addition, it expanded its operations through its spacious, modern headquarters at the Regent Centre in the Gosforth district of Newcastle. In 2006 the company undertook a redevelopment of the Gosforth site, which saw the demolition of the original 1960s office block and its replacement by a new tower block, due to be completed by 2008, to act as the main entrance.

The huge Gosforth campus speaks volumes for the Rock's pretensions to northeastern grandeur. It is made up of the Kielder and Prudhoe buildings, completed in the early 1990s, behind which lies the distinctive glass-fronted Alnwick building. The main atrium reception is adjacent to this, opening out on to the recently completed Baker Street, a large, covered mall that houses a restaurant, shop and on-site branch. A number of other buildings, all named after the region's castles, are joined to Baker Street. Northern Rock's headquarters were a potent symbol of the economic revival of the northeast in the post-Thatcher era. Elsewhere, the Rock has a customer contact centre operations in Sunderland; a branch was opened in Guernsey in February 1996, handling offshore savings and investment accounts; and major branches were opened in Ireland, Denmark and Northern Ireland.

These, then, were the visible signs of the company's growth by the start of 2007. But what had enabled its relentless expansion to take place? Quite simply, Adam Applegarth had been determined to grab a much bigger slice of Britain's mortgage market, and caution was not part of his make-up. Bob Bennett, the finance director who stepped down in February 2007, observed: 'The credit crunch that was obviously coming should have led to more restrained [mortgage] volumes.' But Applegarth would not listen to his cohorts. He was the champion of ultra-competitive deals, and through an aggressive business strategy he drove the company forward to the point where, by 2007, it had annexed some 20 per cent of new mortgage lending at a time when bigger rivals, like the Halifax, part of the HBOS group, were battening down the hatches. Northern Rock's Together loan was central to the bank's drive for growth and became its signature product. With this innovative mortgage, young customers especially could borrow 125 per cent of the value of their new home plus up to six times their annual income. The old days, when loans were worked out on the basis of two and a half times income and no more than 75 per cent of the value of the property, were long past. Now borrowers could combine a home loan and wrap up their existing debt in one arrangement.

Northern Rock would be quick to point out that most of those taking out a Together mortgage did so for only two years, before switching to a more orthodox repayment mortgage. It also insisted that default and arrears levels for its products were very low and highlighted the quality of its lending. Despite its popularity, though, the Together loan had its critics in the industry. One of Northern Rock's biggest rivals condemned the loan as a 'racy product' and said it raised serious questions about the bank as a responsible lender. Such criticism reached fever pitch, of course, when Northern Rock ran into difficulties.

Northern Rock's rise up the mortgage lending table was driven almost exclusively in the latter days by the Together loan. As house prices climbed, the loan raked in first-time buyers desperate to get their foot on the property ladder. Northern Rock's decision to allow so many people to 'go large' on their borrowing – granting mortgages at six times income when other lenders were holding the line at between three and four times – raised eyebrows across the industry. But the fact was that Together helped Northern Rock raise its market share, and, despite the critics, it soon had its imitators. Competitors followed suit, and rules on lending eased across the industry. Mortgages of five times salary or more became commonplace in 2006, helping to stoke the UK property market. Britain was building up a debt mountain for itself unlike any other in western Europe. Total borrowings stood at more than £1,300 billion, as much as the nation's total output, its gross national product.

The 'new kid on the block' had arrived. In the midst of a £19 billion lending spree, the bank was, for a while, Britain's biggest mortgage provider, elbowing aside the traditional giants such as the Halifax and Nationwide. Its shares hit an all-time high of £12 and it won praise from City analysts who were delighted by the bank's ultra-low cost, high-profit business approach. Northern Rock, it seemed, was the business model to follow.

With Northern Rock flying high, investors piled in and drove up the share price to an astonishing £12.60 by February 2007, giving the company a total valuation of over £6 billion. At that stage it was the fifth largest mortgage lender in the UK. The gamble seemed to be paying off, and the City bought into the story. Sandy Chen, equity research analyst at stockbroker Panmure Gordon, commented: 'At one point they were bigger than the Halifax, which was the biggest mortgage lender in the UK. Northern Rock was an amazing growth story.'

Boasting stellar earnings and a chief executive now a big shot in the south as well as the north, Northern Rock, it seemed, could do no wrong. David Buik noted: 'Jacket off, white shirt, clean shaven, bald head, beaming like a Cheshire cat and giving it plenty. It sounded good. It was good. It was a lovely tale. The analysts lapped it up. He did a brilliant job.' The success was based on keen housekeeping, too. As its lending volumes soared, Adam Applegarth kept a tight rein on costs, so ensuring that growth and profits went hand in hand. In early 2007 the bank reported annual profits for 2006 of £587 million, more than double the £245 million recorded six years earlier. The company brushed aside worries about rising interest rates, maintaining that they would not affect lending in 2007, and it authorised a record dividend for shareholders.

Amid this heady atmosphere, the first danger signals flashed – though few realised it at the time. One potential danger arose when the Rock's finance director, Bob Bennett, who had led the flotation and was seen by many as a steadying influence in the organisation, retired in February 2007. This, however, seemed to raise few concerns: Bennett's eventual departure had been on the cards since 2001, when he had been edged out by Applegarth in the battle to succeed Leo Finn in the top job. More seriously, though, questions were beginning to be heard in some quarters, not only about the Rock's ability to sustain its huge dash for growth but also, more fundamentally, about its business model. As Conservative MP Michael Fallon, a leading member of the Treasury Select Committee, was to comment later: 'It was a very aggressive strategy. In one sense, Northern Rock wasn't really a traditional bank at all. It was more financial engineering: it was borrowing 75 per cent of its money from the wholesale market and lending it out in the form of mortgages.'

The wholesale markets are where banks lend to one another, and although it was not alone among UK banks in funding its mortgage lending in this way, Northern Rock was unique in how heavily it relied on it. Just how bizarre this was is underlined by comparing Northern Rock's approach with the conservative one adopted by Lloyds TSB, owners of Cheltenham & Gloucester and one of Britain's most respected lenders. Three-quarters of Lloyds TSB's funding comes from retail and business customer deposits and only one-quarter from the wholesale inter-bank markets. Its balance sheet is the reverse of Northern Rock's. It should come as no surprise that when the Rock started to sink, Lloyds TSB was the first call for Matthew Greenburgh at Merrill Lynch, the American investment bank hired by the company to sort out the mess. He believed that Lloyds was the ideal candidate for a rescue takeover of the Rock.

Northern Rock adopted a highly risky strategy that totally depended on the liquidity of the wholesale market for its continued borrowings and the validity of its business model. In the summer of 2007 the Geordie bank's luck ran out as the chill economic winds that were already gusting in America crossed the Atlantic. In the US there had been a boom in mortgages for poor people – known as the sub-prime market, as in below the standard or 'prime' market. Some borrowers were being offered loans that they had no hope of repaying, and problems arose when far more people failed to pay back their mortgages than the banks had bargained for. By the spring of 2007 the industry was facing a crisis. Former Bank of England insider Danny Gabay, now of Fathom Financial Consulting, said: 'Banks very quickly began to question not only what they were holding in their own accounts, but what their counterparts in other banks were doing, too. And when you don't trust your own accounts, you're very unlikely to trust other bank accounts.'

This was all very bad news for Northern Rock. Banks were now becoming increasingly reluctant to lend to each other, and, when they did, it was at much higher rates of interest. The Rock had huge difficulties raising any kind of decent money from the wholesale inter-bank market as the loans it had already taken out fell due. It was becoming apparent that Applegarth's team was hugely over-stretched. The first crack appeared in June, when the bank issued a warning that profits would fall below market expectations: the race to grab market share had begun to misfire. Even then, Applegarth boasted to reporters that even though bank profits would be hit in 2007, the increased market share would pay off in subsequent years.

The City regulator, the Financial Services Authority (FSA) – created in 1997 by then Chancellor of the Exchequer Gordon Brown – seemed to be convinced of the bank's soundness, and in July 2007 it felt confident enough about the Rock's prospects, despite a plunging share price and City and press whispers, to allow the payment of a special dividend of £59 million to shareholders, to be paid directly out of capital. The numbers involved were small compared with Northern Rock's mortgage book, but it nevertheless sent out a message that all was well at the very time the Rock's funding model was imploding. The FSA had made a huge blunder in approving the payment of a dividend by a company that had the liquidity, the ready cash, to sustain itself for days only, not the long weeks and months of crisis that lay ahead. Under pressure from the Treasury – which was feeling the heat from the media – the FSA eventually persuaded the Rock to cancel the payout. But as the Treasury Select Committee noted in January 2008: 'It was wrong of the FSA to allow Northern Rock to weaken its balance sheet at a time when the FSA was concerned about problems of liquidity that could affect the financial sector.'

Northern Rock was now in deep trouble. To some, this came as a shock. Its growth and share performance had made the bank a favourite in the City for quite a while, and many analysts saw few problems with its business model. But the more sceptical had never been taken in. They had thought for some time that the bank's risky, high-percentage lending would leave it exposed to arrears and repossessions. For those prepared to look, the bank had long been an accident waiting to happen. As far back as April 2002 I noted in the *Daily Mail* that the increasing complexity of the mortgage market posed dangers: 'A number of lenders, including Northern Rock, have been repackaging mortgage debt in the American markets to raise funds and keep the cost of loans lower. It is a great business idea, but one where caution is called for.'

This was not a message that Applegarth, someone used to grinding people into submission during internal debates, wanted to hear. He was not a person given to self-doubt and did not take criticism lightly. He personally disputed my column, the first of several I wrote on these lines, and then took me to a sumptuous lunch at the Royal Garden Hotel in Kensington where, as the small talk began, he quickly made it clear that he was a fanatical Newcastle United supporter – the football club being one of several northeast-based sports teams sponsored by the Rock. Then he moved from football chat to the subject of banking in an effort to persuade me of the safety of the model he was using to super-charge the expansion of his bank. 'Northern Rock's success is based on the securitisation of loans,' Applegarth told me. 'It has given us an extra source of funds that is much cheaper than cash deposits.' It was among the factors that had allowed the Rock to reduce costs. As it turned out, the problem at Northern Rock was precisely at the 'wholesale' end of the business, from where it borrowed to drive its huge mortgage expansion. It had committed the classic banking error of relying on short-term borrowings in the money markets and lending long. It was this that brought the mortgage bank to its knees.

Although Northern Rock would become the highest-profile UK victim of the credit crunch, many across the globe had been following a similar business model. But there is an inherent problem at the core of this model, and it lies in the practice of 'securitisation', by which banks package up mortgage loans and sell them on. Over the past ten years there has been a growing split between the originator of the mortgage and the end user. Lenders need only hold on to loans for a month or two before they pass them on to an investment bank, which packages them up and sells them. It puts cash back on to the balance sheet of the bank, which can then start lending again. But if for any reason the source of funding is disrupted, then the banks involved suffer immediately. This is what happened on 9 August 2007: on that day, banks, fearful about the amount of bad debt each was carrying, stopped lending to one another. The result was panic.

Reflecting on the days that followed the markets meltdown and the start of the credit crunch, Applegarth was to tell the BBC: 'We're certainly not alone in being affected by the global liquidity seizure. It was a strange thing on 9 August to see all banks stop lending to each other worldwide. That will take some time to unwind. We are all being affected, but because Northern Rock raises so much of its money on the wholesale markets, we've been affected first.'

Applegarth's self-serving gloss on events was only part of the story. Certainly, Northern Rock was a victim of the quake that shook global financial markets in the summer of 2007. But it was also a company that had lost touch with reality. Applegarth had become so used to giving the orders and leading the way that he found it all but impossible to heed warning voices, such as that of Bob Bennett, who had helped to bring the Rock to the public markets. He was powerful enough to ride roughshod over the bank's board of directors, which lacked the confidence or ability to call a halt to the imprudent expansion. Applegarth and Northern Rock falsely believed that the only path was onwards and upwards, but he and the bank had badly miscalculated.

CHAPTER 2

Mortgaging the Future

The sub-prime bonanza

Northern Rock's spectacular collapse arose directly from the bursting of the bubble of so-called sub-prime mortgages in America. These derived their name from the cut of meat that is less than best. Prime mortgages went to the better off; sub-prime went to the far end of the market, to those who had never qualified for a mortgage before. In a nutshell, when these mortgages went bad, the banks got into trouble with bad debts and poor investments. These shockwaves eventually reached Britain and prevented Northern Rock from borrowing for its own mortgage lending.

The sub-prime debacle had its origins in US financial policies that went back to the 1990s and the low-interest rate regime that had been established by Alan Greenspan, chairman of the Federal Reserve – a policy that he saw as the panacea for all economic ills. Greenspan, who headed the US central bank from 1987 to 2006, was admired around the world for his ability to read the economic runes and for his skill in steering America safely through a series of financial shocks from the 1987 crash to 9/11. He liked to act in a pre-emptive manner by lowering interest rates and flooding the markets with cash at the first sign of trouble.

In 1997–8 the US and the Western banking system had been threatened by a financial crisis that started in the newly emerging markets of Asia, from Indonesia to Korea, and eventually spread across the world to Russia. In the US, meanwhile, the huge volatility of financial markets proved too much for the super hedge fund Long Term Capital Management (LTCM), based in Greenwich, Connecticut, which invested $125 billion on behalf of wealthy clients and institutions. Greenspan, together with Bill McDonough, head of the New York Federal Reserve (the operational arm of the American central bank), moved speedily. McDonough convened an urgent meeting of 16 of the world's largest banks, including Britain's Barclays, and persuaded them to inject $3.5 billion of capital into LTCM, buying it the time to unwind its complex dealings in an orderly fashion. So large were its commitments that a failure to do so could have brought the whole financial system crashing down. It was a model for dealing with financial emergencies that, ten years later, might have served the British taxpayer better had the Tripartite authorities in the UK acted with the same decisiveness when Northern Rock ran into difficulties.

Despite the Fed's strong action, the credit crunch that hit the US wholesale banking markets was far from over. Greenspan told an audience of economists on 7 October 1998: 'I've been watching the US markets for 50 years and I have never seen anything like it.' Greenspan followed up the LTCM rescue with three quick-fire reductions in American interest rates, and European and Asian central bankers followed his lead. Keeping the credit markets open and steering America away from slowdown or recession became Greenspan's preoccupation. The Fed boss, as had been the case after the 1987 collapse, lowered interest rates and eased monetary conditions – the classic answer to avoiding financial crisis.

There was an even bigger challenge on the horizon. No sooner had the world weathered the fears about the Millennium Bug than Osama Bin Laden and al-Qaeda shattered confidence on Wall Street with the 9/11 attacks on that beacon of capitalism, the World Trade Center in Manhattan. The New York Stock Exchange was put out of action, and the plumbing of global finance clogged up, despite an unprecedented secret action by central banks to flood the money markets with cash. Greenspan once again resorted to his trusted weapon of interest rates to prevent al-Qaeda from scoring a victory over the Western economic system. In an effort to stimulate the economy Greenspan slashed interest rates again and again until they stood at just 1 per cent.

What happened after 2001 was also the natural outcome of events a few years before. Lenders' relaxation of mortgage credit standards had been on the way since 1977, when a federal law, the Community Reinvestment Act, prodded banks into extending more credit to the communities in which they operated. That made them popular with lower income and minority borrowers, and the banks began to take market share from established bodies, such as the government-backed agencies. The banks lured these mostly first-timers with the promise of loans involving less paperwork, faster approval and no-money-down loans that seemed more affordable. In return, they were charged the highest possible rates of interest for the privilege.

The housing market, one of the great drivers of US growth, took off like a rocket. But this housing bubble had a different feel to it. This time, Greenspan's low rates had the effect of creating a home loans market that was boring for mortgage originators and lenders. Low interest rates meant less than exciting returns, and the money men began to crave new ways to make high yields in an otherwise humdrum market. Greenspan was, in fact, to be the midwife to the credit crunch of 2007–8, but it was several years before he realised it.

As in Britain, America's traditional housing market, dealing with prime borrowers, had worked along well-established lines for many years. Banks financed mortgages through deposits received from customers. At the same time, potential home buyers were scrutinised closely for their ability to meet repayments, and there was a vigorous valuation of the house they planned to buy. In other words, proper precautions were taken. Lenders would extend home loans only to those who were deemed good risks. Borrowers needed to have a sufficient income, to possess a good credit record and to have reasonable job prospects. All this was rather obvious and sensible.

The nation's two largest lenders of mainstream mortgages were Fannie Mae (Federal National Mortgage Association) and Freddie

Mac (Federal Home Mortgage Corporation). These colourfully named government-sponsored agencies had their origins in the Roosevelt New Deal of the 1930s that followed the housing market collapse in the Great Depression. The agencies had come into their own in the past 40 years with a mixture of private and public funding, which had allowed banks to lend at low rates at the bottom end of the market. They both have a mortgage ceiling of around £200,000, however, and this traditional model limited both the amount that could be lent and the type of person who could borrow. Thus, a gap existed in the market for potential new borrowers: lending to people who normally couldn't afford to borrow and to people who needed a larger sum. So, the banks moved in to fill the gap. At the same time, banks and other lenders were finding it was hopeless looking to prime borrowers with a large amount of equity in their homes, secure jobs and rising incomes. Such borrowers could demand the finest rates in a highly competitive marketplace and were busy re-organising their existing home loans so that they could benefit from the record low interest rates. The prime market was losing its allure.

Instead, real estate agents, mortgage originators and bankers turned their sights on the millions of people with less collateral and lower incomes who were dying to climb the housing ladder. The era of low interest rates bred new types of mortgage lender who attracted a new breed of borrower into the market. Suddenly, with the invention of sub-prime loans, there was a way to reach out to these borrowers. And, to complete the picture, house builders and construction firms could cater for the boom by building millions of cheap homes in a country where neither land supply nor zoning, the American equivalent of planning laws, was a problem.

Sub-prime loans appeared to be a winner, offering great possibilities for everyone in the housing chain. People with no prospect of fulfilling the 'American Dream' got a chance to own their own homes, while everyone else made piles of money along the way. It was easy to see why sub-prime was attractive to lenders fed up with low returns. Here was the latest chance to make a lot of money in an otherwise jaded market. Never ones to heed a lesson, the banks, fresh from burning their fingers in the dotcom boom, had marched straight into the enticing world of sub-prime lending, barely stopping to pass 'Go'.

For the banks, this latest gravy train had fees, commissions and bonuses to offer all the way down the line as the mortgages were eventually packaged up and sold on to investors. In the first place, bankers raked in a huge amount of business from groups of people who had been previously unable to get mortgages. The traditional underwriting rules were thrown away to reel in these borrowers. Bankers would get commissions for setting up new loans business, or 'affordability products' as the industry termed them. The new borrowers who were signing up to sub-prime deals were seduced by easy-to-get loans that came at attractive short-term interest rates – 'teasers' as they were known – only then to find themselves locked into higher rates, reset to often double the original rate after two years – a rate they could not possibly afford.

For now, though, all self-control was lost as new business boomed with the 'new' wave of borrowers eager to grab the mortgages on offer. Driven by the desire to expand their reach and their profits, banks urged mortgage brokers to sell more and more of these mortgages. Brokers and bank loan officials were under no obligation to find their customers the best possible deal. On the contrary, their commission was based on the size of the loan and the interest rate charged. A large number of borrowers were also being advised to re-mortgage, thereby incurring early repayment charges, even though the adviser was unable to demonstrate why this was needed. This, too, was profitable income for the lenders. The rapid rise in the amount borrowed against a property's value showed how willing lenders were to stretch things. According to Bank of America Securities, the average loan to a sub-prime borrower in 2002 was 48 per cent of the value of the property. A few years on, and just before the sub-prime bubble began to burst, that figure would soar to a jaw-dropping 82 per cent.

Millions of mortgages were dished out in a 'new market' that awoke one day to an array of new products catering for high-risk borrowers with sketchy credit histories. Essentially, these new products were exotic mortgages designed simply to suck in borrowers. There were loans that required low documentation ('low doc') or no documentation ('no doc'); some needed no proof of income or credit history – and all were known as 'liar loans'. One study soon showed that in a third of cases the brokers and intermediaries who were selling mortgages on behalf of lenders were failing to assess whether the buyers could afford the loan, while in nearly half of cases they were not making sure the mortgage was suitable for the customer. Other types of mortgage included 'jumbos', which, as their name suggests, were particularly large loans, disproportionate to a borrower's income and house value. Virginia consultants the Mortgage Asset Research Institute reported that nine out of ten borrowers stated different incomes for mortgage purposes from those declared to the tax authorities. All these sub-prime products took an increasing share of the US mortgage market from 2002. According to Deutsche Bank figures, 'liar loans' actually accounted for 25 per cent of all the sub-prime mortgage business in 2001, rising to 40 per cent in 2002.

Even where income could be proved, the banks simply lent more money than was prudent. At one time high-rate borrowers weren't allowed to stretch as much as conventional borrowers on loan amounts, a reflection of their higher credit risk. But as home prices rose throughout the US, lenders grew more willing to let high-rate borrowers get bigger loans as measured against their annual incomes. In 2005 borrowers who obtained high-rate mortgages to buy family homes were loaned, on average, 2.1 times their reported annual income, according to the data. That was 4 per cent higher than regular borrowers.

To give sub-prime a veneer of bogus credibility, lenders said new, modern credit-scoring systems meant that risk could now be more finely calibrated, thus embracing a whole new area of borrowers.

This was nonsense, of course. Sub-prime borrowers did not qualify for prime loans because they were high risk: they were often unable to offer a down payment, they had a record of not paying debts, and they could not prove their income. This point was noted by Paul Ashworth of Capital Economics: 'As house prices continued to rise ever higher, relative to average incomes during the housing boom, more and more potential borrowers fell into those categories.'

Using these credit-scoring techniques, lenders claimed they could better sort applicants by credit-worthiness and offer them appropriately risk-based loan rates. Holding such large volumes of these risky loans in their portfolios would normally have presented a problem for the banks that lacked the necessary equity capital needed to cover possible losses. But the emergence of default protection, a form of insurance against bad debt, meant they were not held back in the usual way. Lenders could, ultimately, sell on these loans to investors in the form of residential mortgage-backed securities (RMBS). The spread of new products offering default protection was a crucial element in the growth of sub-prime lending.

But the sub-prime boom was not solely connected with the poor who were previously unable to get home loans. Brokers also found rich pickings in equity release among the working classes who had already achieved homeownership. These owner-occupiers were persuaded that they could raise cash by refinancing their homes. As ever, it was not fully explained to them how the 'teaser' rates worked.

With the banks cashing in on sub-prime, it was small wonder that many Americans wanted to get in on the act. It was a bonanza that swelled the ranks of the lenders, as the man and woman in the street sensed 'pay dirt'. At one point the boom was so great that people with no banking qualifications or lending experience were joining in. Tens of thousands of people enlisted in the real estate industry, working as realtors, mortgage originators and sales people. It seemed like a licence to print money – and anybody could do it. It was a form of selling that wasn't difficult to learn, and in an industry with little or no regulation Americans lined up to 'sell the dream' and realise their own in the bargain. As *Newsweek* reported graphically, hundreds of thousands of ordinary folk left their jobs to join in the 'new Klondike' and earn themselves a fortune in the process. The demand for mortgage brokers in Las Vegas, for instance, was so strong that 'every stripper, waiter and bartender on The Strip had a broker's licence'. Between November 2001 and April 2005 housing and housing-related industries created an amazing 788,300 jobs across the US – 40 per cent of the total increase in employment during a period of sharp growth.

Reflecting this explosion of sub-prime home loans, analysis by the *Wall Street Journal* indicated that from 2004 to 2006, when home prices peaked in many parts of the country, more than 2,500 banks, thrifts, credit unions and mortgage companies issued a combined $1,500 billion in high interest rate loans. Inevitably, sub-prime became a particular force in the poorer parts of America, such as the old industrialised north and the Deep South, and in low-income districts in wealthy cities such as New York and Los Angeles. Old industrial cities like Philadelphia, which had a pronounced problem with poverty, saw its residents turning to sub-prime loans. For many years Cleveland, Ohio was the sub-prime capital of America. The poor, working-class community there was hit hard by the decline of manufacturing and sharply divided along racial lines. Sub-prime borrowing spread out from the inner cities right across America, and many immigrants took advantage to buy in the 'hot' housing markets of southern California, Arizona and Nevada.

What was happening in the real estate boom in America had its parallels in Britain. A credit explosion saw dozens of mortgage lenders competing for the same customers. Special low-start mort-gage offers, two-year fixed-rate deals and offers that allowed borrowers to roll up credit card debt with their home loans abounded. Northern Rock, particularly in the early part of 2007 when the housing boom was reaching its peak, was at the heart of this lending free-for-all. This may not have been sub-prime, in the

American sense, but there can be no doubt that traditional lending standards had been relaxed and interest charges cut to the bone. The Rock tended to lend to young, professional first-time buyers, who already had some personal debt. With annual salary increases and clear career paths, these people were regarded as sound, long-term credit risks. The old lending disciplines may have been discarded, but care was taken to check the credit-worthiness of the borrowers – which is more than could be said of the American experience. Even so, the bank came under fire for making it easy for its young customers to borrow large sums of money, typically through its Together mortgage.

Much of the Rock's business came through brokers, such as Staffordshire-based Simple Mortgage Solutions, whose boss Chris Mayor, said: 'Northern Rock took great pains to make sure they were lending to people who could meet repayments. In turn, borrowers were attracted by their products, particularly the Together loan.' Northern Rock's Adam Applegarth would later defend Together as performing something of a social function for young people who were trying to buy their first home. He rejected claims that Northern Rock was cashing in on people's greed and that it was not being responsible. 'I would disagree with that strongly,' he told the Treasury Select Committee in October 2007. 'We've found out that the vast majority of people borrowing from us for a mortgage already had other borrowings. So, it makes financial sense to them to combine their loans into one attractive rate.'

James Atkin was typical of the new wave of Northern Rock borrowers. He was a young, ambitious graduate professional, carrying a little debt and looking to take his first step on the property ladder. James had left university in 2000 and began training as a landscape architect. Within a year he was keen to buy his first property, but he had only a smallish income, a bit of debt and no savings. 'I earned £11,500 and had no scope for a deposit. I borrowed £52,000, which enabled me to buy a two-bedroom house for £40,000 in Burton upon Trent. The Together deal transformed the situation for me. There's no way I could have afforded to get my foot on the property ladder without it.'

Northern Rock has always been at pains to point out that its mortgages were, in no sense, sub-prime. For the most part its mortgage book was high quality, and its repossession figures were among the lowest for lenders in this country. However, it certainly lent a lot of money to borrowers whose existing debts took up a major part of their disposable income. And when higher interest rates began to bite late in 2007, these borrowers were clearly getting into difficulties, reflected by the growing number of repossessions Northern Rock was dealing with. A survey conducted in early 2008 by BBC's Radio 5 Live found that the Rock was among the leading lenders seeking court orders to begin the eviction process against defaulting home buyers.

Back in America, the sub-prime market had taken off like a rocket, the number of borrowers was rising, and the level of homeownership grew with them. Among the most ambitious of the US-owned lenders was the Seattle-based Washington Mutual's Long Beach Mortgage. It armed itself with the company slogan 'The Power of Yes' and made $48 billion in high-rate loans between 2004 and 2006 by using armies of outside brokers to push sub-prime loans into the suburbs. Another major player for much of this period was Countrywide Financial, which, in 2006, accounted for 20 per cent of this market. By 2005 high-rate mortgages accounted for 29 per cent of the total number of home loans – up from 16 per cent the year before. In the three years from 2003, about 10 million high-rate loans were made out of a total of 43.6 million mortgages. High-rate lending jumped by an even larger percentage in 68 metropolitan areas right across the country, from such places as Lewiston, Maine, and Ocala, Florida, to Tacoma, Washington.

Sub-prime loans were not unknown either among the more affluent living away from the inner cities. US mortgage figures covering the boom years show that high-rate lending climbed sharply in middle-class and wealthier communities. As home prices accelerated across the country, more affluent families turned to high-rate loans to buy expensive homes they could not have qualified for under conventional lending standards. Second homes proved a popular idea, too. In 2005 13 per cent of all high-rate home loans were for properties not occupied by owners, a rise from about 9 per cent in 2004. Experts believed that such properties were actually higher foreclosure risks than homes lived in by their owners.

Kristine McMahon was typical of the middle-class drive for second mortgages. A mortgage broker herself, she earned a six-figure salary and lived in a four-bedroom home in East Hampton, New York, valued at more than $2.7 million. Yet Ms McMahon chose a sub-prime loan when she refinanced to turn some of her home equity into cash, because her prime lender wouldn't allow her to raise so much money.

Different social groups with different means and different needs – sub-prime served them all. The result, though, was that the eventual fallout of this market hurt a far broader array of Americans than many could have imagined, cutting across differences in income, race and geography. From the working poor chasing the homeownership dream to investors hoping to strike it rich by speculating on condominiums, sub-prime loans burrowed into the heart of the American financial system, and they would soon take their toll.

For now, though, all seemed well. From the vantage point of 2004 and 2005 the wobbly early days of sub-prime in 2001 – when risky borrowing by risky borrowers brought mortgage defaults almost as soon as the loans had begun to take off – seemed a distant memory. These teething troubles were put down to unemployment brought about by the US recession. After 2002 two factors helped mask sub-prime loan problems. First, this was a period of rapidly escalating house prices as the economy recovered. Sub-prime borrowers who encountered financial problems could either borrow against their equity to make house payments or sell their homes to settle their debts. Second, interest rates declined significantly in the early 2000s. This helped lower the base rate to which adjustable mortgage rates were indexed, thereby limiting the increase when the initial, teaser rates ended.

Soon defaults were on the retreat. And, the theory went, as long as unemployment remained low, so, too, would default and delinquency rates. Sub-prime mortgages were gaining a firm foothold in the market, and by 2004 they accounted for some 35 per cent of all mortgages issued – at its height the value of sub-prime mortgages reached $6,000 billion. Official US statistics showed, too, that between 1996 and 2005 the number of sub-prime lending specialists surged.

By 2006 Countrywide Financial was funding nearly one in five of all mortgages in the US. It was comparable in size to Northern Rock in the UK and had a similar proportion of the home loan market. Nearly all of its mortgages, many of which were issued to inner-city ethnic minority groups, were packaged up and sold on to a secondary market as asset-backed securities. Another major player was First Century Bank, formed in 2004, which catered for customers in middle-class America who were ignored by the larger banks.

Even the redoubtable HSBC, one of the largest global banks, allowed itself to get caught up in the mess. In November 2002, just as the sub-prime lending fiasco was starting to shape up, the British-based bank, which had roots in Hong Kong, made a bold move into the American marketplace by buying credit company Household International in an all-share deal that placed a £9 billion valuation on the bank's new toy. But Household was no ordinary lender. Its customer base was crudely described as 'trailer trash', and its job was to supply loans, credit cards, car insurance and credit insurance to 50 million Americans, many of whom were at the lower end of the social scale.

The group's swashbuckling chairman Sir John Bond boasted to investors: 'This deal brings together one of the world's most successful deposit gatherers with one of the world's largest generators of assets. It is an extremely good match.' He was not alone in lauding the transaction. Mark During, an analyst at stockbrokers Brewer Dolphin in the City of London, applauded the foresight of HSBC. 'Over 75 per cent of all return on equity is derived from the US,' he purred. 'It's where you have to be if you want to be a global player.' But Household International was way outside the HSBC experience. The British bank's greatest expansion in recent times had been in the exclusive world of private banking for the very wealthy, at the opposite end of the socio-economic scale to Household. Moreover, most of its consumer banking experience was in Hong Kong, where a fantastic work ethic meant that even in hard times people found the wherewithal to keep debt payments up to date.

HSBC had bought a dud. At the very height of the sub-prime lending boom its employees at Household, now renamed HSBC Finance, saw a chance to profit rapidly from the mortgage boom, making a huge volume of loans in 2005 and 2006, just as the first signs of strain were beginning to emerge.

Indications that things were beginning to go wrong first became more evident as 2005 wore on. Borrowers were getting into difficulties with their mortgages – payments were being missed and the banks were foreclosing on the loans. The 'For Sale' signs were going up everywhere. The experience of Darla Ball, a printer and copier saleswoman from Las Vegas, reflected what a lot of borrowers went through. She purchased a $460,000 home using an adjustable-rate sub-prime loan with an initial rate of 8 per cent. At the time, Darla expected to refinance before her interest rate reset to 14 per cent within two years – pushing up her monthly payments from $3,700 to $8,000 – but she was beaten by events as prices of comparable homes in her district fell to $310,000, which meant she would not qualify for a new $460,000 mortgage. So, she stopped paying her mortgage. 'I'm going to lose my home anyway,' she reflected. 'So, why pay?'

On the east coast, Fort Myers, Florida, with its palm tree-lined boulevards and once the home of inventor Thomas Edison, also experienced the type of sub-prime lending that went wrong and helped deepen the US mortgage crisis. Between 2004 and 2006 more than $8.5 billion worth of sub-prime mortgages were granted in and around Fort Myers. The loans encouraged borrowers to stretch more than ever, which, in turn, helped inflate property values. The area's average sales price for existing homes then fell by 22 per cent from the end of 2005, and foreclosures ran at an all-time high.

One of the toughest stories, though, was to be found in New York City, as revealed on the BBC business website. When Cynthia and Douglas Brown arrived with their two young daughters at their new home in the borough of Queens, they thought they had at last found a haven from the inner-city life that had so troubled them in the past. 'We used to live in a violent building in Harlem, troubled by rape and drugs,' said Cynthia. 'One of my daughters was too frightened to go to the store. I was worried about leaving them alone.' The 43-year-olds decided they had to leave their small apartment in order to survive as a family. Cynthia contacted real estate agents in Queens, and after a long search she eventually fell in love with a spacious, redbrick house, with three large bedrooms and a garden where her children could play. The family signed what they thought were the appropriate documents and moved in a month later.

However, their hopes for a new life were soon dashed when they received threatening calls from their bank. Financial misery followed as the Browns discovered to their horror that they had fallen into a trap that ensnared other low-income families looking to get on the property ladder. They had unwittingly taken out two costly sub-prime mortgages. The couple's first loan was for about $381,000 (£190,000) with a variable interest rate of 8.2 per cent, which could balloon to a maximum of 14.2 per cent. The second was for $96,000 at a fixed rate of 11 per cent. According to industry estimates, the average for a family in the US would be about $275,000 at a fixed rate of 6 per cent.

'The contract was not explained to us thoroughly,' said Cynthia. 'They just said sign here and sign there and the house is yours.' The family started to receive payment demands from their bank for $3,100. They had been expecting something closer to $2,000. Douglas, who works in the paper industry, earned only $23,000 a year. If he had paid what the bank wanted, he would have nothing to meet the rest of the household budget. Fearing the worst, the family expected the loan to be foreclosed and waited to be evicted. However, with the help of a local lawyer, they discovered irregularities in the original processing of the mortgage, and, after protracted negotiations, the bank agreed to a sensible re-financing, which meant they wouldn't lose their home. The Browns' hard-luck story had a happy ending, but many other borrowers were not so fortunate and had their homes taken away when they defaulted. 'I wouldn't want to see anybody else go through this experience with sub-prime mortgages,' said Cynthia. 'Rich or poor, everybody needs a place to live.'

What happened to one woman in Milwaukee was not uncommon either. A divorcee from a white, middle-class family, she had run up large medical bills and was forced to meet day-to-day expenses by using her credit card. Salvation appeared to arrive on her doorstep one day in the shape of a mortgage seller who offered her a re-financing package on her house that would consolidate her bills and pay off her credit card. Life, it seemed, would be easier.

Welfare workers had seen this time and again. 'These were brokers selling sub-prime loans who offer a friendly face and promise to do all the paperwork and at very tempting loan rates. Why wouldn't you do it?' one commented. But the paperwork was complex – often running to 50 pages – and buried in it was the fact that, a couple of months after the loan began, the 'really low' rates would jump dramatically. The inevitable happened. Foreclosure by the bank was followed by 'For Sale' boards outside the house and eventual eviction. The security from hardship she craved was replaced by even more desperate poverty.

Another seeking the American Dream, as reported by the BBC, was Myra Riggs. She lived in a neighbourhood dominated by drug addicts, rape and gang crime, and to escape this she bought a house on the outskirts of Baltimore. To do so she was drawn into the world of sub-prime mortgages, and, like a lot of other borrowers, she was shocked when her initial rate of repayment suddenly shot up. 'It's a rip-off. That's what it is. Adjustable rate mortgages are for people with money, not the likes of us,' she said. As for so many others, her dream had turned sour.

By 2006 house prices had topped out and were on the slide, fore-closures were gathering pace, and the property market boom was over. The sub-prime genie was now out of the bottle. From the beginning, it had been obvious that 'liar loans' would become a disaster for someone, but it took a near meltdown in the mortgage market to bring the point home to the financial industry. They didn't seem to realise that house prices wouldn't go up forever. Indeed, they didn't seem to see that some day they might even go down. And when they went down, lenders would have neither a strong borrower to make payments nor decent collateral to sell, and nor would there be a buyer with any money to sell the property to.

In early 2007 investors and lenders began to realise the ramifica-tions of easy credit. Delinquency rates for six-month-old sub-prime and near-prime loans underwritten in 2006 were far higher than for those of the same age that had originated in 2004. Other signs of deterioration also surfaced. The past-due rate for outstanding sub-prime mortgages rose sharply and neared the peak reached in 2002, with the deterioration much worse for adjustable than for fixed-rate mortgages. In the first quarter of 2007 the rate at which residential mortgages entered foreclosure reached its fastest pace since tracking of these data began in 1970. Lenders reacted to these signs by initially tightening credit standards on riskier mortgages. In the Federal Reserve's April 2007 survey of senior loan officers, 15 per cent of banks indicated that they had raised standards for mort-gages to prime borrowers in the previous three months, but a much higher 56 per cent had done so for sub-prime mortgages. By January 2008 repossessions were running 90 per cent ahead of the previous year, with defaults mounting particularly in Nevada and California.

All the signs of distress were there, and the collapse of the sub-prime bonanza in the US had a number of immediate effects. The very people whom sub-prime had brought into property ownership for the first time were now losing their homes. In addition, those taking out equity from their houses or buying second homes were also getting into trouble. The Centre for Responsible Lending reported: 'Sub-prime loans made during 1998–2006 have led, or will lead, to a net loss of homeownership for almost one million families.' By the autumn of 2007 the tidal wave of repossessions was threatening to double that figure. In the US, unlike Britain, there is far less tolerance among lenders towards homeowners who fail to keep up payments.

The sub-prime collapse also hit house prices in a number of ways. People who couldn't afford their mortgage put their homes on the market, either voluntarily or through foreclosure. However, as the crisis deepened it got harder to get a mortgage, so there were fewer buyers, exerting downward pressure throughout the housing market. A glut of 4 million unsold homes in 2007 further depressed prices. The sunshine states of California, Nevada and Florida had switched from enjoying the biggest boom in property prices to becoming the worst-hit areas, followed closely by the so-called 'rust belt' states, such as Ohio, which have weak manufacturing economies. Recent years have seen the first nationwide decline in house prices since the 1930s, with the bill for homeowners put at $71 billion, plus $32 billion as the cost of its effects on depressing neighbouring properties.

The property boom had the further effect of damaging local and national economies. More money going to banks and hedge funds from domestic budgets meant that less went to local businesses and shops. And, as those families got into trouble with their loans, they had even less to spend. The cost of this will be worked out for years to come.

Sub-prime lending has been likened to selling used cars in bad neighbourhoods – that is to say, it's definitely not for those with delicate scruples or refined manners. From this vantage point it can be seen as a seedy tale with a sleazy cast: a bunch of snake-oil salesmen, hucksters and crooks fleecing millions of vulnerable Americans in an attempt to keep the housing bubble going, to make themselves fat commissions, to create new financial instruments that could be used as speculative plays on Wall Street, and to pick up property on the cheap when loans were foreclosed.

Others might argue, of course, that the boom was really about an innovative American financial services industry finding a way of providing loans so that those on relatively low incomes could join the property-owning democracy. But if this were so, why did do many borrowers lose their homes and become worse off than they had been before? As financial guru Fred Schwed had shrewdly asked in his 1940 classic on investment: 'Where are the customers' yachts?'

Although the sub-prime bubble had burst, some banks carried on issuing sub-prime mortgages, and this sort of lending still continues in the US today. Wells Fargo & Co. ignored a flagging market to become the biggest provider of sub-prime mortgages. And when other lenders were in retreat, Wells Fargo was still charging ahead, increasing its lending to the least credit-worthy buyers.

The sub-prime bonanza was a house-buying frenzy based on a totally false prospectus for which the banks were largely responsible. Their madcap lending brought misery to US home buyers, reverberated through financial markets around the world, damaged the property market and pushed economic expansion to an abrupt and dangerous halt. Common sense in terms of lending had gone out of the window, and the old banking aphorism that 'the trick was not lending money: it was getting it back' had been turned on its head.

But the effect of the banks' actions didn't end there. As if the dodgy mortgages were not sufficient, greedy banks had seen another way to make even more money by making sure that they didn't come to grief by holding useless bits of paper when the sub-prime 'day of reckoning' came. They devised a complicated wheeze to protect themselves: they would play 'pass the parcel' with their loans – which included credit card debt, student loans and much else besides – by selling them on in a disguised form to other investors. As one market analyst put it: 'In the Alice-in-Wonderland world of financial deregulation, a Wall Street bank could turn the loan into a bond; a credit rating agency using obscure alchemy could bless the bond with a triple-A rating; and some consenting adult could be found to buy it.'

It is what the banks did with the sub-prime loans that caused a financial crisis that spread far beyond America's shores. Regulators were reassured that because these sliced and diced, bundled up, sold-on loans were reaching right across the financial system there was no general risk to global stability. But the loans would become the second main link in a chain that not only brought about a crisis in the US property market but also led to the international credit crunch.

CHAPTER 3

Pass the Parcel

Banks and debt bundling

One bitterly cold day early in March 2007 an analyst's report flashed up on computer screens and landed on desks up and down Wall Street. It was intended to warm up the flagging mortgage market. The analyst, who worked at investment group Bear Stearns – which eventually became one of the biggest losers in the sub-prime debacle and the subject of a rescue by bankers J.P. Morgan Chase – issued an upbeat report on the prospects for California-based, sub-prime mortgage specialist New Century Financial. His over-the-top optimism chose to overlook two crucial facts: that the company had already disclosed that more and more borrowers were defaulting and that its shares had plunged to around $15, halving in value in three weeks.

This episode, with its blatant exaggerations and deceptions, sums up the complete folly of the sub-prime bonanza in America. Bear Stearns, like so many financial firms, had lost its moral compass. It had bet huge amounts of investors' cash on the sub-prime horse, yet at the same time it was extolling the virtues of investment in the deeply damaged American mortgage market, while being aware that the bank's very survival depended on the sub-prime crisis blowing over. What Bear Stearns was doing was nothing new for the investment banks, however. It echoed the last days of the dotcom boom seven years before, when analysts breathlessly urged investors to buy technology stocks just as the bottom was about to fall out of that market.

Not long after the Bear Stearns report was published, the inevitable happened. With the sub-prime crisis sending the housing market into freefall and taking the securities market with it, New Century – which describes itself as America's 'largest non-prime mortgage lender' – stopped offering loans and revealed that it needed emergency financing just to survive. Its shares collapsed to $3, and it was forced into protective bankruptcy on 2 April 2007, less than a month after the Bear Stearns analyst had been extolling its virtues.

Financial bubbles of the kind that led to the credit crunch are nothing new and can be traced back as far as the tulip bulb mania of the 17th century and even earlier. In his classic work *Manias, Panics and Crashes: A History of Financial Crises* MIT economist Charles Kindleberger describes the financial crisis as a 'hardy perennial' associated with the 'peaks of the business cycle'. At the peak of the boom all sense of reality is lost and speculation takes over. Crowd psychology drives people and firms into a feckless hunt for profits, and they borrow heavily to feed their financial addiction, leaving them totally exposed to collapse when the boom comes to an end. Most booms, Kindleberger observed, are fuelled by the expansion of money and by credit. This kind of monetary explosion has been seen on both sides of the Atlantic in the past decade.

When the technology bubble burst in 2000 Wall Street office shredders worked overtime to get rid of the wildly optimistic, wildly inaccurate and ultimately worthless share analyses – similar to that about New Century. As was the case in the dotcom boom, vast fortunes were made in the sub-prime bonanza, but this time the mania was based on the creation of highly questionable new securities, which in turn were based on home loans taken out by risky borrowers. The work of bullish stock and credit analysts for some of the same Wall Street firms that profited in the underwriting and rating of those investments lulled investors with upbeat pronouncements even as loan defaults ballooned. In both the 2000 dotcom boom and the sub-prime crises regulators stood on the sidelines, issued the most non-specific of warnings and did precious little to prevent the collapse.

Central to the housing boom in the US was the new form of residential financing – sub-prime borrowing. Its eventual collapse would prove more troubling than its dotcom predecessor because it would hit the real American economy of growth and jobs much harder than the dotcom crisis. It would also spread further and wider, until almost every Western financial institution was affected. The sub-prime bonanza helped to spawn the enormous $6.5 trillion mortgage securities market. This was a sum larger than the mighty official treasury market where the US government funds all of its operations, from the Pentagon to the social security safety net. At the heart of this mortgage boom there was, of course, a central paradox: how was it possible to make money by lending large sums to people who had not a hope in hell of paying it back? Sub-prime borrowers were, by definition, an appalling credit risk. Yet it was on this fragile base that a most elaborate financial superstructure was shabbily erected.

Exploiting a perceived gap in the market, a significant number of US banks moved away from traditional plain vanilla, prime mortgages with their low returns and turned to a new, sexy, multi-flavoured lending model. This model led to a new relationship between borrower and lender: the mortgage broker introduced buyers to the bank, which granted a loan, and the buyer then made monthly repayments. Unbeknown to the home buyer, however, the mortgage loans were being parcelled up by the banks into neat packages and sold on to investors. Loans made against that historically solid security bricks and mortar had been turned into readily traded assets, which, remarkably, offered high returns in an era of low interest rates. Endorsing these loans were the credit rating agencies – firms with solid and respected names like Standard & Poor's and Moody's – which lent their stamp of approval to packages of structured mortgage debt. The alchemy was now complete. Sub-prime mortgages had been disguised as first-class assets and, best of all, yielded far better returns than better quality debt.

After all, it was the banks that paid the credit rating agencies, not the consumers and investors they were meant to protect. The banks sold on the packaged mortgages to clients in the bond markets or created special units known as structured investment vehicles (SIVs), conduits or special purpose vehicles (SPVs) in which investors could park their money. SIVs were a useful device. Because they can be kept off the balance sheet, SIVs and conduits do not have to appear in the annual accounts and are notionally self-funding; they do not count against a bank's capital requirements for prudential purposes. Financial institutions can therefore expand their lending without putting undue strain on their capital, and in many cases, the shareholders, the ultimate owners of the banks, will be ignorant of their existence. In the summer of 2007 Halifax Bank of Scotland (HBOS), Britain's biggest mortgage lender, disclosed for the first time that it was stepping in to take Grampian, a conduit with £18 billion of commercial paper on its books, back on its balance sheet after it had encountered funding difficulties. Because it has a strong balance sheet, HBOS was able to handle the transaction and restore confidence in Grampian. But there is no escaping the fact that a financial institution that sells itself as a different kind of bank, focusing on the needs of the consumer, had blundered into a sophisticated area of finance without feeling the need fully to disclose either its decision or the amounts of cash tied up in the enterprise to its shareholders.

The whole sub-prime and securities process has been likened to meat processing. Because the low-priced, sub-prime cuts could not be sold over the counter, they were mixed up with other cuts, put through the grinder and made into sausages. These could then be sold, and the customers would be unaware of, or unconcerned about, their content. They ended up as assets in the balance sheets of banks like Britain's Alliance & Leicester, in the portfolios of investments held by insurance companies and pension funds, in money market funds and in mutual funds and unit trusts on both sides of the Atlantic. And, so the argument went, with these bits of meat spread around in lots of sausages, if there was a problem no single consumer would be seriously ill, even though a large number would have a stomach upset.

Not only were Wall Street banks skilled at securitisation, they were also adept at creating thousands of new products, known as credit derivatives, on the back of them. Among those at the forefront of all of this were some of the most famous names in investment banking, including American firms Lehman Brothers, Bear Stearns, Merrill Lynch and Morgan Stanley, and the Deutsche Bank of Germany and UBS of Switzerland. Tens of thousands of mortgages were placed in pools to spread out the risks and then divided into slices, known as tranches, based on quality.

The profits that could be made from packaging these securities and trading them on in these complex investment pools, known as collateralised debt obligations (CDOs), were phenomenal. At Lehman Brothers, for example, mortgage-related businesses contributed directly to record revenue and income. According to the Bond Market Association, the market for these mortgage-related securities, including those backed by home-equity loans (deals that allowed people to raise cash from the equity in their houses), peaked in 2003 at more than $3,000 billion.

Pooling risky sub-prime loans within loan portfolios at first mitigated the chances of defaulting loans hurting the bottom line. CDOs were, after all, neat, certified packages with a rich debt content, including corporate bonds and junk bonds – sub-prime was just one ingredient. CDOs also allowed investors to choose a level of return and risk. At the top of a CDO – where the best quality debts were held – were investors who accepted more modest returns for what they believed to be low risk. These top tranches were designed to be sound, even if a number of loans in the pool went bad. At the bottom were the tranches that were attractive to investors seeking the highest possible returns for the higher risk. These were also, of course, the ones most at risk if mortgage payers defaulted on their loans.

In the ever-present search for high yields it was the securities at the bottom of the pool, containing a high proportion of sub-prime mortgages, that proved most attractive. It was Wall Street's philosophy to give investors what they wanted rather than to offer unsolicited warnings about the quality of what they were buying. The dollar bills that came with surging profits and ever higher bonuses were too mesmerising to ignore. In the past, investment banks would not have considered anything as lowly as becoming involved in mortgages – that was for the lower order commercial banks and mortgage houses – but the opportunity was too tempting. If there were profits to be made lower down the chain, why should they not be shared? Mortgage companies were taken over in the name of synergy.

By directly soliciting the loans, investment banks were able to provide a ready supply of raw product for their existing packaging and sales operations. The ambition to reach ever further down the ownership chain continued right up to 2006, when the mortgage boom passed its peak. Morgan Stanley – a huge loser in sub-prime – bought Saxon Capital Inc., described in the press release as 'a premier servicer and originator of residential mortgages', for $706 million, and Merrill Lynch took over First Franklin Financial, 'one of the nation's leading originators of non-prime residential mortgage loans', for $1.3 billion. Even Goldman Sachs, which was one of the few investment banks to emerge from the credit crunch relatively unscathed, dipped its toes in the water. 'We were curious to better understand how the mortgage origination business worked,' a Goldman Sachs insider told me. However, as soon as Goldman Sachs realised what a quagmire the mortgage origination market had become, it secretly and unceremoniously disengaged from the business, offloading a bunch of duff loans on its rivals at the same time. Continental banks, too, jumped on the band wagon – banks like UBS, BNP Paribas and Deutsche Bank. Even small banks and insurers became willing holders of sub-prime-based packages because of the enticing returns.

So complex was the system that no one quite knows where all this structured debt has ended up. One senior British banker, whose company came seriously unstuck in the sub-prime imbroglio, told me: 'No one ultimately knows where the losses lie. So far [end of 2007] banks have written down $100 billion of losses out of an estimated $300 billion of bad loans. That means that there is at least $200 billion of bad stuff out there and I would not be surprised to find it had ended up with mutual funds.' (In fact, Ben Bernanke, chairman of the Federal Reserve, subsequently revised the potential loss from $300 billion to $500 billion; the IMF has put it even higher, at $945 billion.) Many mutual funds are favoured by smaller investors because they allegedly protect the holders from the higher risks associated with holding assets directly. It was the search for high yields, at a time of extraordinarily low interest rates, that made the sliced and diced sub-prime loans so attractive to investors.

To get an idea of how all this worked in practice, and to understand why it was built on such shaky foundations, take the fictional example of Mr and Mrs Jerome Smith of downtown Cleveland. They are persuaded by Fast Talking Mortgage Brokers Inc. (FTMB) to buy their shabby clapboard property with a $100,000 mortgage. The interest rate of 10 per cent is being waived for the first two years. In fact, interest has not been forgiven but is being rolled up with the original mortgage, increasing the debt to $120,000. FTMB, having taken an arrangement fee from the Smiths, then sells on the mortgage to Grasping Investment Bank (GIB) of New York, which pays the broker a commission for the mortgage. GIB wraps up the Smiths' loan with dozens of other loans to other Smiths from poor neighbourhoods around the country and renames it Smith Mortgage Obligation (SMO), and then it pays its favourite credit rating company, Stamped & Correct, to certify SMO as good quality debt. The attraction of this SMO or security is its 10 per cent return at a time when government bonds are paying between 2 and 3 per cent.

But rather than selling SMO directly to clients, GIB takes another route. It creates a new company – a special-purpose vehicle called GIB Capital – and this borrows from other banks cheaply and uses this money to buy Smith Mortgage Obligation. GIB then offers shares in GIB Capital, now the proud owner of SMO, to clients, who lap up the shares because of the high return.

Grasping Investment Bank benefits from the process in several ways. It has collected profits and commission on the sale of the SMO and also benefits from leverage (borrowing) because it is using someone else's money. GIB has also cleverly placed the SMO off its balance sheet in the special purpose vehicle, which it does not have to disclose on its accounts as a liability. It can stretch its capital further and will not have the regulator on its back.

Two years pass, and the Smiths in Cleveland receive a demand from Fast Mortgage Brokers for payment on what is now a $120,000 loan. Jerome's welfare payment has been cut, and there is no way the couple can meet the monthly charge. The warning letters start to appear, and three months later Nasty Collections arrive and threaten to throw the Smiths on to the street if they don't pay up within 14 days. In truth, the various Smith mortgages that make up SMO are rotten, but the people now holding them are none the wiser because their investment has the stamp of approval from Stamped & Correct to prove its quality.

But on 9 August 2007 GIB admits that it can no longer value SMO inside GIB Capital because so many of the underlying mortgages have gone wrong. The banks that had lent to GIB Capital call in the loans. Grasping Investment Bank admits that it has made a terrible mistake. It will be taking the assets of GIB Capital back on to its own books and writing them down to next to nothing. GIB is now in trouble, but never mind – the Federal Reserve, America's central bank, steps in to save it. The boss of GIB is forced to resign but is allowed under his contract to collect millions of dollars in compensation.

The whole edifice of securitisation was based on dodgy foundations like this. The very fact that original loans were hived off meant that lenders no longer had any clear responsibility for them, and by packaging the loans into parcels and gaining a credit rating for them the lenders managed to turn household mortgages into traded securities, which could be bought and sold on the open market, like shares or government stocks. Just how dodgy even the very first part of the foundations was is shown by a lender such as California-based Countrywide Financial Corporation. It looked perfectly respectable, but its model was based on a poorly designed incentive structure by which employees were rewarded with free shares (a scrip issue) if they induced target customers, often families with a disposal monthly income of just $1,000 a month, to take out loans. Nor surprisingly, Countrywide was among the earliest American casualties of the sub-prime crisis, coming close to bankruptcy in August 2007 before the Bank of America stepped in with a cash injection of $2 billion in exchange for preference shares. Depositors who wanted out were rapidly repatriated by the Federal Deposit Insurance Corporation (FDIC), thus preventing an unseemly retail run of the kind that took place at Northern Rock. So rotten was Countrywide's loan book that it was still close to collapse in early 2008 as America's worst housing market in a generation fuelled new concern. Bank of America boss Kenneth Lewis stepped in for a second time, taking over the fast-sinking lender for $4 billion.

For a while, though the system appeared to be working well. Everybody took on a fraction of the risk, and all seemed well in the sub-prime meat plant. New borrowers got their homes; brokers and banks made money up front; and investors received the higher returns they longed for in a low interest rate environment. There seemed to be winners all round. The investment banks were re-cycling the surplus savings in the world, most of them owned by the emerging market economies of Asia and the Middle East, into the poorest sections of US society – America's very own third world. And bankers continued to draw their bonuses.

In Britain Northern Rock did not have enough retail or high-rolling, long-term savers to fund Adam Applegarth's fast-expanding mortgage book. So the ambitious chief executive bought into the new model. He determined to raise the cash he needed to expand the Rock's loan book by turning to the money markets and using the complex financial techniques beloved of the American banks. Northern Rock's loans were generally better secured than those in the US because they were based on good quality mortgages with low default rates, but when all hell broke loose in August 2007 the distinction between good quality mortgage securities and sub-prime toxic debt was not one that the panicked markets recognised.

Northern Rock's main funding came from Granite, a Jersey-based financing vehicle set up as a trust, through which it raised half of its resources. Mortgages to the value of £49 billion, taken out by ordinary British families, were siphoned off into Granite. These home loans would be parcelled up and turned into traded securitised bonds, providing the funds for a new round of lending by the Rock. A second technique used by the Rock from 2004 onwards was to turn mortgages into so-called covered bonds and keep them on its own balance sheet. It all looked safe enough, especially as the Rock's mortgages were generally solid, but it did mean that the former building society, which lacked the sophisticated Treasury expertise of Britain's high street banks, had become hooked on footloose finance, which could vanish as quickly as it arrived.

The first signs of the cracks that would eventually cause the whole building to totter came with the early reports of mortgage defaults and arrears throughout America in 2003. Foolish loans made shortly before and after the millennium had started to go wrong, but lenders and the investment banks, with their insatiable demand for high-yielding securities, turned a blind eye. This line of business was far too good to be switched off by a few poor Americans being cast out from their homes. As the bad debts started to accumulate, there were fewer lenders. Fewer lenders meant it was harder to get loans; nevertheless, the locomotive rolled on.

In his pre-retirement appearance at the monetary conference held at Jackson Hole, Wyoming, in August 2005, the chairman of the Federal Reserve, Alan Greenspan, offered a foretaste of the trials ahead. In one of his most forthright warnings since he had railed against 'irrational exuberance' in 1996, just as the technology boom was taking off, he told the gathered central bankers and economists that people were investing in houses as if they were a one-way bet and were not allowing for the risks of house price falls. 'History has not dealt kindly with investors who kept ignoring risks,' he said.

But Wall Street and bankers across the globe were not really listening and would later seek to blame Greenspan and his low interest rate regime for its own serial mistakes. This became known as the 'Greenspan put' (as in a put option that allows an investor to sell shares at an advantageous price even when they have fallen below it), because in the eyes of the critics it encouraged the very same one-way bet he was warning against, a bet on never-ending low interest rates and rising house prices. In a conversation with me in Washington, D.C., in September of 2007 Greenspan, as intellectually rigorous as ever, firmly rejected this interpretation of events. It was fears of recession and deflation that led him to keep interest rates low after 9/11, and Wall Street, with its voracious appetite for yield, that drove sub-prime lending.

Before leaving office in January 2006 Greenspan began the process of returning interest rates to a more natural rate amid concerns that inflation was starting to build. The key American federal funds rate began to rise again in the summer of 2005 and was like an arrow aimed at the housing balloon. The residential market suddenly stalled, tens of thousands of homes were repossessed and 'For Sale' signs sprang up like weeds across the United States. The vast housing construction sites on the edge of America's cities gradually ground to a halt. The residential market, which, along with car sales, has long been a driver of America's economy, was now caught in a vicious downward spiral.

Arrears mounted among sub-prime borrowers. By 2006 13 per cent had fallen behind with their payments, and eviction misery reached right across America. None more so than in Stockton, California, which gained the reputation as the USA's 'foreclosure capital'. In 2005 alone the banks repossessed over 8,000 properties – accounting for one in every 27 households in the town. Miami, Detroit and Las Vegas – areas where sub-prime lending had surged – suffered from high foreclosure rates, too.

But there was an extraordinary mismatch between the reality of what was happening on the ground and the behaviour of house prices and Wall Street. Indeed, it was not until early 2006 that the high-water point of the housing boom was reached. With investors still showing a strong appetite for mortgage-backed securities, lenders continued to relax their underwriting standards, and sub-prime borrowing went on, despite the flood of foreclosures. That summer some observers did warn of the worst housing recession in decades and its financial fallout in the mortgage market. Some likened it to watching a train crash in slow motion. Even so, the prevailing wisdom was still that any sub-prime problem would not affect the better secured mortgages or spill over into the credit market and the wider economy. How could a crisis that erupted in America's trailer parks and poorest estates be expected to have an impact on the people whom novelist Tom Wolfe had called the 'Masters of the Universe', people who lived comfortably in their luxury apartments on the Upper East Side of Manhattan and enjoyed the good life in exclusive beach houses on the Hamptons? Little did they suspect that their comfortable world, cosseted from the reality of the continental United States, was about to come apart at the seams.

The cutbacks by lenders were increasing, and by early 2007 housing activity began to falter again while the rises in arrears and fore-closures escalated. Defaults on loans issued just 12 months earlier were rising at their sharpest rate in history as an abrupt end to the housing boom curbed the ability of the riskiest borrowers to refinance their homes. The stupidity of the lending practices was becoming evident for all to see, but no one was really aware of where this was going to end.

Then there was a bombshell. In February 2007 the new chairman of HSBC, the lay preacher and alumnus of McKinsey & Co. Stephen Green, revealed to shocked investors that for the first time in the history of the 142-year-old bank it would not meet profits forecasts and was writing down its sub-prime loan book by a massive $10.6 billion (£5 billion). Green was being refreshingly honest, and HSBC was among the first of the major Western banks to reveal the scale of the problem now stalking the financial world. Yet the markets did not seem to be watching.

This was not the end of HSBC's troubles. In November 2007 it revealed another $3.4 billion of write-downs. The American adventure had turned into a disaster for a bank that clearly had no idea what it was getting into when it initially purchased Household Financial Inc. in March 2003 and allowed executives to plunge into mortgage origination. It was only because of HSBC's vast scale and global reach that it was able to absorb the losses from its foolish adventure in the highly volatile American credit markets.

US lender New Century Financial, which had relaxed its underwriting standards in a bid to preserve its volume of business, reported larger than expected losses and on 2 April filed for Chapter 11 bankruptcy, announcing that 3,200 jobs would have to go. Meanwhile, Freddie Mac – the government-guaranteed supplier of mortgages – revealed that it could no longer buy those sub-prime mortgages that were most sensitive to increases in interest rates and that were, therefore, the most likely to suffer foreclosure. It would invest in mortgages only where a borrower made the highest possible monthly payments, so minimising the risk of arrears and defaults. One of the last lines of defence, the government-backed secondary market, had been removed from the equation.

Distress signals were now going off all over the place. The following month, D.R. Horton, America's largest house builders, warned of huge losses from the sub-prime fallout. In May – in a foretaste of much worse to come – Swiss bank UBS closed its American sub-prime lending arm, Dillon Read Capital. It was now obvious that some big players were affected, particularly those that had blithely decided to play directly in the mortgage market, cutting out the middle men. But the full dimensions of what was happening and the financial trickery in which most of the big investment banks had been involved were still wrapped in mystery.

The American banks faced huge losses from the sub-prime melt-down, but they were not alone – the sub-prime mess had been exported overseas, and banks across Continental Europe and in Britain were affected too. The potential losses ran into hundreds of billion dollars, but no one could really tell because of the way the sub-prime loans had been converted from conventional mortgages into exotic financial instruments, such as SIVs.

Banks initially denied that they owned these SIVs and sought to disclaim liability for any losses, but it was clear that they had a moral responsibility to the clients who had invested in these funds. Regulators started to place pressure on them to own up to their expo-sures, and many were forced to take them back on to their balance sheets, picking up huge bills along the way. The stock market began to react to the scale of the catastrophe befalling the financial world, and by the summer of 2007 shares in the major banks were falling fast. Merrill Lynch shares slumped by 15 per cent from their January high, Morgan Stanley and Citigroup fell almost 13 per cent, while Goldman Sachs dropped nearly 10 per cent. This was just the start of a revaluation of banking shares that would eventually see the stocks of some of the most blue-blooded banks decimated and their leaders going cap in hand to wealthy Gulf and Far Eastern investors for bail-outs.

The truth was finally dawning elsewhere. Credit ratings agencies, which had played a huge part in the sub-prime saga by giving debt parcels far higher ratings than they deserved, finally decided that a dose of reality was needed. Fitch Ratings and Standard & Poor's issued downgrades for sub-prime-linked debt. Although this was the right thing to do, their timing was unfortunate because it made much of the sub-prime debt look even more toxic than had been recognised.

At the height of the boom the agencies had conferred the highest AAA (triple-A) rating on packages of mortgage-backed securities, even though they were clueless about the poisonous mixture of debt inside those packages. Now, these securities were downgraded to three Bs, the second lowest grade. There was a feeling that securities taken out in 2006 and now given a triple-B rating would soon be little better than junk. I was shocked when one shrewd hedge fund analyst in London told me during a business lunch, in a dining room overlooking the lush gardens of Buckingham Palace, that he had conducted his own audit of some of the asset-backed securities that Britain's banks were still holding in their balances sheets. In some cases large parcels of the collateralised debt obligations (CDOs) held were worth just a few cents in the pound. They were close to worthless.

Despite this, several banks sought to maintain the fiction that they had been ruthless in marking down their value to reflect the new reality. Clearly they had not and were vainly hoping that by the time they next reported to investors values would have started to recover and the losses would be less severe. This was both disingenuous and misleading at a time when politicians and regulators were demanding openness and transparency.

Bond-holders, including pension funds, that had bought sub-prime mortgage bonds were also suffering huge losses. These fell sharply – between 20 and 40 per cent – in value in 2007 for most classes of asset, even those considered safe by the ratings agencies. If banks were to be forced to reveal losses based on current prices, their losses would be even greater. In early 2008 it was estimated by the Group of Seven finance ministers that the losses suffered by all financial institutions involved could eventually be as high as $400 billion.

In the bond markets, too, Wall Street's biggest and best were being marked down. The price of credit default swaps (CDS), the insurance contracts used to protect investors against non-paying bonds, leapt. In the first six months of 2007 the cost of CDS insurance on Goldman Sachs's debt rose by 52 per cent. The market thought that this debt had become riskier, even though the company had developed a smart strategy that saw it quietly exiting from sub-prime in early 2007, at the expense of its rivals.

High summer of 2007 saw great nervousness among investment bankers about their own finances even though Wall Street – and the City of London for that matter – had earned record sums in the previous 12 months. No one was quite clear where the real risk in the financial system lay, so everyone was tainted in the same way: the guilty, the innocent and those simply on the sidelines. The big players began to look insecure, with global asset values tumbling as the flood of easy money started to dry up in the face of rising interest rates in Japan, higher real rates in the US, the threat of rising rates in Switzerland and a jump in UK rates in July 2007. The market was becoming increasingly concerned about potential losses. Huge amounts of money had been made by selling mortgage-backed securities. However, the actual risk of mortgage default was going to be borne by a far larger group of institutions, and no one was quite sure who would be left holding the bad debt when the music stopped.

A sign of this disruption was the fact that traders in the leading financial houses began to mark down their own shares, with Goldman Sachs, Lehman Brothers and Bear Stearns on Wall Street and Deutsche Bank and the Credit Suisse Group in London suffering particularly from market contagion. Quite simply, their exposure to sub-prime was known to be great and credits were going bad. Worse still, some investment banks also kept back a little of these asset-backed insecurities for themselves. At Bear Stearns this was calculated to equal about 13 per cent of the firm's 'tangible equity'.

The investment banks were also suppressing commissioned

reports that revealed growing risks in sub-prime loans. Amid the housing frenzy, and in a bid to keep up with the market, many Wall Street firms ignored due-diligence warnings about problem mortgages. They eased the guidelines that these firms followed in checking that mortgages conformed to certain standards. As a result, investors were starved of vital information and failed to understand the true nature of the mortgages that formed the underlying assets. As August arrived and the bankers headed for the Hamptons and their yachts in the Mediterranean and Caribbean, the fallout from the sub-prime collapse was becoming increasingly apparent in the US. The facts seemed pretty clear.

In early August there were signs that the financial misery was likely to persist in those areas where sub-prime loans had surged. It was thought that many loans would be at risk of going bad in 2008 as they were reset to higher rates, causing more borrowers to fall behind with their payments. Indeed, in the hardest hit areas the numbers could batter borrowers, lenders and builders for years to come. As for lenders, it seemed that the story would go on for a good deal longer. They can be forced to buy back bad loans if it can be proved that the borrower was never remotely able to make monthly repayments or if the loan application involved any fraud, such as falsifying income. It is now becoming clear that there was fraud on a pretty massive scale. There will be more mortgage lenders filing for bankruptcy and, no doubt, some class-action lawsuits.

Industry repossession figures far outstripped the White House's official estimate of 500,000. This heightened concern that slumping house prices would shatter consumer confidence, causing a drop in high street spending and pushing the USA into recession. That prospect was not made any less likely when Congress estimated that in all $103 billion would be lost by homeowners; that 2 million sub-prime mortgages were expected to increase in cost; and that $917 million was likely to be lost by states in property taxes. Democrat Senator Charles Schumer commented: 'From New York to California, we are headed for billions in lost wealth, property values and tax revenues. The current tidal wave of foreclosures will soon turn into a tsunami of losses and debt for families and communities.' The feckless lending and unacceptable level of foreclosures would prove a ripe issue for Hillary Clinton and Barack Obama, the leading Democrats slugging it out for the 2008 presidential nomination.

Only the rapacious bankers made money out of these devastating events. In the case of the blue-blooded Morgan Stanley bonus pay and bonus levels shot up to $16.55 billion in 2007, some 60 per cent of the investment bank's income. This was despite the fact that it had dropped a cool $9.4 billion in the sub-prime market, making the first quarterly loss in its history. The group's chief executive John Mack, known as 'Mack the Knife' for his ruthlessness in cutting jobs, had waived his bonus for 2007, but this was hardly self-sacrifice since he collected a $40 million payout in 2006, a year in which Morgan Stanley was up to its neck in sub-prime dealings.

Raghuram Rajan, Professor of Finance at the University of Chicago and a former chief economist of the IMF, remarked early in 2008: 'Compensation practices in the financial sector are deeply flawed and probably contributed to the ongoing crisis.' Greed had triumphed over the traditional banking virtue of prudence.

The sub-prime meltdown was devastating for lenders, for the property industry and for the record number of families throughout the United States who lost their homes. It was morally reprehensible that the poorest people in America had been exploited by those who had the most. But it was a much bigger crisis than that. The toxic debt built on the rickety foundations of sub-prime had been turned into investment quality bonds and exported to every corner of the globe. Assets held in banks, insurance companies, pension funds as well as in exotic off-balance sheet funds were decimated, and investors and savers everywhere suffered.

The capacity of capitalism for self-deception and manias was once again fuelled, as has been true across the centuries, by the availability of easy money. The globalisation of the world economy has brought with it huge benefits in terms of more open trade and cheaper production, but it has also allowed US bankers to export the results of their greed and mistakes. The toxic fallout from the implosion of America's sub-prime residential market did not stop at the water's edge of the Atlantic or the Pacific. When the rest of the globe finally woke up to the crisis in August 2007, it would quickly become evident that global financial markets were in deep trouble. As Rachel Lomax, the shrewd and plain-speaking Deputy Governor of the Bank of England, observed the world was facing the worst peacetime cash crisis since the Second World War.

In April 2008 the International Monetary Fund went a step further in the spring edition of its highly regarded 'World Economic Outlook', shockingly describing the events surrounding the credit crunch as 'the worst financial crisis since the Great Depression'.

CHAPTER 4

When the Lending Stopped

9 August 2007:
The day the markets froze

Thursday, 9 August 2007 dawned like any other quiet summer's day in the world's financial centres. The City of London and Frankfurt were dry and cloudy. Even New York was not as hot and humid as is normal in August. The dealing rooms in the big investment banks flickered to life in the usual way – although, because it was August, trading seemed less frenetic and there were more empty desks. And on the upper floors, from where the Masters of the Universe normally plied their trade, there was an eerie silence. Bankers put aside the concerns that had pulsed through financial markets since the spring and went on their annual leave. But as the sun shone and they cavorted in swimming pools in St Tropez or skippered yachts off Cape Cod, nasty things were happening behind their backs.

It was not unusual. August is often a tricky month for finance. The run on the pound that eventually led to Britain's humiliating exit from the exchange rate mechanism (ERM) on 16 September 1992, Black Wednesday, and led to a calamitous loss of confidence in John Major's Conservative government, began in August. Six years later the devaluation of the Russian rouble, which was to trigger the meltdown at the super hedge fund Long Term Capital Management, took place in the same month, paving the way for Boris Yeltsin's eventual replacement by hardliner Vladimir Putin. In the words of novelist Edna O'Brien, 'August is a Wicked Month'. And August 2007 was no exception.

Jean-Claude Trichet, the publicly austere Frenchman who heads the European Central Bank (ECB) in Frankfurt, was holidaying in his favourite spot of St Malo, the rocky seaport where he skippers motor and sailing boats. Trichet, like any banker worth his salt, was accompanied by his Blackberry but, in common with many of his generation, was not entirely certain what to do when it started bleeping and flashing madly. Like most central bankers, Trichet is someone who plays it by the book and, being highly traditional, feels more comfortable with the fax and mobile phone, technology of a slightly earlier generation. At the same time, he is savvy enough to know precisely what to do when the markets turn sour.

Trichet might have escaped briefly to the beach, but he was still better prepared than his counterparts at the Bank of England and the Federal Reserve. Mervyn King, the assiduous Governor of the Bank of England, an owlish intellectual who thinks in whole sentences, was still at his desk overlooking the courtyard of the solid Bank building in the heart of the City of London. He was sheltered behind architect and designer Sir John Soane's famed curtain wall. Like his American counterpart Ben Bernanke, King could not entirely desert his post in August, since both the US and UK central banks hold interest rate decision meetings at the start of the month.

Nerves had been jangling on the financial markets for several months, with the sub-prime losses revealed by British bank HSBC in the early part of the year only a sign of things to come. Tension was growing at America's new-wave mortgage lenders New Century and Countrywide Financial, which were up to their necks in fore-closures and finding it increasingly difficult to fund operations. In Paris France's largest bank BNP Paribas was struggling to work out the value of billions of euros of sub-prime mortgages held in off-balance sheet investment funds it controlled. And in Germany the authorities were acting behind the scenes to prevent a developing cash crisis at several of its second-line banks from infecting the larger commercial banks that were essential to the smooth operations of the financial system.

Financial markets are driven by electronic pulses that are the collective wisdom of tens of thousands of traders, who, in turn, act on the information they have on their screens, the terse conversations and message exchanges they have with colleagues and, finally, sheer instinct. The fabulous salaries and bonuses they collect reflect their ability to read the runes and take positions valued at tens of millions of pounds within seconds of receiving the vital intelligence. On 9 August the system appeared to be broken. Distrust was in the air. The paper and promises of even the world's biggest banks no longer looked fully secure. The wire services, which monitor the markets for financial players and the media, started to go crazy. Market interest rates, the price at which money changes hands among banks, soared to more than one point above the official rates at which banks lend to each other. No one was going to be doing business at these kinds of elevated rates. The world's financial plumbing was starting to seize up as it had on Black Monday, 19 October 1987, when the stock market crashed, and on 9/11, when terrorists struck at the heart of Wall Street.

The world's financial capitals in London, New York and Frankfurt were about to witness the most dramatic 24 hours in the whole international credit crisis. On 9 August the full exposure of major European banks to sub-prime was revealed, causing the world's finance system to glue up and leaving central banks to pump in vast sums of money to avoid its total meltdown.

The first public signs of serious distress had come a week earlier, on 2 August, when three German banks revealed severe problems arising from their exposure to sub-prime loans. IKB Deutsche Industriebank, Sachsen LB and West LB were near to collapse from the strain of losses on mortgage-based investments. The first of these, IKB, was a lender to one in ten of Germany's small to medium-sized companies, but, growing over-ambitious, it had looked elsewhere for higher yields and became deeply committed to the US property market. The German magazine *Der Spiegel* reported that IKB and its affiliates had run up an amazing $10 billion of loans in the US mortgages sector.

German authorities moved rapidly to stem the crisis, acting in sharp contrast to what would happen at Northern Rock in Britain just a few weeks later. An emergency 3.5 billion euros bail-out, underwritten by a consortium of banks, was assembled. It involved Germany's main player, Deutsche Bank, and was organised by the Bundesbank (Germany's central bank) and the state-owned KfW Group development bank, which had a 38 per cent stake in IKB. As immediate investigations began into the IKB affair, both its chief executive officer and chief finance officer resigned. This was not the end, however: IKB needed two further funding rescues in the months that followed. Karl Nolle, a member of the Saxon state parliament, commented: 'The IKB affair was the result of disastrous decisions by the bank and the state government.'

The second German bank in difficulties was Sachsen LB, one of Germany's old regional Landesbanken. Over the decades the Landesbanken had often overstretched themselves as they sought to shed their old-fashioned regional image. Sachsen, based in Saxony, had become one of Europe's biggest operators of off-balance sheet funds. Suddenly it was playing in a league with global players, such as British bank HSBC, which had 25 times its equity. An investigation by the *Financial Times* revealed that much of Sachsen LB's sub-prime exposure was connected with its investment offshoot, a Dublin-based company, Ormonde Quay. Various sub-prime loans in Ormonde Quay's portfolio were over-rated and when creditors began to call in their loans at the same time, Sachsen, having guaranteed the loans, was forced to come to their aid. The bank could not meet its obligations and, in turn, needed rescuing via a 17 billion euros credit line from a consortium of banks. Sachsen was later taken over for a paltry 300 million euros by its biggest rival, LBBW (Landesbank Baden-Württemberg).

The third bank in trouble was West LB, the state bank of North

Rhine Westphalia, which was also rescued after reporting difficulties arising from US sub-prime loans. West LB had a history of over-ambition and had become deeply involved in leveraged buy-out deals and private equity in the cut-throat City of London. The bank's boss, Alexander Stulmann, believed that the German banking system was in a 'critical situation'. There were other signs of instability, too. On 3 August Union Investment, Germany's third biggest mutual fund manager, stopped withdrawals from one of its funds after investors pulled out 10 per cent of the assets, while Frankfurt Trust, mutual fund manager of the private, Frankfurt-based BHF-Bank, halted redemptions from one fund after clients removed 20 per cent of their money. Germany had famously been highly critical of the get-rich-quick culture of private equity, hedge funds and investment banking, labelling them 'locusts' and seeking to tighten up on regulation. Yet even as ministers were looking to do this, it was estimated that the German banks were nursing 'trailer trash' securities worth as much as £54 billion.

In the space of just seven days, these German banks had come clean about the extent of their sub-prime exposure and the terrible mess they were in. Jochen Sanio, head of the German regulator BaFin, admitted that the country was going through its worst banking crisis for over 70 years. Having lived through the terrible effects of hyperinflation and the chain reaction of runs on banks during the Weimar Republic, German banking regulators and the healthy banks were taking no chances that the financial system would implode. They moved with remarkable speed and skill to shore things up, ignoring the petty bureaucracy of European Union rules governing subsidies and riding roughshod over the rights of investors. It was a case of addressing the immediate cash needs and worrying about the consequences afterwards – unlike in Britain, the German regulators were not caught like rabbits in the headlights. A bank collapse 'could create difficulties for confidence and economic growth,' Peter Steinbruck, the German finance minister, remarked in the spring of 2008.

The German authorities regarded the rescue of the three banks as vital because of their central role in the economy. Any bank failure would have a knock-on effect, bringing about a system-wide crisis and huge economic disruption. Even so, the need to rescue the banks did raise serious questions about the regulatory process – about the ability of those who own, supervise and manage public banks to understand and monitor the activities of specialist offshoots dealing in mortgage-backed securities packages.

Events in Germany, however, proved to be just the prelude. What really precipitated a disaster was the revelation on 9 August by French heavyweight BNP Paribas that three of its investment funds worth 2 billion euros, with 700 million euros of sub-prime related investments, were now in trouble, having fallen in value by one-fifth over the previous two weeks. So bad was the scare that BNP admitted that it did not have a clue about how much the investments held in these funds were worth. The level of ignorance and the apparent lack of understanding and regulation give us some insight into how, some five months later, Jérôme Kerviel, a rogue trader at Société Générale (SocGen), could go on a mad gambling spree in which he bet the capital of the whole bank on the recovery of European stock markets. When his trades went disastrously wrong, it left SocGen nursing losses of £3.7 billion, in addition to an enormous write-down of sub-prime loans.

With a complete collapse of demand for the type of securitised debt held by the three BNP funds – Parvest Dynamic ABS, BNP Paribas ABS Eonia and BNP Paribas ABS Euribor – the Paris bank could not properly value the fund assets, even though they carried credit ratings of AA or higher. BNP blamed the 'complete evaporation of liquidity in certain market segments of the US securitisation market' for temporarily halting redemptions on the three funds. It immediately suspended the three funds, arguing it was the best way to protect the interests of investors. Commenting on the move, one money manager echoed former US Defense Secretary Donald Rumsfeld's feelings about the Iraq invasion: 'There are known unknowns and unknown unknowns. Now we are discovering that there are a lot more unknown unknowns than anyone thought.'

Interestingly, a few weeks before the funds' suspension, the bank's chief executive officer, Baudouin Prot, said its exposure to US subprime was 'absolutely negligible' when the bank reported a second-quarter rise in net income. The announcement on 9 August that the funds were being suspended hit the European stock markets hard, and BNP's shares tumbled by 6.5 per cent, valuing the bank at 77.3 billion euros.

The day before, on the evening of 8 August, Trichet travelled to France for a long-planned, one-day leave from the office. But over breakfast in his St Malo home he must have been contemplating the turmoil ahead – a feeling confirmed by a telephone call from colleagues attending the bank's executive board meeting at the ECB's Eurotower headquarters in the heart of Frankfurt's Kaiserstrasse. They brought news of BNP's fund suspension and the extreme volatility of the markets.

Trichet, a former governor of the Banque de France, knew only too well that for financial markets to function properly securities had to be cheap and easy to buy and sell. On the rare occasions when they fail to operate, liquidity rapidly dries up and the markets cease to function. This was the case now. The summer's credit squeeze had worsened considerably. The credit crunch had arrived and it was time to act. The problem was how to handle it. European bankers had traditionally adopted a 'hands-off' approach to banking crises, concerned not to cause what is termed 'moral hazard' – that is, they want to make sure that financial institutions bear the full consequences of their actions. The fear is that, knowing they could be rescued by central banks, lenders might act recklessly. Moral hazard, as it transpired, was this time an issue that concerned the Bank of England alone.

The ECB regulated liquidity in the markets, but, unlike the US Federal Reserve, it did not inject or withdraw funds on a daily basis.

It usually conducted fine-tuning from time to time, when it would carry out its liquidity regulation. What made its moves on 9 August highly unusual was that it did not coincide with any planned cash injections. Since the ECB began operations in 1999 it had largely adopted the practices it had inherited from the deeply traditional German central bank, the Bundesbank. It also had wide and little used powers derived from the central banks that made up the membership of its board. These allowed it to accept mortgages as collateral from commercial banks in exchange for cash injections, a facility not available either to the Bank of England or to the Federal Reserve at that time.

The ECB was disdainful of the quick fixes used by what it regarded as the Anglo-Saxon economies of the US and Britain to hold off recession. If the choice was between controlling inflation and lowering the growth rate it would always opt for the latter. It monitored the money supply – the expansion in the amount of cash and credit across the eurozone – carefully and cautiously and was not given to sudden rushes of blood.

But to the ECB team this time was different: it was a crisis that required special action, and there could be no further delay in moving into the markets to calm the volatility. After consulting Trichet, ECB officials decided to intervene immediately by opening an eye-watering 96.8 billion euros ($130 billion) line of credit into the overnight money market. It was an extraordinary decision and one that caught financial observers totally by surprise. Large amounts of cash would now be pumped into the eurozone, making funding available to commercial banks and so alleviating any shortages due to the unprecedented demand for money. This huge hunger for money had forced overnight interest rates to rise to an unacceptable 4.7 per cent, far above the bank's target 4 per cent.

By pumping liquidity into the market, the ECB sought to ease the first signs of the credit crunch, although its public utterances were that it was seeking to 'assure orderly conditions in the euro money market'. The level of the initial injection far exceeded the

ECB's only previous intervention after 9/11, when it lent 69 billion euros followed by 40 billion euros over subsequent days. Even more notable was its one-day pledge to offer unlimited support – that is, to meet 100 per cent of all funding from financial institutions. The scale of the ECB's intervention gave everyone involved in the markets an enormous jolt. If the super-cautious ECB was behaving like a lottery winner, conditions must be really appalling. After a highly nervous day on the markets, during which 49 banks took up the offer, it became clear that more money was needed. The following day the ECB ploughed in an additional $84 billion to soothe the continent's shaky banking system. Even so, the markets were still unsettled after the weekend, so the bank added 47 billion euros ($65 billion) on Monday, 13 August, and 25 billion euros ($32 billion) the next day.

Bruce Kasman, economist at bankers J.P. Morgan, concluded: 'The concern that short-term liquidity for financial institutions might dry up became something of a reality in European markets. The drying up of short-term liquidity to financial institutions is a more serious concern to central banks than the shutdown in term credit financing. As a result, the ECB took action to protect the functioning of the Euro area money markets.'

The level and speed of the ECB's intervention was completely unprecedented and, in total, it was three times as much as the Federal Reserve would commit to the US market. Europe's liquidity problems spilled over to the US, where the benchmark federal funds rate moved 0.5 per cent above the Fed's target rate of 5.25 per cent in early trading on 9 August. The Fed's overall line to begin with was that the situation was not too serious. Indeed, only two days previously its board of governors had decided to leave interest rates unchanged, issuing a statement that inflation, rather than financial instability, was the greater threat to the US economy. But with shares on Wall Street plunging 387 points, at just before 8.30 a.m. the Fed, led by its unseasoned chairman Ben Bernanke, was forced to inject liquidity into the American markets.

The Fed's Open Market Trading Desk – known as the Desk – pumped in $24 billion in two scheduled open-market operations. This was not a huge amount, compared with similar operations after 9/11 when it was difficult to trade even US Treasury securities, usually the most liquid of markets. The Fed immediately put out a statement:

> The Federal Reserve is providing liquidity to facilitate the orderly functioning of financial markets. The Federal Reserve will provide reserves as necessary through open market operations to promote trading in the federal funds market at rates close to the Federal Open Market Committee's target rate of 5.25 per cent. In current circumstances, depository institutions may experience unusual funding needs because of dislocations in money and credit markets. As always, the discount window is available as a source of funding.

This was about as close as Bernanke could go to promising the banks a cheap ride. He was not going to risk presiding over a chain reaction of US banking collapses reminiscent of the Great Depression, on which he was one of the world's greatest experts. The Fed system had been created largely to prevent a cascading series of crashes from crippling the American economy, and as chairman he would do what was necessary to keep the US growing. His predecessor, Alan Greenspan, had told me in September 2007 that in financial panics you should not worry about punishing 'the greedy and the egregious'. The job of the Fed was to do all in its power to prevent collapse. The more collegiate Bernanke was following in the maestro's footsteps.

However, the Fed's intervention failed to do the trick, and the next day, after Asian and European markets had plunged further, the Fed decided another $38 billion was needed. It came in three operations – $19 billion in the morning, $16 billion in early afternoon and $3 billion towards the end of the day – creating the feeling that it was monitoring the markets hour by hour before reacting. These funds were pumped into the system via repurchase agreements known as 'repos'. A repurchase agreement is a short-term collateralised loan in which a security is exchanged for cash, on the understanding that the transaction will be reversed for an agreed price on an agreed date. The Desk does such trades almost daily, with most agreements being overnight, although some are for as long as 14 days.

What happened on Friday, 10 August, however, was highly unusual. The $38 billion pumped into the system by the Fed was entirely directed at purchasing mortgage-backed securities, which might, otherwise, have had no buyers. Normally, when the Desk sends out a message it tells dealers exactly what it wants in collateral. Each category of collateral – Treasury, agency and mortgage-backed securities – is treated separately. On 10 August the Desk merely said that it would accept whatever the dealers wanted to deliver. Obviously, the move was designed to show that it considered mortgage-backed securities as good collateral and that the authorities were trying to get the financial markets to value mortgage pools sensibly. And as mortgage-backed securities were the cheapest to deliver – having the lowest price in the market – that's precisely what the Desk received. This was an episode that was to be repeated in March 2008, when the Fed, in common with other central banks, pumped enormous sums into the markets to boost liquidity in return for whatever collateral was on offer.

The two-day Fed rescue operation totalled $62 billion and was a powerful indication of Bernanke's concern. It was on a somewhat smaller scale than the interventions after the 9/11 attacks on New York, when there had been a one-week daily average of $75 billion and a single-day record of $81.25 billion. But the August intervention would not be enough. In the coming months far more dramatic steps would be needed as the whole American banking system teetered on the edge of a precipice.

With two of the major central banks committed to action, the spotlight fell on London. Here the Bank of England had decided to stick to its normal policy of inaction. The Governor, Mervyn King, did not believe in pumping liquidity willy-nilly into markets to get banks out of trouble. King's approach was different from that of his counterparts because of his concern about 'moral hazard'. He wanted to avoid a situation in which banks took too many risks because they were certain that the central bank would intervene to rescue them.

The Bank of England was the only one of the world's leading central banks to take this approach, and it found itself under strong fire in the City for its seeming indifference to a once-in-a-lifetime financial event. King and his colleagues took an altogether tougher line on the seizing up of the inter-bank markets and decided not to change the system that was broadly agreed with the London banks. Instead of the Bank pumping cash into the inter-bank market, any bank in London that was short of cash had to lodge bids for extra reserves, for which it would pay a penalty charge of one point above the official bank rate.

The system was fine in principle, but in the crisis conditions in which banks found themselves it backfired. When the mighty Barclays Bank twice found itself short of cash in August, it was identified by its competitors and immediately 'stigmatised' in the press, suffering a sharp fall in its share price as a result. Instead of contributing to stability, the carefully calibrated system put in place by the Bank of England perversely added to the volatility, jumpiness and fear that were stalking the City of London, which was far and away Europe's dominant financial centre.

When the crisis broke, King was at his desk in Threadneedle Street, not least because his deputy in charge of monetary stability, the aloof former Home Office civil servant Sir John Gieve, was away on leave because of a family bereavement. Gieve, who was in contact by telephone, was later questioned by MPs about his absence at such a sensitive moment. He said that he had asked the Governor if he should return to work immediately but had been told it was not necessary. Gieve's stuttering performance before MPs in the Treasury Select Committee some weeks later did not inspire confidence. It came as no major surprise when, months later, the Committee recommended the creation of a new all-powerful post of 'Deputy Governor of the Bank of England and Head of Financial Stability' with the powers and ability to operate across the spectrum of government in the case of financial emergencies.

Unlike his colleagues at the ECB and the Federal Reserve, King was not aware of any specific problems with British banks on 9 August, so he did not immediately feel compelled to act. It was later claimed that had he joined other central banks on that day the immediate difficulties at Northern Rock could have been mitigated. But then responsibility for supervising British banks rested with the Financial Services Authority (FSA), and it was not until five days later, on 14 August, at a meeting with the Treasury and the FSA that King was first informed of the potential difficulties at the former building society.

The events of Thursday, 9 August, had devastating consequences for Northern Rock as it felt the full blast of the credit crunch. The bank's risk committee, headed by former NatWest banker Sir Derek Wanless, had failed to act as a restraining force on the strategy of the executive members. Throughout the summer the Rock had been finding it increasingly difficult to fund its mortgage lending, relying as it did on short-term borrowing from other banks in the wholesale markets. Now that the credit markets around the world, on which it depended for 75 per cent of its funding, were freezing up it found itself caught in a perfect squeeze, unable to fund the loans on its mortgage book, many of which had been sold too cheaply.

Even the massive intervention by the ECB in the wholesale markets failed to jump-start inter-bank lending, and Northern Rock was left high and dry. Adam Applegarth now found himself short of the billions he needed to balance the bank's books. In the most dramatic fashion, the Rock's business model was about to implode.

Unlike other British lenders, which had substantial operations on the Continent and in New York, Northern Rock could not draw on the largesse of Trichet or Bernanke, and its Irish and Danish arms were not fully functional branches. But the Bank of England wouldn't help either. King firmly rejected the view that the Bank of England should have followed the ECB and the Fed and simply provided money to all and sundry in the markets. On 16 August he received a direct request for financial assistance from Matt Ridley, the chairman of Northern Rock, but was unbending in his response. The Bank of England could only be 'a lender of last resort, meaning lender of last resort'.

In a dramatic appearance before the Treasury Select Committee on 20 September King was defiant. Asked why he had not injected funds into money markets to attempt to get them working again, the Governor said that the Bank would have been required to inject much more than anything attempted by the ECB or the Fed. 'To have announced measures on that scale would have been irresponsible,' he said. Under questioning, King said that he had had no advance knowledge of the Rock's problems. 'Nobody I know said on 9 August that these events would occur,' he replied.

King told the MPs that his preferred route, once he knew the size of the problem, would have been to put together a secret rescue package for Northern Rock – 'in the way we would have done in the 1990s' – but that he had been advised that this was not possible under the 2005 Market Abuses Act. 'The way I would have wanted to do it … is to have acted covertly as lender of last resort,' he said. King was accused by the Commons Select Committee of simply being prepared to let Northern Rock 'hit the buffers'. He said that it was right to wait to see if Northern Rock could be rescued by the market. 'At that point, I didn't see much point blowing up the train before it hit the buffers.'

The Bank of England was out of line, then, with the other major central banks from the start of the crisis on 9 August, and it showed. Mervyn King was adamant that foolish commercial banks should pay for their mistakes, and banks bidding for extra resources from the Bank of England could have the extra cash only if they were willing to pay a premium of 1 per cent above the official bank rate. Elsewhere around the world, although levels of support varied, the approach by central banks to the credit crisis was to follow the lead of the ECB and the Fed – the world's two most powerful central banks – and to intervene with additional credit. The Bank of Japan, which had had more than its fair share of banking troubles in the 1990s, added $8 billion of support to the markets. Central banks in Australia and Canada mustered even greater support.

Although the sums expended by the central banks were far larger than their everyday operations, the amounts were small compared with the overall scale of the international financial markets, and the immediate effect on the share markets of the central banks' intervention was mixed. On 10 August the world's stock markets remained under intense pressure over sub-prime fears. In London the Stock Exchange's FTSE-100 Index had its worst day in four years, closing 3.7 per cent lower. The banking sector led the way down, and the first criticism of the Bank of England's inaction in the face of co-ordinated support elsewhere was heard.

Similar falls were registered in the Asian markets and in Germany and France. New York, meanwhile, rallied after a fall of nearly 200 points, with the Dow Jones average ending 31 points down. Japan's economy minister, Hiroko Ota, commented: 'The effect of US sub-prime loans is spreading to financial markets around the world.' At the same time the ECB's move prompted a sharp rise in eurozone and US government bonds and a corresponding decline in yields. There was a flight to the safety of official bonds, and commodity prices, notably gold and oil, began a long trajectory upwards, hitting record levels before the end of the year. Early in 2008 gold reached $1,000 an ounce and the oil price moved through $100 a barrel. Traditionally, in times of financial crisis investors look for safe havens like gold to preserve the value of their investments.

The events of 9 and 10 August demonstrated that even though

they shared a desire to forestall a chain reaction collapse of the global system, in practice the central banks have differing, and in some cases conflicting, agendas based on contrasting national concerns. This lack of coordination was to become a feature of the credit crunch and eventually led to calls by Gordon Brown and others for the International Monetary Fund to have a greater 'policeman' role to bring about a more coordinated global approach.

Financial experts around the world soon had their say about the way the central banks had reacted. Some analysts applauded the ECB for its prompt action. Erik Nielsen, economist at Goldman Sachs, remarked: 'This is outstanding central banking by the ECB and ought to provide a lot of comfort to the market.' But there were also some concerns and criticisms. Some critics condemned the fact that central banks had acted at all, citing that intervention can make panicky markets even more uneasy. The ECB, in particular, was seen as having acted rashly and out of character and, in the process, spreading the fear and panic ever wider.

In the confusion that followed the 9 August intervention the ECB and the Fed also came under fire for failing to react more quickly to the strains in the European money market. 'Asleep at the wheel' was the charge the central bankers faced. But there was no escaping the fact that as soon as they became aware of the dangers they had acted and more decisively than anyone could have imagined. Certainly, few international policy-makers had spotted the impending meltdown and its consequences; or, if they had, they had kept very quiet about it. Warnings by the 'central bankers' club', the Bank for International Settlements in Basle about the scale of debt accumulation and the risks involved had been studiously ignored, although it has to be said, in fairness, that the role of policy-makers is, partly, to underpin confidence, and this can make it difficult for them to speak up. In a speech only nine days before the markets froze, IMF deputy managing director John Lipsky had said optimistically: 'The fundamental underpinnings of the current global expansion appear to be reasonably solid. If so, the current market strains most likely will help set the stage for both financial and fundamental adjustments. This, in turn, will help set the stage for a new leg of global expansion.'

Gordon Brown and Alistair Darling offered a similarly optimistic message, arguing that Britain and the world could buck a financial market crash. Downing Street believed that because the UK had managed to avoid the worst impact of the 1997–8 emerging market difficulties, the aftermath of 9/11 and the dotcom collapse it could do so again. But there was a big difference this time: the problem lay right at the heart of Britain's financial system, which had been cosseted by New Labour since it took office in 1997 and had been gobbling up an ever larger share of the economy ever since. Financial services were estimated to account for at least 12 per cent of national wealth alone. If ancillary activities, such as consultancy and legal services, were included, the figure was closer to 30 per cent. If financial services proved to be sickly, the British economy could become seriously contaminated.

A few days after the central bank interventions, the *Financial Times* questioned whether the ECB's bold move merely masked a deeper problem in the European financial system. As far as the US was concerned, the jury was out on whether the Fed was dangerously behind the game or simply keeping its powder dry for an even more serious liquidity crisis. Many analysts compared the circumstances of the bursting of the dotcom boom with the sub-prime mortgage collapse and its effects on the real economy, but the big difference was that in the late 1990s, in stark contrast to 2007, the US economy was in a far better position in terms of growth potential. Albert Edwards, global strategist at Dresdner Kleinwort, commented:

When you have a run on the money markets like this, it is bound to spill over into the real economy. We already thought that there was a 40 per cent chance of a US recession before all this happened. But the risks are now much higher. Don't forget that the rates on adjustable mortgages will keep rising until a peak in March, so the maximum pain will be in the second and third quarters of 2008. There will be large bankruptcies. A lot more bodies are going to float to the surface before this is over.

Some commentators took a more extreme view. The economist and activist Ann Pettifer – architect of the Jubilee 2000 movement on African debt forgiveness – had previously warned of the dangers of the debt and credit mountains that were building on both sides of the Atlantic. She argued convincingly that 9 August would go down in history as 'detonation day', the beginning of the end of the deregulation and privatisation of finance that had marked the era of globalisation. Essentially, this somewhat extremist and apocalyptic argument blamed deregulated finance, among other things, for drowning the world in debt through gambling and excessive risk-taking, so sparking a world markets crisis, which needed state intervention to bail-out a financial sector meltdown.

Central banks, which were mostly committed to the role of the 'invisible hand' in the markets, were forced to intervene because commercial banks no longer trusted the solvency of other banks. The situation that Pettifer was describing was worrying in the extreme, but the authorities were doing their best to play down its severity. There were no secret gatherings of central bankers at the Bank for International Settlements in Basle, no emergency meeting of Group of Seven finance ministers and central bankers, and no effort – until the very end of the year – to put in place coordinated actions to try and make the money markets function again.

Whatever the interpretation of the events of August 2007, it is clear that the world financial system had undergone its worst crisis in a generation, with banks unwilling to lend to one another and central banks having to step in to keep the markets afloat. After 9/11 the determination of the Western states not to be bullied into submission by terrorists meant that urgent actions were taken to make sure that the plumbing of the financial system did not clog up. There was no such coordinated action this time around. Each of the central banks took the action they considered necessary. No one appeared prepared to admit the scale of the problem. Nor did they explain why early warnings signs had been complacently ignored.

This failure was partly because central banks have, since the 1980s, been far more focused on the fight against inflation than on financial stability. This was certainly the case at the Bank of England, where the top expert on stability, the burly Alistair Clark, had been allowed to retire in 2007 and was not replaced. (Clark was, in fact, called back to service as a consultant when the credit crunch arrived.) All around the world banks were flailing around, and Britain, with its failure first to detect and later to clean up the mess at Northern Rock, found itself in the firing line with a disaster that threatened the future of the government itself.

There had been a terrible failure of regulation and coordination, which contributed to the severity of the catastrophe. When the crisis exploded with the big money market freeze on 9 August, it seemed as if no one had really understood the potential for rotten subprime mortgages to blow up in the face of the world's banking system. The greed of commercial and investment bankers had allowed an enormous edifice to be built on the most flimsy of foundations. It should have been the job of regulators, such as the FSA in Britain, to see this coming. But they were blindsided, and it was left to the central banks to come in and clear up the mess as best they could.

The crisis for the Bank of England, the Treasury and the FSA was just beginning. While other central bankers and regulators were applying balm in the hope of calming the markets, the situation for at least one British bank, Northern Rock, was just starting to unfold. The Rock's apparent advantages turned out to be its fundamental weakness. It had a low-cost base, but that meant it also had a meagre branch network and little in the way of retail savings to fall back on. Against advice, it foolishly over-traded in the first half of 2007, grabbing more than a fifth of the entire British mortgage market from its larger high street rivals with their vast network of branches and leaving itself over-stretched as a result.

Applegarth had committed the cardinal banking sin of raising most of the bank's borrowings in the short-term money markets but lending long – in some cases, for as long as 25 years or more. It was a terrible mismatch and a dangerous mistake made possible by the fact that the Rock had allowed itself to be dominated by one person, Applegarth, who was surrounded by boardroom members who refused to stand up to him. The way it raised its money led it to become the British victim of the rogue sub-prime mortgage lending that had taken root some 3,000 miles away across the Atlantic in the trailer parks and inner-city tenements of America.

Unlike the Continental European banks that had got into trouble with sub-prime mortgages, Northern Rock could not count on an immediate bail-out by the Bank of England. Britain's humiliation – in the shape of a run on the branches of a retail bank – which was beamed around the world on round-the-clock television, was only just beginning.

CHAPTER 5

Aftershock

The implosion at Northern Rock

The shock to the system set in motion by the events of 9 August was to lead to the anxious and untidy queues that formed outside Northern Rock branches up and down the country some five weeks later. But Northern Rock's own anxieties were immediate. Adam Applegarth and the Northern Rock board recognised straightaway that, with the inter-bank market closed for business and the company's share price plunging, it was facing an urgent liquidity crisis. The game was up. 'We were hit by an unexpected and unpredictable concatenation of events,' the subsequently displaced chairman Matt Ridley, reaching into his best academic lexicon, would tell the Treasury Select Committee when called to provide evidence on 16 October 2007.

The following day, 10 August, the Financial Services Authority (FSA) was finally alerted to the potential for disaster at the Newcastle bank and opened urgent discussions with the lender. The Rock, aware of its vulnerability and seeking to protect investors and depositors, called its investment bank advisers, Merrill Lynch, and asked them to identify a potential buyer for the bank that would be capable of taking on its mortgage liabilities.

On 14 August the FSA alerted the other members of the Tripartite system of regulation (the Bank of England and the Treasury) of potential funding difficulties at Northern Rock, and at 10.30 a.m. on that day a teleconference was held between the FSA's smooth-talking chief executive Hector Sants, the Bank's fiercely intellectual executive director responsible for markets Paul Tucker and the slim and bright Treasury official Stephen Pickford, who had mountains of experience of handling crises on the international front. It was not until the following morning, 15 August, that Treasury officials, led by Clive Maxwell, the director for financial services, first warned ministers that Northern Rock could be in difficulty but had enough funds to hold on until September without government assistance.

The first that Chancellor of the Exchequer Alistair Darling knew of the credit crunch was on 9 August. He was on holiday in Majorca, and his office called to brief him about the extraordinary intervention on the money markets by the European Central Bank and the Fed. The following morning he read more about their actions in the *Financial Times* and realised that something serious was happening. There was no hint at this stage that any British bank was in difficulty. But by the time Darling had returned to the Treasury on 14 August word of the Rock's potential difficulties had filtered through. There was no immediate sense of panic. It was known that although the Newcastle bank was running short of cash, it had enough resources to see it through until the end of the month, and there was optimism that some kind of private-sector deal could be put in place, with Lloyds TSB and the Royal Bank of Scotland seen as possible saviours.

As the Rock board had requested, Merrill Lynch started to try to find a buyer in the hope of doing a quick deal before the cash ran out. The banker put in charge of the operation was Matthew Greenburg, a terrier-like deal-maker, who was also up to his neck in advising the Royal Bank of Scotland on its record-breaking bid for the Dutch bank ABN Amro. Greenburgh identified Lloyds TSB as among the UK banks least affected by the credit crunch and contacted its chief executive, Eric Daniels. Lloyds TSB was up for the challenge, and the bank's shrewd finance director Helen Weir, advised by investment bankers UBS, took charge of operations.

Lloyds TSB offered to buy Northern Rock at a price of £2 a share – a generous bid given what eventually happened to the Rock's share price. Applegarth and the Rock board, desperate for cash, agreed to the deal. But Lloyds TSB was not prepared to make an unconditional offer. Having examined Northern Rock's books, its chairman Sir Victor Blank and his fellow directors made it clear that a guarantee that up to £30 billion of Bank of England loans, made on commercial terms, would be necessary until such time as the Rock was trusted enough again to be able to finance its book in the money markets. It had fixed on £30 billion because the examination of the Rock's books had revealed that this huge volume of loans would fall due by 2009 with a very heavy repayment schedule over the next year.

Both parties believed that the deal was possible. James Murgatroyd, an associate at Finsbury, the City agency that handled Northern Rock's financial and corporate public relations, drew up a detailed press release, outlining the terms of the deal, ready for release to the financial markets on the morning of Monday, 10 September. All that was needed was the approval of the Bank of England. The Rock received the distinct impression from its regulator the FSA, its first point of contact, that this was a deal that could be done.

The Bank of England was not willing to play ball, however. It saw a number of difficulties. The cash involved far exceeded anything that the Bank's own balance sheet could handle, so an indemnity from the government would have been necessary. Moreover, there was no way in which a behind-the-scenes deal, between the Bank and a private lender like Lloyds TSB, could have been done without raising the curiosity and hackles of the European Commission, with its strict regime on state aid to failing businesses. With the deal all but signed and sealed, the Bank's Deputy Governor Sir John Gieve telephoned Applegarth on Tuesday, 11 September and said it was 'no go'. There was visible shock and anger at the Rock's Newcastle head-quarters. One insider openly voiced the fear that everyone else was thinking, that the 'bank could go under'.

It subsequently emerged that Mervyn King informally advised Alistair Darling against such a deal, arguing that to provide Lloyds

TSB with loans to support the Rock would distort the market in mortgages and provide unfair advantage to Lloyds over its competitors. Darling was not convinced that there was a real deal on the table or that any such transaction could be done without the approval of the European Union. He nevertheless remained in contact with Lloyds chief executive Eric Daniels, who took another brief look at the Rock after the Bank of England had stepped in. Privately, it turns out, FSA boss Hector Sants believed that the Lloyds offer should have been pursued. After all, he told colleagues 'there is no moral hazard involved in protecting consumers'.

With the benefit of hindsight, the Shadow Tory Chancellor, George Osborne, would later attack Darling and the Labour government for its 'incompetence' in failing to pursue the deal with Lloyds TSB. Osborne believed that a speedy, Bank of England-sponsored rescue would have been best. The Prime Minister told the House of Commons that 'no offer' from Lloyds TSB had formally been made. The shuttle-cock over the Lloyds rescue plan took place in secret, and it wasn't until four weeks later that it became clear the approach had failed.

A second private-sector solution was being pursued with the support of the FSA. Northern Rock had approached Sir Fred Goodwin, chief executive of the Royal Bank of Scotland (RBS), one of Britain's most ambitious banks, about providing several billions of cash in exchange for taking over a chunk of the Rock's uncommitted mortgage book. The talks were going well, but in the end the need for RBS, like other banks, to build and conserve liquidity scuppered the deal. RBS was also involved in a highly complex takeover of Dutch bank ABN Amro and decided to call off the negotiations over the future of the Rock.

The Tripartite authorities – the Bank of England, the FSA and the Treasury – now had a real problem on their hands. No 'voluntary' private-sector answer to the Rock's problems looked possible. The crisis in the money markets had deepened as August progressed, and criticism of the Bank's reluctance to act to relieve the tension reached a crescendo. It was pointed out that King and his team at the Bank could hardly have failed to notice that Northern Rock's shares had plunged nearly 10 per cent on 10 August, attracting huge headlines on the financial pages of the national press. The panic was spreading. Bob Diamond, the Chelsea-supporting, American boss of Barclays Capital and the highest paid banker in Britain, made a thinly veiled call for the Bank to ease the liquidity crisis on 3 September. By then, Northern Rock shares were falling heavily, and in the two days that followed the bank was London's biggest faller. The panic in the markets was spreading, but the Bank of England gave the appearance that it was impervious to what was happening all around it.

On the morning of Wednesday, 12 September, Mervyn King gave the first public hint that something dreadful might be happening. He wrote to the Treasury Select Committee indicating for the first time the conditions under which the Bank of England would intervene if a bank were to run into difficulty. His comment was buried deep in a much longer statement about deteriorating conditions in the credit markets and the Bank's hard-line attitude to providing assistance to banks that had lent foolishly. 'The provision of large liquidity penalises those financial institutions that sat out the dance, encourages herd behaviour and increases the intensity of future crises,' he stated in a letter to MPs. The reality was that King, having advised against using public money to back the Lloyds TSB bid, was now preparing to offer Northern Rock assistance using the Bank's lender of the last resort facility – one of the oldest functions of a central bank.

By Thursday, 13 September, matters had reached crisis point. Merrill Lynch had failed in its effort to secure a commercial buyer for Northern Rock, and its position was so bad that Adam Applegarth had no choice but to throw himself on the mercy of the Bank of England. There Mervyn King's response to the credit crunch had given rise to tensions within the Bank's Court. Some members had wanted to challenge King's view on 'moral hazard' in the banking system and the timeliness of information provided to the Court on the Northern Rock affair. They were also angry that the Bank had failed to provide them with guidelines on the

Court's role in maintaining financial stability, which had been requested in May 2007, long before the credit markets stalled. But King, backed by Court member Sir Peter Jay, the BBC's former economics editor, managed to fend off angry and disillusioned dissenters. Now after concealed negotiations, Mervyn King agreed that the Bank would make an emergency loan facility in its capacity as lender of last resort. Darling consented to the move, which would eventually require tens of billions of pounds of funding from the taxpayer. On the evening of the 13 September King called an emergency session of the Bank's Court (the Bank's non-executive directors, responsible for the governance of the Bank's affairs) for 9 p.m. He informed them that a request had been received from Northern Rock for a lender of last resort loan and that it had been granted. Not all Court members were present, but there was a quorum. The meeting lasted an hour.

The terms of the rescue and the way it would be communicated to the market and the public had still to be settled. The Tripartite authorities originally wanted to release the information on Monday, 17 September, before the stock market opened. A 'communications strategy' would be put in place, and this, accompanied by the necessary government assurances to depositors, borrowers, shareholders and other interest groups, would help to ensure that the emergency loans could be announced with the minimum of disruption. But Alistair Darling was not convinced that the arrangement would remain secret until Monday, 17 September, and it was agreed that an announcement would be made at 7 a.m. on Friday, 14 September.

Darling's instincts were right. On the evening of 13 September news was carelessly leaked to the BBC's business editor Robert Peston, Gordon Brown's biographer and a reporter with unusually close links to Downing Street. Peston had been pursuing the story of the Rock's difficulties intensely for three days. He had made several inquiries of the regulators and the mortgage bank's financial PR advisers, Finsbury. Until then he had had no joy. But that evening his persistence paid off. As soon as he had confirmation of the Rock's lender of last resort loan he went on television to broadcast details of Northern Rock's travails and posted the news on the network's website.

There has been much debate about how Peston learned of the bail-out. When I asked him about this he rightly maintained a studious silence – journalists do not disclose their sources. The finger has been pointed in Whitehall at Finsbury, which might have felt that releasing the information would have brought an end to the speculation and halted the calamitous fall in the bank's share price. Others have suggested that it was an official leak, authorised by Downing Street to demonstrate that it was in charge of crisis management. If this was the case it would be the supreme irony, given the eventual costs to the taxpayer and the political price that was paid. Whatever the source, the release of the information turned out to be disaster for all those involved. Far from calming anyone, Peston's delivery, oddly drawling and breathless at the same time, gave rise to panic, despite his careful assurances to depositors, particularly as deposit guarantees for retail investors were clearly inadequate. (The existing government guarantee plan for savers, the Financial Services Compensation Scheme, only offered a 100 per cent guarantee for the first £2,000 of savings and 90 per cent for the next £33,000. Any savings above that level were liable to be wiped out.)

The BBC's business editor had a brilliant scoop, but the normally cautious broadcasting network had inadvertently precipitated a crisis. Peston's sensational disclosure was quickly picked up in the later editions of Friday morning's national newspapers, many of which changed their front pages to lead with the story. Rock chairman Matt Ridley was so angered by the leak that he fired off a personal letter of protest to Alistair Darling.

Pandemonium broke out on the morning of 14 September. Amazingly – and unthinkably for a bank – Northern Rock appeared to have run out of cash, and depositors panicked. Fearing that they could lose their savings, customers started a run on the bank as they attempted to withdraw their money. Northern Rock's branches were poorly staffed and not used to a rush of cash withdrawals, and crowds built rapidly. The bank's management now faced twin crises. Not only could Northern Rock no longer obtain wholesale funding in the money markets, but its retail branches were under siege from its own terror-stricken customers. Northern Rock was the first casualty in Britain of a crisis that was shaking the global banking industry.

Queues outside branches snaked along Britain's high streets, while the bank's website was almost permanently seized under the sheer weight of customers trying to access online accounts. Between 14 and 17 September no less than £2 billion was withdrawn by savers who feared for their money. TV images of worried savers queuing in the street were flashed around the world. Angela Knight, the elegant and fearless director general of the British Bankers' Association, was horrified, fearing that the City's reputation would be tainted. She was outraged at the inability of the Tripartite system of regulation to act more decisively. The Treasury Select Committee's Michael Fallon commented: 'It looked appalling. The first run on a British bank for over 100 years – something that we always managed to prevent before.' Certainly, Britain's reputation for financial excellence was now well and truly in tatters. The government had saddled itself with billions of pounds of support funding, Alistair Darling was stumbling on with his 'policy on the hoof' as the government sought to stem the flow of funds out of the bank and prevent a chain reaction to other institutions, and the Bank was having to offer to lend billions of pounds on three-month terms to hard-pressed banks, starting with a £10 billion injection. King said the injection of liquidity was a 'carefully designed and judged' decision. Northern Rock's predicament had increased the risks of damage to the economy, which now outweighed the potential 'moral hazard'. His words, though, cut no ice.

As the chaos outside Northern Rock branches was flashed around the world on 24-hour television reports, bank shares in London went into freefall. The Rock's own shares tumbled 40 per cent, but just as worrying was the fact that other lenders were dragged into the crisis, with Alliance & Leicester shares dropping by almost one-third and Bradford & Bingley by 15 per cent.

There has been much disagreement over the whole issue of who recommended that retail deposits should be guaranteed and who didn't. The Governor of the Bank of England says that he had recommended that the Chancellor guarantee Northern Rock's retail deposits, but that the advice was ignored in Whitehall. Darling and the Treasury, however, have a different memory of events. Even though King and Darling spent the day together at a financial summit in Lisbon on 14 September, according to one insider, 'The word "guarantee" never crossed his [King's] lips.' It was not until Sunday that the Bank first raised the issue of providing depositors with some kind of assurance. Even then there were reservations in Downing Street. Gordon Brown demanded to know exactly which depositors would be guaranteed and what would be the likely exposure of the government.

The chaos on 17 September was the moment that Labour's reputation for economic competence vanished. It was widely seen as the government's 'Black Wednesday' moment – a reminder of the humiliating failure of John Major's government when the pound exited from the exchange rate mechanism (ERM) in October 1992. After three days of panic, and amid growing fears that the run would spread to other banks, the government finally stepped in. Late on Monday afternoon, after a tumultuous day on the streets of Britain and the stock market, Alistair Darling, who had been holding talks with the US Treasury Secretary Hank Paulson, hastily called lobby reporters to the Treasury and issued a portentous statement:

> Following discussions with the Governor of the Bank of England, should it be necessary, we and the Bank of England will put in place arrangements that would guarantee all the existing deposits in the Northern Rock during the current instability in the financial markets.

In answer to reporters' questions, Darling also made it clear that should similar problems arise at other banks the government was prepared to offer the same guarantee. Extraordinarily, the Chancellor had inadvertently guaranteed the deposits of the whole British banking system, a position that was subsequently clarified by officials. They made it plain that should other banks suffer the fate of Northern Rock the Tripartite regulators (the Chancellor, the FSA and the Bank of England) would look at the position of depositors on a case-by-case basis. In addition, the government was looking at a new deposit insurance scheme, on American lines, where retail deposits up to £100,000 would be fully insured.

The Chancellor guaranteed over £20 billion worth of consumer savings, and this shored up the bank. But while the queues outside Northern Rock melted away, many people thought that Darling had come along four days too late. In Kingston Pam Hilleard, having rescued her £780,000 savings, reflected: 'If Alistair Darling had guaranteed every depositor's money at the beginning, when the announcement was first made, there would have been nothing to panic about.' Financial experts were equally critical. 'It may shore up confidence in the short term, but what if he actually has to do it?' they asked.

Meanwhile, Northern Rock began to borrow billions from the Bank of England's loan facility at a punitive rate of interest – believed to be around 7 per cent. This was more than a point above the official bank rate, which then stood at 5.75 per cent. With the interest likely to take a heavy toll of its profits, the City began to revise forecasts for the company from several hundred millions of profit to losses of over £100 million. The slide was under way. The share price had dropped from a high of £12.60 to £1.22 (and subsequently lower) – a loss of over £4 billion to shareholders. Analyst Danny Gabay remarked: 'The scale of that loss and the speed of that decline was something that the markets probably hadn't seen – at least in a bank of that size and certainly in the UK – for well over a generation.'

The company's shareholders took a bath. Roger Lawson, spokesman for the UK Shareholders' Association (UKSA), which claims to represent small investors, was seriously hurt. 'I lost more than £10,000. Many people buy shares to get dividend income in their retirement. They often buy substantial amounts and now they won't be getting a dividend. So, that will affect them severely.'

But he was not alone among those with sorry tales to tell as their investment nose-dived. One former Northern Rock employee, with 24 years' service, held company shares, which she planned to cash in to pay for a new kitchen booked for the autumn of 2007. And even when the shares began to dip a few months before work was due to start, the pensioner still saw no reason to sell, preferring to stay 'loyal' to her old firm. How she regretted that decision when they plunged in September, leaving her to find the money for the kitchen out of her meagre savings. Then there was a Newcastle couple's investment of £90,000 in Northern Rock shares to meet their children's college fees and a few comforts in their retirement. Now their whole future seemed to be in jeopardy.

With its shares on the floor, the company was propped up by borrowings from the Bank of England – which neared £25 billion by the end of the year – and put up for sale. Taxpayers' exposure was more than £55 billion when the guarantees were added to the loans made. Inevitably, therefore, the spotlight now turned on the management shortcomings of Northern Rock's directors, who had presided over this disaster and who had paid themselves a total of £30 million in salaries, bonuses and share-based incentive schemes over the five years to 2007.

From its earliest days, the Northern Rock board had reflected its local community – particularly the local aristocracy. The days of the 'keen amateur' seated alongside 'prestigious names from industry' continued to be a feature of Northern Rock's hierarchy, even after the advent of Adam Applegarth – the first meritocratic, career businessman in the boardroom, who spearheaded the company's dash for growth. Applegarth himself was a life-long 'Northern Rocker'. Starting his career there as a graduate trainee, he was a driven marketing man, who dreamed of overtaking the high street clearing banks. In 2006 he earned £1.3 million, half as a basic salary and half in bonuses, and his pension pot increased by £266,000 each year – indeed, the last pension payment was made just days after the FSA warned of a fallout from the sub-prime crisis.

Along with Applegarth, other key members of the board – the chairman, the Hon. Matt Ridley and non-executives Sir Ian Gibson and Sir Derek Wanless – were called before the Commons Treasury Select Committee on 16 October. The four would be spared no mercy by MPs. As Michael Fallon put it to them: 'Do you realise what damage you have done to British banking?' The committee accused them of failing to ensure that Northern Rock 'remained liquid as well as solvent, to provide against the risks it was taking'. They were also accused of failing to act as an 'effective restraining force' on Applegarth and his fellow executive directors. MPs were particularly unimpressed with Applegarth's oft-repeated mantra that: 'Nobody could see the squeeze on global liquidity.' As Michael Fallon observed witheringly:

It's quite extraordinary. The board of a British bank has been allowed to destroy £4 billion to £5 billion worth of value. This is the fourth strongest economy in the world. We shouldn't have people queuing outside banks trying to get their money out as they did in the Weimar Republic and in Zimbabwe.

Given the mess the company was in, it was obvious that heads would have to roll. Sir Ian Gibson, the senior independent director, revealed that the whole board had been considering its position since August. However, after the Treasury Select Committee humiliation, the last rites were issued, and not long after most of the discredited board resigned. Matt Ridley was the first to go on 19 October.

The 49-year-old Ridley had been Applegarth's chairman during Northern Rock's dash for growth. He was a member of one of the great Northumberland families (his uncle Nicholas, his father's brother, was best known as an irascible, right-wing member of Margaret Thatcher's Cabinet), and when he took over as chairman of the Rock, he was following in the footsteps of his father, the 4th Viscount Ridley, who was chairman some years before. In the days before many building societies became banks it was customary for the chairman to be drawn from the local aristocracy to add a touch of lustre to the headed notepaper, the reports to members and the shindigs organised by executives at the annual conferences of the Building Societies Association, but it was unusual for a public company, especially one with such a sophisticated business model as Northern Rock.

Ridley had become a non-executive director in 1994 and moved up to become chairman in 2004. He was paid £315,000 a year, a generous amount for a non-executive chairman. A former journalist with the *Telegraph* and *Economist*, and a prolific science writer and expert in the field of genetics, it is unclear how, other than through his hereditary claims, he rose to become chairman. I personally knew Ridley as a fellow Washington correspondent in the 1980s when, as far as I can recall, he had shown no particular leaning towards finance and banking.

When he was questioned about his qualifications and assumption of the chairmanship by MPs on the Treasury Select Committee, he replied that the board had asked him and he had said 'yes'. In 2006 he had attended 14 formal meetings at the bank. He had a high profile inside the company, but when the 2007 crisis hit he earned the nickname of the 'the invisible man'. Indeed, after his appearance before the Select Committee he made no further public statements about Northern Rock.

The lack of a strong chairman during the crisis, one who could give Applegarth guidance, had increased the strains on the chief executive, who was in out of his depth and up against it on both the personal and business fronts. None of the executive directors appeared strong enough to challenge him. The retirement of finance director Bob Bennett after 13 years at the top meant that the only executive capable of standing up to Applegarth was off the scene. Bennett had been seen in the City as a 'calming influence'. He had told Applegarth that the housing market was slowing and that the 'appetite for securitisations would be lower. So lending should be restrained'. But the single-minded Rock boss had not listened. Nor did he receive sensible advice from his deputy, David Baker, who, within days of the crisis, 'went home ill'. The irony was that the only properly functioning executive, with the inner toughness to see through the affair, was Applegarth himself – the person directly responsible for the debacle.

Nor did the independents seem to want to question Applegarth's drive for glory. In fact, the board appeared to be populated by non-executives who were in place as much because of who they were as for what they knew about banking. Among those who might have been expected to ask the right kind of questions was 44-year-old Nichola Pease, chief executive of J.O. Hambro Capital Management. She was a scion of one of the founding families of Barclays, and banking blood coursed through her veins. Her brother-in-law, John Varley, is the current chief executive of Barclays; her father, Sir Richard Pease, was chairman of Yorkshire Bank; her brother was a high-flier at New Star Asset Management; and her husband, Crispin Odey, runs one of the City's more successful hedge funds. Yet when Northern Rock imploded Pease, who might have brought some calm and experience to events, failed to deliver.

Although Pease has said very little publicly about her time at the Rock, she has been anxious to defend her role in the whole affair. The job of a non-executive, she told the *Financial Times* in May 2008, 'is to ask questions that might shed light but you can't get as involved in detail as the management.' She has also denied that what happened was forseeable: 'Of course there were a lot of conversations about funding but we never envisaged the level of the [liquidity] crisis we are going through now. It is unprecedented.' 'I wouldn't have been on that board if I didn't think it was full of very able people and I'll say that to my dying day,' she said. Be that as it may, when the new chairman Bryan Sanderson arrived he found Pease's resignation and that of the other non-executives on his desk and accepted them.

Pease was not the only one to be overtaken by events. Executive director and treasurer Keith Currie, the person responsible for organising Northern Rock's dealings with the wholesale money markets, had declared himself sick soon after the crisis began and had not been seen at the company's offices since.

The position of another non-executive director, Rosemary Radcliffe, raised further questions about the way in which they were appointed. Radcliffe had worked for the Independent Complaints Commission at the FSA, and was also a former chief economist at PricewaterhouseCoopers (PwC), Northern Rock's accountants. The Treasury Select Committee pointedly noted that there was a 'conflict of interest' over PwC, which was in receipt of £700,000 a year in consulting fees, in addition to its payment for audit. At the moment Radcliffe was most needed she was ill and trying to do what she could from her sick bed. 'Poor girl, she bears no responsibility,' an insider remarked. But there were serious questions about whether a former employee of PwC should have been recruited to the board in the first place.

Another local northeastern dignitary, Adam Fenwick, of the eponymous department store family, which has large premises in Newcastle and a landmark store on London's New Bond Street, lacked the skills to make an impact. He had to start learning on the job when the Rock struck the iceberg.

Amid the amateurism and illness it might have been thought that Sir Derek Wanless, the former chief executive of NatWest, would have shown his mettle. He was director chairman of Northern Rock's audit and risk committees, and so one could argue that he, if anyone, should have understood the gravity of the situation and how best to handle it. Then 59, Sir Derek had grown up in Newcastle upon Tyne and was educated at the city's Royal Grammar School – where Adam Applegarth became a governor – before going on to King's

College, Cambridge, where he gained a first-class degree in mathematics. A genial, likeable man, he had a gold-plated CV, which included working as an adviser to Gordon Brown on the National Health Service and other directorships, including the chairmanship of Northumbrian Water. He was also vice-chairman of the Statistics Commission and a member of the Board for Actuarial Standards at the Financial Reporting Council, which, paradoxically, set the rules for the way in which companies draw up their accounts.

Wanless, as head of the audit and risk committee, should, in the view of the new team that took over at Northern Rock in the wake of the immediate crisis, been more fully aware of the potential dangers of the wholesale funding model, stress-tested it to the limit and made sure there was adequate liquidity around to deal with any impending problem. After all, the risks of failing to maintain a liquidity cushion, which could be called upon in emergencies, were widely known – a former Deputy Governor of the Bank of England, Sir Andrew Large, had sounded the first warnings on liquidity before he left Threadneedle Street in 2005. Consequently, when he took control of the Rock in October 2007, Bryan Sanderson had little choice but to include Wanless in his boardroom clear-out. 'It was brutal, but we couldn't see how we could keep him,' one insider noted. Indeed, nobody at Northern Rock had bothered to put in a contingency plan under which the bank would close its branches to savers and arrange for the efficient repatriation of depositors. Such a plan was eventually put into place at the end of 2007, but only at the insistence of the Treasury, which was astounded that no emergency measures existed.

Amid all this boardroom chaos, one of the few who kept his head was the bustling businessman Sir Ian Gibson, the board's senior independent director. Gibson, as chairman of Trinity Mirror since May 2006 and with a slew of other non-executive directorships at GKN, Greggs and Asda, had more than enough on his plate. A member of the Court of the Bank of England from 1999 to 2004, Gibson had built his reputation as boss of Nissan Europe and architect of the Japanese car group's famously efficient Sunderland plant. Yet when most of the rest of the board was wobbling, Gibson appeared to show a steady hand. It was he who helped organise the search for a replacement chairman for the Rock, calling on the services of head-hunter Anna Mann, who identified the BP veteran and former Standard Chartered chairman Bryan Sanderson. The moustached North-Easterner was the ideal candidate. He had extensive banking experience (albeit on the international stage) and good connections with New Labour. He found immediate favour with Gibson, and won rapid approval from the Tripartite authorities. Yet, although Gibson made some good moves, he had his critics, too. When advisers from London arrived in Newcastle, in the middle of the run, they found him determined that as little information as possible about the travails of the bank should be disclosed.

With this odd boardroom mix of ambition and lack of it, experience and inexperience, and gentleman and players, the directors had witnessed the very best and the very worst of times. The board had supervised vast expansion and presided over the company's virtual demise. An unsustainable business model had been pursued, and no check appears to have been applied to some of Applegarth's wilder ambitions.

'He had come up from the ground and was an old-fashioned, hard-line martinet of a manager who was difficult to challenge,' one of the new team observed. Another insider who had seen him in action over the years said: 'Any rival plan or idea was rejected by those close to him on the basis that "Adam wouldn't like it". He had an iron grip on the company. There was no feedback. He surrounded himself with "yes men" who worked their way up the company and who were dependent on him. Northern Rock ended up with people in senior positions who were not fit for purpose.'

After initially resisting calls for him to go, Applegarth resigned on 16 November, with a view to staying until the end of January 2008 to help with the takeover process. Once seen as the youthful, vigorous leader of a go-ahead company, he was now in disgrace.

Not only was his national reputation in tatters, but his local esteem in the northeast had never recovered since it became known that he had made two large share sales in 2006 and 2007, raising just over £2.6 million. Even after the bank ran into difficulties, he continued collecting his salary. In Newcastle, where he was once regarded as a hero, his name was now mud.

Applegarth finally left on 16 December. Some commentators expressed concerns that he would walk away with a large sum of money, and they were right to be worried. When the Rock's 2007 accounts were published on 31 March 2008 they showed that Northern Rock's directors were too timid to challenge Applegarth's contract. Remarkably, the man who had led Northern Rock over the precipice was awarded his full salary of £760,000 plus £25,000 extra in non-cash benefits. This was like kicking sand in the eyes of the shareholders, employees and taxpayers who had been so badly hurt by his actions. As if this were not enough, he had also accumulated a pension pot of £2.6 million, enough to keep him in clover on £305,000 a year once he reached the retirement age of 55 years.

Applegarth is said to have left with a 'broken heart' – though the immense wealth he had accumulated no doubt made the transition easier – and soon his private life was in a shambles, too. The Northern Rock board received an anonymous letter making sensitive claims that he had acted in breach of company rules and that his actions were also a threat to his marriage. The *Mail on Sunday* reported that he had had a secret relationship with Amanda Smithson, from the company's buy-to-let lending division. Suspicions of an illicit relationship were aroused when Ms Smithson booked holiday time to coincide with Applegarth's six-times-a-year trips to New York to meet with Wall Street firms. In addition, the anonymous letter, which was also sent to his home in the village of Matfen in Northumberland, contained allegations about his management style and suggestions that he was deeply unpopular with staff. His eventual early departure was hastened, according to senior insiders, by his 'belief that he might save his marriage by getting out' after two national newspapers, the *Mail on Sunday* and the *News of the World*, investigated his alleged infidelities. 'He really left because of persecution by the press,' a senior insider told me. Applegarth became so obsessed by these inquiries that his usefulness to the new team leading the bank was seen as negligible.

As a momentous year drew to a close, Applegarth's time at Northern Rock had come to an ignominious end. Bruised by his experiences, he retreated to the privacy of his £2.5 million home, where he was protected from a prying media and an angry public by a burly minder and bodyguard, ironically known to locals as 'The Rock'. When he did venture out in his sleek Aston Martin – which, along with a Ferrari for his wife, was bought with a share sale at the beginning of 2007 – Applegarth would have plenty of time to contemplate the past as he drove along Northumberland's leafy country lanes. Without doubt, he would be reflecting on his part in the rise and fall of one of the most aggressive brands ever seen in the UK financial markets. With his dreams of high street domination now in ruins, how was it, he might ask, that Northern Rock had become such a stretcher case?

Accompanying Applegarth out the door were several other executives, including the bank's treasurer, Keith Currie, who earned £415,000 and had been on sick leave during the crisis, and David Baker, the almost invisible deputy chief executive, who earned £530,000. The non-executive directors were also cleared out, with Pease, Radcliffe, Wanless and Fenwick being shown the door. The last person standing was a tough Dutchman, treasury director Andy Kuipers, who was slotted into the job of chief executive on 19 December.

With Ridley and Applegarth gone, his successor Bryan Sanderson tried to move Northern Rock on. He came with a good business pedigree. He was the former chairman of the international bank Standard Chartered and of the health insurer BUPA. Brought up in a colliery village in the northeast, Sanderson spent most of his career at BP and is a former chairman of Sunderland Football Club and director of Durham Cricket Club. He had also been a regular adviser to New Labour and served on several committees advising the Department of Trade and Industry. Two new non-executive directors, former Marconi boss John Devaney and Simon Laffin, a consultant with private equity firm CVC, were also appointed.

Sanderson immediately set about damping down expectations of a deal for Northern Rock that would please all stakeholders – from taxpayers and shareholders to employees and regulators. 'There's not going to be any ideal solution,' he said. 'We've got to find the least damaging outcome.' In a later interview with the *Daily Mail*'s Lucy Farndon he said: 'This is a big business challenge. So, of course, there is enjoyment in that. It is stimulating and very worthwhile. We have got to find a way of managing ourselves out of all this. Naturally, the banks are a bit wary of somebody that is in Northern Rock's position.' Privately Sanderson believed there was only a 50/50 chance of saving the bank from nationalisation.

But Sanderson did have his City detractors, who believed he was unfamiliar with the complexities of running a mortgage bank. Nevertheless, his six months at the helm did not go unrewarded. He was contractually entitled to £315,000 for six months' work and a further £85,000 to cover the cost of his West End office in London. Shareholders might be taking the pain, but directors were not shy about collecting their fees.

The end of 2007 brought much uncertainty for the bank, its shareholders, savers and employees. The Northern Rock brand, which had had such a strong market presence, had been severely damaged by the autumn's storm. But it was far from clear whether it would disappear from the high street – and, if it did, what would replace it?

The government meanwhile was searching desperately for a solution that would avoid nationalisation, a course of action that was being advocated by the Liberal Democrats, the *Financial Times* and the *Economist* among other illustrious voices. On Monday, 21 January 2008, it embraced a complex financial scheme devised by investment bankers Goldman Sachs, the Treasury's chosen advisers.

The plan involved slicing and dicing the £25 billion or so of mortgage collateral taken by the Bank of England, stamping it with a British government guarantee and selling it off in the marketplace – an ironic strategy given that this was how Applegarth had funded the Rock's operations (though, obviously, he had not had the benefit of a government guarantee). The possibility of a private-sector rescue involving one of three main bidders – Sir Richard Branson's Virgin Money, Luqman Arnold's Olivant consortium and an internal offer led by new director, Paul Thompson (formerly of insurer Resolution) – looked to be on the cards, and the Rock's share price duly almost doubled to just under £1.00. Other potential bidders, including the US-based private equity firms J.C. Flowers and Cerberus, also circled.

Bryan Sanderson recruited a team from another private equity group, Blackstone, which was headed by renowned investment banker and philanthropist John Studzinski. With the support of accountants PwC and City lawyers Freshfields Bruckhaus Deringer, they helped to prepare the company for the restructuring that would inevitably follow. Sanderson had come to know 'Studz', as he was known in the City, during his period at BP when he had worked closely with the group's then chief executive, Sir John Browne.

The presence of Branson as a preferred bidder had already helped to stabilise the situation, and weekly withdrawals by savers fell from billions of pounds to a few millions. This was something that the fastidious Studzinski, who had dropped everything to head the negotiations with the government and buyers, had counted on. 'The honey has to be spread over the toast,' he cryptically assured his fellow financial advisers.

While executives and staff at the Rock awaited their fate, there was an unreal air of 'business as usual'. Despite everything that had happened, Northern Rock House, the company's elaborate headquarters in Gosforth on the edge of Newcastle, continued to undergo an expensive extension. By December 2007 a new circular tower block, seven storeys and rising, was being added – which could be seen as a gesture of optimism for the future. Reassuring in such testing times was the fierce local loyalty and affection that the company enjoyed.

On the national and international stage it had become a laughing stock, a potent symbol of failure for Britain and Gordon Brown's government. But it was still popular in the northeast. After all, the bank had become the symbol of the region's rejuvenation and renaissance. It engendered fierce support through its lavish sponsorship of local sports teams – Premier League Newcastle United, rugby's Newcastle Falcons and the Durham County Cricket Club – and in an area full of sporting heroes, such as Kevin Keegan, Alan Shearer, Michael Owen and Jonny Wilkinson, it was easy to see why the local public had taken the company to its heart.

Not least, it enjoyed an elevated status because of the good work carried out by the Northern Rock Foundation. The company channels 5 per cent of its profits into the Foundation, which is a huge giver in the northeast and is involved in 1,500 projects there. The past decade has seen Northern Rock donate £175 million to a range of charities and community ventures, including youth football teams in Newcastle, opera in Leeds and local homeless projects. One of those who has benefited is Ray Spencer, director of the Customs House Theatre in South Shields. 'Northern Rock has given us something like £250,000 over the years. The entire cultural scene in the region would be vastly different if there was no Northern Rock. People need to support this company to ensure it doesn't leave the region,' he said.

John Shipley, Liberal Democrat leader of Newcastle City Council, summed up Northern Rock's contribution: 'The Foundation had provided the fundamental link for social welfare in the area through its donations to charitable and community causes. The difference it has made has been massive. And, inevitably, this has generated a wealth of good feeling.'

It's not surprising, then, that even in its darkest moments in the autumn of 2007, the stricken bank enjoyed great public backing in the northeast. Support came in immediately from the business community, summed up by Margaret Fay, chairman of the regional development agency, One NorthEast: 'Northern Rock is a landmark northeast business – a success story which has contributed greatly to the economic welfare of our region. We fully support the bank.' Meanwhile, large unions, such as Unite, nailed its colours to the mast, by issuing a charter aimed at rescuing the company and preserving its business and jobs, of which there were 4,300 based in Gosforth and 1,200 in Sunderland.

Local politicians were quick to point out the company's importance to the area. John Shipley said: 'We were happy to see Northern Rock grow. Firstly, because it was a major employer; and, secondly, because it was the region's major financial institution. Ten to 15 years ago, the region needed to recreate itself out of the decline of the old manufacturing and extraction industries. We had watched Leeds grow its financial services and decided we should do the same.'

Ironically, only a week before the company first hit trouble, Newcastle councillors had agreed to recommend that it should receive the freedom of the city, mainly in recognition of the Foundation's work. Despite the national furore over the business fallout that followed, the council stayed behind the company and later confirmed its intention to bestow the honour, although the ceremony has yet to take place. Backing for Northern Rock also came from much-loved figures such as Sir Bobby Robson, while ordinary Tynesiders, led by the local media, rallied around, too. Brian Aitken, editor of the Newcastle morning newspaper, *The Journal*, launched a 'Rock Steady' campaign. He explained the motives behind it: 'To a large extent, to the London-based media this was a banking story. To us, this was about a friend in trouble. What we have not done is look into the "blame game".'

Northern Rock, once a provincial also-ran, was one of the region's two flagship FTSE-100 companies and its single biggest employer, so it is important not only to the economy of the northeast but also to its pride and sense of itself. Its ten-year sprint for glory proved a magnet for bringing other business to the area and, just as importantly, attracting thousands of young professionals. Newcastle's regenerative quayside development, with its bustling shops, restaurants, bars and small businesses alongside the Tyne, is a testimony to that. 'Northern Rock's 150-year history is part of the Newcastle psyche,' explained John Shipley.

If there was any anger on the part of the northeast community it was directed at the company's management team. Incompetence and a series of catastrophic blunders were blamed for bringing down what had been the star of British banking. Northern Rock had turned into Northern Crock, and the investors were naturally furious. Robin Ashby, a spokesman for some 100,000 small shareholders, who include the former police chief Lord Stevens and Sir Neville Trotter, the former Tory MP for Tynemouth, summed up their feelings: 'While the directors were cashing in shares worth millions of pounds before the company got into trouble, they left small shareholders and employees, who have remained loyal to Northern Rock for more than a decade, facing financial ruin. They obviously had no long-term faith in the company.'

What would happen to Northern Rock would be a key issue in the coming months, as the government and its advisers looked for a buyer for the stricken bank. In the meantime, the recriminations continued. While it was clear that Northern Rock executives had to bear much of the blame for what went wrong, they were not the only ones at fault. Fingers were left pointing at the responsibility of the regulators for the mess that had been created. In dealing with the crisis, the three bodies whose specific responsibility it had been to avert disaster – the FSA, the Bank of England and the Treasury – also showed themselves to be woefully inadequate.

CHAPTER 6

Asleep at the Wheel

Why the regulators failed

Amid the soaring banking towers of Canary Wharf, Britain's new-wave financial centre built on the Isle of Dogs to the east of the City of London, nestles the Financial Services Authority. The glass-fronted headquarters of the FSA and its open architecture are designed to reflect the image of the modern regulator – accessible, flexible and practical. This is a world away from the formal and legalistic regulation of financial services seen in other capitals, from Washington to Frankfurt, and many people believe that the success of London as a financial centre in the early 21st century is down to the FSA's light-touch regulation. It was this regime that encouraged many of the world's biggest investment banks to move their global headquarters to London, some employing more people in the City and Canary Wharf than in their home headquarters. The investment banks brought with them the big firms of international lawyers, accountants and consultants, and they were soon followed by the migration of private equity and the burgeoning hedge fund industry to the more civilised environs of Mayfair and London's West End.

The FSA's mission is enormously complex. It is required to regulate some of the biggest financial institutions in the world, ranging from HSBC, which reaches into every cranny of the globe, and medium-sized mortgage banks, such as Northern Rock, to retail mortgage and insurance brokers operating from high street shops and, in some cases, local garages. It is both a retail and wholesale regulator rolled into one, with a mission to protect the consumer, encourage competition in the financial system as well as making sure that firms – banks, insurers and regulated exchanges – behave prudently.

The FSA was created in May 1997, amid the euphoria and high-octane energy of New Labour's early days in office. It was the result of one of the most important pieces of legislation to be passed by the new government, affecting the lives of every consumer in Britain and reaching deep into the fastest growing sector of the British economy – financial services – and it came about because New Labour was critical of the Bank of England and wanted to give it a more specific, limited role. The FSA's creation, however, went largely unnoticed by a British public basking in the youthful reforming zeal of Tony Blair's government. Driven by the new Chancellor of the Exchequer Gordon Brown, his right-hand minister at the Treasury, the businessman-turned-MP, Geoffrey Robinson, and Brown's economic adviser, Ed Balls, financial regulation in Britain was now to be split three ways between the holy trinity of the Treasury, the Bank of England (the traditional regulator) and the FSA. This Tripartite arrangement received its first serious test during the Northern Rock crisis, and the shambles it made of decision-making when the credit markets froze is now a familiar story to many beyond the narrow confines of the City and Westminster.

The new regime was born of much behind-the-scenes controversy and strife. When New Labour gave independence to the Bank of England soon after it took office, it wanted nothing to detract from its enhanced role of controlling inflation and setting interest rates. Labour blamed the Bank for the serious mistakes made in the regulation of the Bank of Credit and Commerce International (BCCI), which closed down in 1991, and the collapse of Barings Bank four years later. It thought it best that the Bank be insulated from such events so that it could concentrate on becoming a monetary authority with a reputation for the same kind of intellectual rigour as the Bundesbank in Germany (before its functions were taken over by the ECB) and America's Federal Reserve.

In setting up the FSA, therefore, the Treasury wanted to cut the Bank down to size, while also taking the view that, as the traditional distinctions between banks and other financial services, such as mortgages and insurance, were breaking down, it made sense to put responsibility for supervision in the hands of a single, all-powerful regulator. In theory this was correct at a time when bancassurance (insurance products sold over the counter in the high street and on internet sites) was all the rage.

The way in which the Tripartite system was expected to work was set out in a Memorandum of Understanding, which was signed in 1997 and has been updated over the years. Until Northern Rock erupted there was almost no public awareness that such a system, designed to protect consumers from damage and to preserve overall financial stability, actually existed. It was occasionally referred to in the days after 9/11, when airline insurance could not be secured on the open market, but as a recognised system on the lines of Cobra, the Downing Street crisis management team, it barely registered on the public radar.

In essence, the Tripartite system, or T3 as it is called inside government, sees the Treasury in charge. It is responsible for the overall structure of regulation, makes decisions and carries the can in Parliament for any problems that arise. But, as we saw with Northern Rock, the Treasury Select Committee expects the FSA, which serves as a single supervisory authority monitoring banks, insurers and financial markets, and the Bank to be accountable and responsible, too. It has repeatedly called their leaders back to provide testimony and, in its final report, held them culpable for mistakes.

The powers and responsibilities of the FSA, as set out in the Financial Services and Markets Act 2000, are wide ranging. The authorisation and prudential supervision of banks, building societies, investment firms, insurance companies and brokers, credit unions and friendly societies are just two aspects of its work. It is also responsible for the supervision of financial markets, securities listings and of clearing and settlement systems. Indeed, given the scope of its operations, it is, in some respects, remarkable that there haven't been more Northern Rocks – although it might have been a close run thing in the autumn of 2007, when mortgage banks Alliance & Leicester and Bradford & Bingley, instead of relying on the money markets, refinanced part of their loan books by doing private deals with other banks.

Under the Tripartite system, the Bank of England's job is to scan the money markets for problems and to be a lender of last resort – a function formally adopted in the 20th century – under which it makes cash available to ailing banks. The Bank's other responsibilities, as outlined in the 1997 Memorandum, include the maintenance of overall financial stability. It does this by running monetary policy through its work in the money markets, where it seeks to maintain liquidity and ensure that payment systems – the plumbing of the global economy – do not clog.

The British regulatory model is unusual among the main Western economies. Effectively, what its authors, Messrs Brown, Robinson and Balls, did, by moving banking supervision to the FSA, was to weaken the authority of the Bank of England. Indeed, as Balls, then Economic Secretary to the Treasury (otherwise known as the City Minister), explained to me in March 2007, this was always the intention. He and his colleagues wanted the City to look to the FSA for leadership and to be its spokesman. Before the Tripartite system was introduced, banking supervision took up much of what the Bank of England did. In fact, for the former Governor, Eddie George, who had spent most of his career at the Bank and was known in the City as 'Steady Eddie' because of his skill in handling financial crises, it was an integral part of its operation. Traditionally, it helped make the Governor's words law in the City, George reputedly being able to signal his dissatisfaction with poor practice with the merest twitch of an eyebrow. No one at the Treasury initially had the courage to tell the former Governor of the government's clear intention to remove banking supervision to the newly minted FSA. When he did find out just a few weeks later, on 18 May 1997, he hit the roof.

George believed that he had been duped and, worse, had misled bank staff about the new government's intentions. The occasionally voluble, Cambridge-educated George took the highly unusual step of admitting to a press conference a few days later that he had considered resignation over the issue.

One person at the Bank, its chief economist and executive director – soon to become Deputy Governor – Mervyn King was, however, 'cock-a-hoop', according to insiders. The former London School of Economics professor could now concentrate on the task of building the Bank's reputation for excellence in guiding monetary policy. It is paradoxical that the greatest test of all, after he took over as Governor in 2003, would be served up by the credit crunch and the bail-out of Northern Rock four years later.

The rift between George and the Treasury was patched up, though not before word escaped from Downing Street that George had compromised himself with New Labour and might not be re-appointed to a second term. Paradoxically, a decade later – after the credit crunch and the run on Northern Rock – Gordon Brown, who had moved on to No. 10, showed similar reluctance to give Mervyn King a second term as Governor. Downing Street eventually relented, announcing on 30 January 2008 that King would be reappointed to a second five-year stint.

Britain has shown a propensity to stage a banking crisis at least once a decade. However, in the ten years of unprecedented economic growth and stability that followed the removal of banking supervision to Canary Wharf, the Tripartite arrangement was never properly tested. That said, even before Northern Rock, the FSA did not cover itself in glory. In 2000 Britain's oldest insurer, Equitable Life, failed under its watch, and the FSA, then led by former CBI chief and Deputy Governor of the Bank of England Sir Howard Davies, was widely criticised for ignoring warning signs and not spotting insolvency problems at the insurer. Davies is a skilled but thin-skinned operator, who always has found it hard to take criticism. He retired in 2003, taking over as director of the London School of

Economics. The FSA would also take a beating over supervision and enforcement actions against 'split capital trusts' – investment trusts that promise capital protection and income gains. The problems came to the attention of the market only after an analysis of their problems by blue-blooded stockbroker Cazenove in 2001. Once again, the FSA was in the slipstream of enforcement rather than the vanguard.

When it came to supervising the banking system, the problem for the FSA was that the City, like financial centres everywhere, has a huge reverence for central bankers and the mystique around their work and so has a tendency to look to the Bank of England, not the FSA, for guidance. New Labour's idea that the FSA would become an alternative power centre to the Bank therefore never really took off. Indeed, bank bosses, called to regular meetings with supervisors, were often nonplussed by the uninformed, mechanical style of the questions and the failure to tackle the big issues – such as liquidity – and close relationships between bankers and supervisors were therefore never really formed. At the same time, the Bank, fearful of treading on the toes of the new regulator, pulled back from its traditional role of friend and mentor to the banking sector and allowed its financial stability wing to wither.

So, when the Northern Rock crisis came along, the system proved it was not up to the job. There had been no shortage of warning voices. The Liberal Democrat economic spokesman, Vince Cable, a former economist at oil giant Shell and one of the most respected voices in British political life, had warned frequently of the dangers posed by Britain's debt mountain built up during ten years of Labour rule, and before leaving his post in 2005, the Bank of England's then Deputy Governor for financial stability, Sir Andrew Large, cautioned financial institutions on the need to maintain liquidity, so that when crises arose there would be sufficient cash on hand to pay out disgruntled investors or depositors. In the US Fed chairman Alan Greenspan left office warning that the price of homes was no longer sustainable. And in Basle the venerable Bank for International Settlements worried publicly in its annual report about the build-up of asset-backed securities and other derivative products. For those with political memories, it all had the feel of the disastrous period in the 1970s when Tory Chancellor Anthony Barber let credit rip with his policy of 'Competition and Credit Control'. But the FSA, quite simply, never saw the Northern Rock crisis coming.

One irony of the situation was that some nine months before 9 August the Tripartite authorities had taken part in one of their regular 'war games' designed to cope with potential crises that would cause a market meltdown. Previous subjects had been a terrorist attack, avian flu and Sars. On this occasion, however, and behind closed doors at the FSA's headquarters, the crisis simulation looked at the impact on the financial system of a banking crisis and discovered that the government's compensation scheme for savers with deposits in banks that collapse – 100 per cent guarantee for the first £2,000 and 90 per cent for the next £33,000 – was inadequate. The Bank and the FSA recognised that this was a serious problem and that if there were problems at a financial institution savers would be panicked into pulling out their money. Even worse, the cash in the Financial Services Compensation Scheme was negligible, the Scheme lacked capacity to act in a crisis, and it was, inevitably, distrusted. The Treasury was informed and experts were put to work … but nothing happened. Out in the real world, and a few months later, it was the very genuine fear of tens of thousands of ordinary depositors that the money they had saved over their lifetimes could be threatened that drove the run on Northern Rock.

More relevantly, as it turned out, the FSA wanted work done on the global reappraisal of risk that might affect emerging markets and high-yield assets. Sub-prime mortgage products and the high-yielding exotic packages of debt created out of trailer trash loans were not specifically mentioned, but the warning signs were there for everyone to see. Similarly, the FSA's Financial Risk Outlook report for 2007 expressed fears about a deterioration of credit quality –

something directly relevant to Northern Rock as Adam Applegarth embarked on a borrowing and lending spree that saw the former building society capture 20 per cent of Britain's mortgage market in the first half of 2007.

Despite this foresight, no one at the FSA seems to have put two and two together and recognised that Northern Rock was endangered by both events. It was highly vulnerable to a repricing of asset prices, and its accelerated lending meant it was offering increasing volumes of credit to a saturated market where concerns about default were mounting. Mortgage brokers were pushing Northern Rock products hard because the bank was undercutting rivals on price. Senior figures at the FSA have told me that they believe that the organisation dropped the ball because it was so focused on protecting the consumer and was obsessed with the formal capital ratios set by experts at the Bank for International Settlements. Liquidity, the access to ready cash in times of crisis, was not on its radar at all. It was a fundamental shortcoming, and one that would damage the reputation of the FSA and the City and cost the taxpayer – forced to stand behind Northern Rock – dear. To add to its miscalculation, in June 2007 the FSA allowed Northern Rock, which was already facing difficulties, to issue a dividend to shareholders. Back in January its Financial Risk Outlook report underlined the profitability – and by implication the safety – of the banking system, although it did urge financial firms to 'stress-test and do scenario analysis' and specifically wanted to see research on the risks of a 'human influenza pandemic' that could disrupt the financial system.

Another important reason why the FSA fell down on the job was that, unusually among regulators, it liked to think of itself as a 'principles based' regulator, not hidebound by legalistic rulings (although it was not unknown for it to turn a principle into a series of detailed rules). In fact, it has often been described as a 'light-touch' regulator. In this respect, the fact that a strong chairman, in the form of Sir Howard Davies, who was not scared of speaking his mind, was followed by the shadowy leadership of Sir Callum McCarthy, who specialised in keeping a low profile, assumed a particular significance. As for the three-person supervisory team from the FSA assigned to Northern Rock, it is now accepted at the highest level within the FSA itself it failed to focus sufficiently. 'We did not challenge the Northern Rock board enough on the risks it was taking,' a senior FSA official acknowledged to me. 'Supervisors visiting Northern Rock were not really particularly focused on liquidity,' the official added.

It is not surprising therefore that in the first high-level report on the Northern Rock affair it was the FSA – rather than the Bank of England or the Treasury, the other parts of the regulatory Tripartite system – that took the brunt of the criticism. The Treasury Select Committee, chaired by blunt, no-nonsense John McFall, Labour MP for West Dunbartonshire, later noted:

> There were clear warning signs about the risks associated with Northern Rock's business model, both from its rapid growth as a company and the falls in its share price from February 2007 onwards. However, insofar as the FSA undertook greater 'regulatory engagement' with Northern Rock it failed to tackle the fundamental weakness of its model and did nothing to prevent the problems that came to the fore from August 2007 onwards. We regard this as a substantial failure of regulation.

Indeed, the FSA's internal audit of its supervisory actions, published in March 2008, read like a script for an episode of the Keystone Cops, though chief executive Hector Sants did gain credit for coming clean, a rare event when it comes to government blunders. The most astounding revelation was that between April 2004 and February 2007, a period in which Northern Rock had expanded rapidly, it had been supervised by insurance regulators, not bank supervisors. This was despite the fact that Northern Rock's model of raising money, through securitisations, was unusual among its peers. When

Sants was pressed on this curious decision he suggested that it had been used as an experiment in an effort to provide super-visors with broader knowledge. Sants also acknowledged that the FSA had been too consumed with a mission of protecting the consumer and, in the process, had not given due weight to the nitty-gritty of banking enforcement.

The 136-page audit inquiry also revealed that the analytical model used to supervise Northern Rock was wholly inadequate. If the firm had been assessed in relation to its peers a comparison would have found that the Rock was very different. It had a high target for asset growth of 15–25 per cent year on year and for profits growth. It operated on a low net interest rate margin (the difference between borrowing costs in the market and the mortgage rate charged to borrowers), a low cost to income ratio and – most significantly – a high reliance on wholesale funding and securitisation. Yet even though the Rock was very obviously an unusual animal, no one paid much attention. 'There was insufficient engagement by the heads of the department responsible,' the report revealed, and no one both-ered to meet with Northern Rock in the period leading up to the catastrophe. A table accompanying the report showed that most meetings with the Rock were at a low level. Of the eight super-visory sessions that took place between 2005 and 9 August 2007 five were held over just one day and two were by telephone. Sensationally, when the internal auditors looked for a paper trail, they found that the sloppy regulators concerned had not even bothered to take notes. The auditor described Northern Rock as 'an outlier' in terms of the inadequate supervision it received. In other words, for a bank of such sensitivity, given its unusual structure, it was the subject of extraordinarily weak regulation.

Excoriating criticism of this kind might have been expected to result in high-level resignations at the FSA. Indeed, before the report was published there were no fewer than four reorganisa-tions of banking supervision leading to countless departures. The highest level resignation was that of Clive Briault, the managing director in charge of retail markets, who left just days before the internal audit report in March 2008. But the highest level leadership of the FSA felt itself inoculated against early change. Its chairman, the very correct but almost invisible, Sir Callum McCarthy, had announced his departure for September 2008. He chose to take a back seat when the disastrous internal audit was revealed. Chief executive Hector Sants had only taken over as chief executive in July 2007, having previously been in charge of the wholesale markets division. To his credit, Sants took the criticisms on the chin, though he rightly pointed out that the serious errors in policing the bank took place before he took over surveillance from his predecessor, the Arthur Andersen-trained financial expert John Tiner. Sants, who, in my experience, tends to behave as if he were doing the FSA a favour by his presence, argues privately that the regulator will never attract high-quality market practitioners from the City if their actions are constantly questioned from outside. In fact, the opposite will have to be the case. The internal audit report demonstrated why the FSA cannot be left to its own devices.

Of course, most of the blame for the international credit crunch must be laid on reckless attitudes to debt and risk and the greed of the world's leading banks. But the failure of the enforcers to see the crisis coming in the wake of unprecedented mortgage foreclosures in the US and an explosion of credit worldwide was a serious contributory factor. Britain's trio of regulators, quite simply, fell down on the job. The FSA failed to grasp fully the potential for a disaster at Northern Rock given the make-up of its borrowings, the weakness of its board and its relentless pursuit of growth in deteriorating credit and housing markets. The government lacked the experience to deal with the crisis head on, worried about the political fallout and then dithered. The Bank of England tried and failed to fight the momentum of events under a system where its former powers to intervene and take control – as in the case of Johnson Matthey Bank in 1984 – had been severely curtailed.

At no point was there clear cooperation in the handling of the Northern Rock crisis. In fact in the immediate aftermath, all three authorities became involved in an unseemly public spectacle of blaming each other for the mess. The FSA was accused of leaking to the *Financial Times*. Downing Street openly briefed against Mervyn King. And when King decided to take to the airwaves to defend the Bank's role, his appearance on BBC's *File on Four* radio programme was interpreted as criticism of the Chancellor. King was described by Treasury officials as having been 'naïve'. For their part, Alistair Darling's team at the Treasury claimed that, when the Northern Rock crisis developed in August, nobody from the Bank or the FSA had raised the deficiencies of the deposit guarantee scheme as a likely cause of a run on a bank. Even when the queues started to form, they said that the scheme was not the issue. It is my understanding, however, that when the lender of last resort arrangements were being put in place for Northern Rock, King specifically warned that the deposit insurance arrangements were inadequate and increased the risks of a run on retail deposits. In fact, the only point of agreement among the three arms of the Tripartite system was that Britain's regulatory architecture needed total refurbishment.

It is fair to say that no matter how good the regulators are, it is impossible to have a watertight system – as was seen in early 2008 at Société Générale in Paris, when a rogue trader took the bank to the cleaners with the apparent connivance of some senior managers. But while there can be no total protection, the banking supervisors should at least be able to see large, systemic crises coming, and seek to avert them. In the case of sub-prime lending and the credit crunch, the regulators failed so miserably that serious questions have to be asked about their role: their alertness, their responsibilities and the way they performed. Warnings about the credit risk and lack of liquidity were certainly available, but there was a leadership vacuum, and no one was willing to assume control and take the harsh disciplinary action that might have restrained the worst excesses and calmed the market. None of the regulators in Britain,

Europe or the US appeared capable of acting to slow or halt the madness of sub-prime lending and the securities and debts invented to disguise their negligible worth.

But while regulators across the globe have to take a measure of blame, there's no doubt that the Tripartite structure in Britain, with its cumbersome system of decision-making, seems to have been less capable of handling the storm when it came than its American and Continental European counterparts. Certainly, the American system had not been pre-emptive. The excess and corruption that allowed the sub-prime problem to grow into a global financial crisis had been picked up late, and it was not until 2008 that the Securities and Exchange Commission, the US's tough Wall Street enforcer, acknowledged formally that laws may have been broken. The FBI was called in to investigate 14 firms in the sub-prime mortgage chain, from the corrupt brokers sponsoring mortgages that should never have been granted to the investment banks that should have known better. 'We have been raising this issue since 2004,' the FBI disclosed. 'We view mortgage fraud as a significant and growing crime. Combating this is a priority given the housing market's impact on the wider economy.'

Yet when it comes to dealing with financial crises, the Americans, scarred by the experiences of the Great Depression, have learned to act decisively. In the 1980s the US launched a massive bail-out of the Savings and Loans system, which performed much the same job as Britain's building societies, to prevent a systemic collapse. The rescue eventually cost the American taxpayer $124 billion, a sum likely to put eventual UK government losses at Northern Rock in the shade. In 1982, when the American banking system over-exposed itself to Latin American debt, the administration of George Bush Snr invented the so-called Brady Bonds, which allowed the borrowers to securitise debts with a US government guarantee. And in 1998 the Federal Reserve Bank of New York pressed a consortium of leading banks, including Britain's Barclays, into the rescue of the hedge fund Long Term Capital Management.

The Americans have opted for a system for regulating and supervising financial institutions that is highly complex and has an array of overlapping institutions. While Britain adopted a highly centralised system with an all-singing, all-dancing regulator in the shape of the FSA, the Americans have a fractured system of financial regulation under which any single firm might have to deal with several regulators, depending on the range of their businesses. At the national level commercial banks are supervised by three agencies: the Office of the Comptroller of the Currency (OCC), the Federal Reserve System (Federal Reserve) and the Federal Deposit Insurance Corporation (FDIC). Mortgage banks known as 'thrifts' are regulated and supervised by the Office of Thrift Supervision (OTS). The federal system also includes regulation of the securities industry by the Securities and Exchange Commission (SEC) and the Commodities Futures Trading Commission (CFTC). Both organisations have extraordinary powers to seize documents and subpoena witnesses, and they have a reputation for kicking down doors and asking questions afterwards. The regulation of the mortgage intermediaries Fannie Mae and Freddie Mac – which have been hard hit by the sub-prime and housing market imbroglio – is carried out by the Office of Federal Housing Enterprise Oversight (OFHEO) … and so on. If this was not enough regulation, most of the states have their own bank and insurance supervisors.

This Byzantine structure came about because financial regulation has been responsive to traditional concerns that run through American history. Principal among these is a distrust of concentrated financial power and a preference for market competition. There is also a belief that credit is an entitlement, like any other, but the consumer has to be properly protected from charlatans out for a quick profit. The reality of the American system is that everyone knows their role, and the culture of regulation is very much enshrined in the national psyche. Far from being regarded with disdain in the financial community, as the FSA was in Britain, the culture of regulation at the SEC is deeply ingrained. The best and the brightest young lawyers regard a stint at the SEC or in the New York Attorney General's office as a critical stepping stone to an eventual political career or job at a top law firm, where they will enjoy rich rewards.

The reality, too, is that in every financial crisis the Fed is *primus inter pares*, willingly intervening to ensure stability. Both the Fed and FDIC played key roles in the rescue of Countrywide Financial, the sub-prime lender rescued by Bank of America in 2007. FDIC seized and protected the depositors, and the Fed encouraged Bank of America to step in. If any breaches of securities laws were to be found at Countrywide it would be the job of the SEC, with the assistance of the Justice Department, to take action. The Fed, under Ben Bernanke, also moved decisively to slash interest rates with large, bold cuts to the key interest rate in a matter of days when the sub-prime crisis threatened to sweep banks and the stock market into the Hudson River early in 2008. There has never been any hang-up over 'moral hazard' when the stability of the financial system or the prosperity of the nation is at stake. Republican President Calvin Coolidge's dictum 'the chief business of the American people is business' is never lost sight of when a financial crisis or recession looms

Europe, of course, operates rather differently. At the core of the European system of regulation is the 'single passport', which allows financial groups to operate across the EU. Home country regulators supervise home country laws and regulations, but host countries specify rules of conduct and supervise compliance. This places a huge onus on the UK's flawed FSA, since so many of the Continental banks, including, Germany's Deutsche Bank and the major Swiss banks UBS and Credit Suisse, have chosen to set up their investment banking headquarters in the City of London. The most recent effort to harmonise practice across the EU came via the clumsily named Markets in Financial Instruments Directive (MiFID), which aims to improve consumer protection.

Being part of the EU imposes constraints, as the British government found with its rescue of Northern Rock. Throughout the crisis it was conscious of the fact that using state loans to support the bank for more than six months would be in breach of EU rules. Similarly, Mervyn King took the view in the summer of 2007 that it would be impossible secretly to rescue Northern Rock, in the traditional way of the Bank of England, because it would be in breach of EU regulations. The reality is that, of itself, a bank rescue would have been permitted. What would have stymied the bail-out was a requirement under MiFID that the markets would have had to be immediately notified of any change in Northern Rock's condition. Clearly, public notification of the liquidity crisis and the likely losses the bank was facing might have had much the same effect as the disclosure of the leaked lender of the last resort facility.

Yet, significantly, none of this seems to have troubled the German authorities when three of their banks ran into difficulty on or around 9 August. Old-fashioned German banking regulation swung into force, and the rest of the system was prevailed upon to do the right thing by providing reserves and capital to the ailing banks and absorbing them into larger, healthier institutions. It was an operation conducted in a matter of days, in stark contrast to the regulatory stalemate that took place in Britain.

While he was dealing with the immediate crisis of bailing out Northern Rock, Alistair Darling recognised that the Tripartite system he had inherited was seriously dysfunctional, and he set about reforming it as quickly as possible. Its failure fully to grab control of the situation as it evolved persuaded him to institute a Treasury equivalent of Cobra, a recognition that coordination during the credit crunch was poor. Similarly, he and senior Treasury officials finally recognised how dangerous it was that Britain lacked a credible bank insurance scheme similar to the one operated by the Federal Deposit Insurance Corporation in the US – with pots of ready reserves to make sure that personal depositors had nothing to fear from bank runs. In what was also an admission that the 1997 arrangements were not good enough, Darling proposed that the FSA would be given powers to take control of failing banks and the Bank of England would have the right to mount secret rescues – something that might, potentially, have avoided the Northern Rock crisis.

The international blame game began in earnest with the arrival of the credit crunch, and everyone, including the regulators, has rightly come in for heavy criticism. Apportioning blame is inevitable when people have been thrown out of their homes, when investors have lost so much money and when the stability of the global financial and economic system has been rocked to the core. Some nasty home truths have come to the fore. In an increasingly global market with ever more complex products and interdependence, there is an obvious need for vigilance and early-warning systems that work as well as sharp-witted and experienced regulators who know how to deal with a crisis when it arrives.

In America and in mainland Europe, central banks play a central part in regulation. That did not happen in Britain when problems arose with Northern Rock. The key role here was with the FSA, which fell down badly on the job. But it was not the only villain. The Bank of England was slow to react, and in this it failed in its responsibilities, too.

CHAPTER 7

Central Bankers

Who got it right, who got it wrong

Most of the time central bankers are the hidden hand of the global economy. They tend to shun the limelight, preferring to work quietly, but effectively, in the background. The buildings they traditionally inhabit are designed to reflect the solidity of their trade. The Bank of England, with its powerful, stone curtain walls, sits at the heart of the City of London and is uniquely stylish with its army of pink-coated waiters – the former military men – who welcome visitors and escort them down wide corridors and through myriad doors to the Court, where the Governor and his deputies overlook one of the finest and best tended courtyards in Britain. The walls are decorated with the portraits of past Governors, City scenes and cartoons, including that of the famous 18th-century illustrator James Gillray, lampooning the Bank as the Old Lady of Threadneedle Street.

Similarly, the Federal Reserve Board, which sits opposite the Department of State in downtown Washington, D.C., is a magnificent building with Doric columns. It lacks the style and artwork of the Bank of England but exudes the same solidity. The headquarters of the European Central Bank, Eurotower, in the centre of Frankfurt, is different. It reflects a different time and a different age. With its twin towers and brightly lit 'Euro' sculpture, it is a creature of the modern era, mimicking the glossy, high-rise architecture of the financial districts of southern Manhattan, Canary Wharf and Frankfurt itself.

When central bankers do speak it is often elliptically. Theirs is a world of mystique, a world of money supply, demand variations, asset values and inflationary expectations. Except in the most exceptional circumstances hints about interest rates are buried in riddles, spawning a whole industry of central bank watchers whose job it is to interpret the jargon and, if necessary, advise the companies for which they work on which way to jump in their investment dealings.

Often the same speech or the same testimony by a central banker is translated as pointing in opposite directions by the chroniclers of their work. It is all part of the mystique. It is unusual for central bankers to become household names. The sheer endurance of Alan Greenspan at the Federal Reserve, his marriage to a glamorous television reporter, Andrea Mitchell, and his mastery of his subject turned the former Fed chairman into a global personality and, when his memoirs were published in 2007, a bestselling author. But he is the exception rather than the rule.

It is when a crisis emerges that central bankers break cover and become objects of public fascination and speculation. The three key players in the sub-prime saga – Bank of England Governor Mervyn King, Ben Bernanke of the Federal Reserve and the European Central Bank's Jean-Claude Trichet – faced the biggest test of their careers when the global markets seized up on 9 August. The personalities, differing political environments and contrasting political agendas of the three men helped shape their actions. In the event – and to the surprise of many – it was Trichet who best recognised the scale of the problem and how to deal with it and who best understood the political fallout that followed. Bernanke, a novice in comparison, was slower off the mark, but he, too, eventually bent to the will of Wall Street. In Britain King was more guarded and has since come to recognise critical mistakes, not least in his communications with the market.

Indeed, it would be more than a month into Britain's worst banking crisis for a generation before King finally lifted his head above the parapet when he was summoned before the Treasury Select Committee. This is not because he had been absent during the unfolding drama. In fact, the owlish and likeable Governor had buried himself in the minutiae of the crisis, and had even been known to pronounce on the dangers of surging house prices, although his tendency has always been to see this more as a social than an economic phenomenon. But he was reluctant to take a firm hand with errant high street bankers, believing that this was a task for the Financial Services Authority. His main concern remained the control of inflation and keeping it below the Treasury's 2 per cent target, even though the credit crunch threatened fundamentally to shift the global economy.

The truth is that for all King's mastery of the workings of the financial markets and his understanding of the way that responsibility for the stability of the banking system was split between the Financial Services Authority and the Bank of England, some felt he lacked the sure touch expected of central bankers in crises. This may partly be because he is the first Governor with a largely academic background. He studied at King's College, Cambridge, and at Harvard, later teaching and researching economics at Harvard, Massachusetts Institute of Technology and Cambridge and Birmingham universities. He eventually settled into the post of Professor of Economics at the London School of Economics in 1984, where he was highly rated.

Among those he taught at Cambridge was Bob Parker, now deputy chairman of Credit Suisse Asset Management, who told the BBC: 'If, 30 years ago, you'd asked me the question: "Did I think that he would eventually end up as Governor of the Bank of England?" I think the answer would be no. He was very likeable, very personable, very friendly, very approachable. He taught economics in a very clear, easy-to-understand way.'

King is certainly no ivory-tower academic, though. He is quick witted and erudite and performs well in the public spotlight. Every quarter, when the Bank delivers its Inflation Report, a document all but invented by King, he happily appears before the world's financial media and takes questions for more than an hour on British and global economic developments with supreme confidence. He is also fantastically enthu-siastic about sport, applying the same clinical analy-sis to the teams he supports, Aston Villa FC and Worcestershire County Cricket Club, as he does to policy-making. I recall a lengthy lunch with him at a restaurant in central London where the then Deputy Governor studiously contrasted the value, pound for pound, of his Villa squad with that of Chelsea FC. Born in 1948, he is a baby boomer who recently married, relatively late in life.

King left the academic world to join the Bank of England as chief economist in 1991, long before anyone had seriously contemplated giving the Old Lady her independence. But soon after the trauma of Britain's exit from the exchange rate mechanism the then Chancellor Norman (now Lord) Lamont put in place a rudimen-tary system of inflation targeting, which paved the way for mon-etary independence. In May 1997, almost immediately after New Labour came to power, the Bank was given its independence to set interest rates, and King was put in charge of the new quarterly Inflation Reports, which would track the progress of prices and output. Fathom Financial Consulting's Danny Gabay, worked with him: 'He adopts a very intellectual approach, and always did, to the Bank of England's work, which I think has borne fruit,' he said. 'He is a serious person, particularly when it comes to policy – but he has a lighter side, as his frequent references to sport in his speeches show.'

After a stint as Deputy Governor, King was appointed to the top job on the retirement of Eddie George in June 2003. Since then his inner toughness, firmness of purpose and attention to detail have been seen in the workings of the Bank's Monetary Policy Committee, where he has mostly been seen as an 'inflation hawk' and someone who has not flinched from voting to raise rates in an attempt to bear down on any inflationary pressures, no matter how unpopular that may make him with a wider audience. Indeed, his willingness, from time to time, to take a minority position is unusual among central bank leaders.

In the first years of King's era the clear focus of the Bank was on monetary policy. Until Northern Rock erupted, everything else was regarded as of secondary importance. Whereas Eddie George knew every aspect of the Bank, including the people and systems used for smoothing payments and the foreign exchange operations, the present Governor appeared to show only intermittent interest in such matters. His concern was tracking the progress of the economy, recruiting the very best economists and developing grand thoughts on the future shape of the International Monetary Fund and the global financial system. He certainly had a rare genius when it came to managing inflation. The record of the Bank was widely admired and became a blueprint for other banks across the world. He was an economic leader who easily understood the economic underpinnings of the credit crunch, its origins and its dangers. He thought through carefully the arguments about 'moral hazard' and articulated them in a most convincing way. Yet when it came to the practical side of banking – the provision of liquidity designed to prevent contagion – King was strangely out of touch. He behaved as if the Bank was able to offer only fundamentalist, free-market solutions and should not pollute its reputation by becoming involved in nuanced activity in the money markets. No two financial crises are ever the same, yet the lesson to be learned from the past is that sitting on your hands at a time when markets are failing to function properly – if at all – is not an option.

When, in 2004, the Bank decided to change the way it operated in the money markets, through an auction system for reserves, it was Paul Tucker, one of the few prominent insiders left at the Bank, who would lead the charge and do the briefing. King was happier monitoring inflation expectations. As for financial stability, King believed that this function, hived off first to Deputy Governor Andrew Large and then his successor Sir John Gieve, was more academic than anything else. The Bank's great thoughts would be laid out in its financial stability reports. Its regular warnings on house prices, stock markets and commercial property would be reported in headlines in the national press, and that seemed to constitute job done. And in fact for some three years before the Northern Rock crisis the Bank of England, along with the Bank for International Settlements and the International Monetary Fund, issued warnings that markets were pricing risk wrongly, and that investments once seen as risky were yielding little more than rock-solid government bonds. The warnings went unheeded.

What didn't make things any easier was the fact that in 2007, just as the sub-prime crisis was enveloping the world, Alistair Clark, one of the most experienced financial stability regulators, left the Bank. He did not cut the most dashing figure on the international financial circuit, and this may well have counted against him in the battle to climb to the very highest level at the Bank. But he is a decent and amusing man with an encyclopaedic knowledge of the world of banking and financial regulation, and the Bank sorely needed his advice. He was eventually recalled to his post in the summer. Privately, King was to acknowledge that as an operational function, financial stability, unlike monetary policy, had been a poor relation within the Bank, and this was partly due to King's own interests. In fairness to King, though, and as I have already pointed out, it also reflected the confusion at the heart of Britain's regulatory system, which came with the setting up of the Financial Services Authority. The FSA's own Financial Risk Outlook in many ways simply duplicated the work being done at the Bank. It was a case of two separate institutions working on parallel rail tracks, with very few points where they came together.

King traced the causes of the credit crunch and the Northern Rock affair back to the Asian financial crisis of 1997. This had proved so chastening to the countries of the region that they embarked on a new strategy, using income from low-cost exports to the West to build up vast war chests of reserves. This glut of savings was recycled into global financial markets, driving down yields on government bonds and hence long-term interest rates and returns. Markets sought higher yielding investments to help them cope with the pressures of ageing populations and to satisfy the demands of high-rolling investors in hedge funds. They then became ever more confident and made ever riskier financial plays.

The Governor was only too aware of this, so when the credit crunch arrived, he therefore decided to play hardball. The Bank, he said, would offer help only to institutions that ran short of cash overnight – and it would punish their recklessness by charging them a penal rate of interest. Critics of King argued that it was inexplicable, at a time when credit markets were still congested, that the Bank continued to demand a one-point premium on an official bank rate of 5.75 per cent. For the banks it was a red rag to a bull, reflecting an unusual level of distrust between the Bank and the high street lenders. The days when clearing bank chiefs and the Governor maintained quiet and cordial relations seemed to have gone.

King's approach to handling the sub-prime crisis contrasted starkly with his counterparts at the European Central Bank and America's Federal Reserve. When the BNP Paribas bank was rocked by losses in the sub-prime market, the ECB delivered massive assistance to the money markets – more than £60 billion on the first day alone. Across the Atlantic, Ben Bernanke did much the same, although he needed some prodding from the Wall Street princelings. But King's attitude was different. The Bank of England made it clear through media briefings that it did not believe in the power of such massive efforts to stabilise markets and lower short-term interest rates. It also turned out, according to a senior Bank official, that it lacked some of the tools.

The European Central Bank had the authority to lend to the markets against almost any collateral – including mortgage debt – but this was not part of the Bank's armoury. It eventually won the authority to operate such a scheme in April 2008 when it offered short-dated British government bonds in exchange for mortgage securities. Such weapons are vital if there is to be a ready supply of money for banks that cannot raise cash. Instead of offering emergency aid, King thought such wholesale bail-outs only benefited those players in the financial markets who had behaved irresponsibly.

King's early approach was quickly exposed as wrong-headed. It increased jittery nerves rather than calming them. When Barclays, one of Britain's best capitalised and strongest banks, asked the Bank for a £1.6 billion overnight loan – a demand that, normally, would not have raised an eyebrow – it found itself the subject of lurid headlines questioning its long-term stability. What King had achieved was to raise fears about the future of a sound institution. Not surprisingly, considering the reaction, the Bank quickly reversed its policy by abolishing the penal rate of interest and releasing more money.

The damage, though, was done and instability set in. According to Alan Greenspan, the respected former head of the Federal Reserve, who had steered the world through the 1987 stock market crash, King's policy was too subtle. He criticised the hard-line approach to bail-outs, telling me in an interview in his office in Washington, D.C., on 11 September: 'You cannot calibrate liquidity to only rescue the deserving.' Greenspan's view was that bailing out the 'greedy and the egregious' is the price that had to be paid for overall economic stability. In plain English, some rogue banks have to be helped as part of the larger picture of securing the health of well-run institutions.

Ultimately, King's refusal to pump money into the markets after 9 August made a bad situation worse. Unlike the European and American central banks, which flooded hundreds of billions of euros and dollars into the markets, he sanctioned much smaller amounts and demanded a punitive rate of interest. Although the Bank of England is clearly a much smaller central bank than its US and European counterparts, it does sit at the centre of Europe's most important financial centre where liquidity is essential. Through much of August the Bank was under intense pressure to ease the terms under which it supplied reserves of cash to the market. Some participants believed that an emergency cut in interest rates might have helped to ease the crush in the money markets. Others felt that the Bank's hurdle for borrowing, with the penalty rate that had to be paid, was too high. There was also a belief that the Bank needed to broaden the range of securities it would accept as collateral – something that had been possible at the ECB in Frankfurt and was later followed through by the Federal Reserve. Had the Bank acted more flexibly earlier on it is possible – though by no means certain – that confidence could have been restored and the high risk of other banks being weakened avoided.

King may well have calculated that the freeze in the inter-bank market was a one-off and that once the banks had accumulated bigger cash cushions there would be a return to normality. But it did not happen. Months after the inter-bank markets clogged up they were still largely closed to business, although interest rate spreads in the City – the cost of short-term and three-month money – did fall back in line with those on the Continent and in the USA in the autumn of 2007.

King has also come under fire for not acting earlier and possibly preventing the collapse of Northern Rock by allowing a rescue bid by Lloyds TSB, which had been approached about a rescue. One member of the Bank's governing Court suggested to me that the whole situation might have been handled differently had King's predecessor, Eddie George, been in the hot seat, with Howard Davies at the FSA and Gordon Brown still at the Treasury. The suggestion is that George would have knocked heads together. This is the way he had acted in 1998. George had summoned high street bankers from their country homes and gardens on a Sunday afternoon to persuade them that they had to act to bail-out the trade credits of Korea or risk a cascading series of defaults that would have ended up damaging their own balance sheets.

The Bank of England, however, rejects the notion that it could have countenanced the Lloyds TSB offer or assembled other bankers in a darkened room and forced a rescue for Northern Rock. The former building society had a vast liquidity requirement of between £20 billion and £30 billion, so any 'behind-closed-doors' rescue would have been on a far bigger scale than anything ever attempted before. The size of the guarantee Lloyds asked for was larger than the entire reserves held by the banking system as a whole. 'Even Eddie George couldn't have whistled that deal through in a weekend,' a senior Bank insider told me. Moreover, the moment the Bank went to the government for permission, the whole EU state aid issue would have raised its head. This rule didn't apply to the ECB's action in effectively rescuing the troubled French and German banks, because it pumped money into the markets and not into the individual banks.

'I don't believe it was realistic at any time to believe the government would agree to collude in concealing large-scale state aid from the Commission,' the official added. It was also noted that it would have been all but impossible for the Bank and Lloyds TSB to have kept a secret rescue from the market. When Barclays borrowed just £300 million from the Bank in August, the information leaked almost immediately and was plastered across the financial pages the following day.

Whatever excuses are made for King, though, the fact is that the hero of the fight against inflation had not proved adept at battling turmoil in the markets and the most dramatic run on a British bank seen in modern times. So questionable had his performance been that for most of the autumn of 2007 his reappointment to a second term as Governor, starting in June 2008, appeared to be in doubt, despite his stellar record as a fighter of inflation. In the end it was Downing Street that blinked, fearing it would be punished on the financial markets if it were to swap King for one of the Prime Minister's favourites, but it was not until February 2008 that he was confirmed in his job for a full five years, an announcement that he had been holding out for in the face of suggestions that he might care to resign before he had served a second, full five-year term.

Banking misery continued into 2008. In the spring it became clear that the money markets in Britain were still not functioning normally. Interest rates in the inter-bank market remained elevated and well above the official rate set by the Bank of England, despite several cuts in the bank rate since 9 August 2007. Almost all the mortgage lenders, the high street banks and the building societies were hurting and finding it difficult to lend to house buyers. The Prime Minister made it clear that he wanted the high street banks to pass on interest rate cuts by the Bank, but in a series of meetings, first, with Mervyn King at the Bank and later at Downing Street, the high street banks requested assistance. They wanted the Bank to take illiquid mortgages off their books and exchange them for government bonds or cash.

The government was determined not to roll over at the demands from overpaid high street bankers. When the Treasury go-between John Kingman had turned to the commercial banks for assistance in the autumn of 2007, as the Northern Rock situation was worsening, the door had been politely shut in his face. It was claimed that the world was a different place from that of previous decades, when central banks and governments could sort out a financial crisis between themselves, including picking up the pieces of failed financial institutions. Britain's high street banks today were global institutions, with a different reach and different responsibilities. So now that the very same banks were in difficulty because of the continued blockages in the money market and were desperately short of capital, they could not expect an easy ride. Attitudes towards the banks had hardened in both Downing Street and Threadneedle Street. King was determined that this should not be a cost free bail-out. If the banks wanted assistance they would have to be prepared to take a 'hair cut'. The collateral they offered would be valued at very cautious rates – that is, there would be no pound-for-pound exchange of mortgages for government bonds.

The Governor also rightly believed this should not be a cost-free exercise. The high street banks needed to behave more responsibly by strengthening their capital. They also had to be encouraged to adopt policies that would see them accumulate capital, reserves and liquidity during the upswing in the economic cycle, leaving them better placed to weather the storm when the financial system froze or the economy stumbled. King was determined that if there was to be a government rescue – which would inject a possible £100 billion into the money markets – it would be in exchange for a new, more cautious approach. A price would have to be paid for rapacious and imprudent behaviour, and this included rebuilding their balance sheets through a massive capital raising exercise, led by the Royal Bank of Scotland. This was soon followed by Halifax Bank of Scotland (HBOS). King might have started out as neophyte when the credit crisis hit, but he had learned some crucial lessons.

His opposite number in America, Ben Bernanke, was also learning on the job through the early days of the credit crunch. Another academic turned policy-maker, he had taken over at the Fed from the legendary Alan Greenspan in February 2006 as the first reverberations from the sub-prime mortgage implosion and the record foreclosure rates on homes were beginning to be felt across the continental United States.

In assuming the reins, Bernanke had found Greenspan an exceedingly hard act to follow, even though his rise to the top had been seamless. His CV was a roll-call of the Ivy League – Harvard, Stanford, Princeton and MIT – and at Cambridge, Massachusetts, he had once shared an office with Mervyn King. Bernanke had a reputation as a leading economic thinker. But he also had little practical knowledge of government and markets. Greenspan, on the other hand, had sat on the board of Morgan Stanley and spent much of his career in the private sector advising America's great companies.

Bernanke was born in Augusta, Georgia, in December 1953, the son of a drugstore owner. He grew up in a traditional Jewish family in the nondescript town of Dillon, South Carolina, where he earned a reputation as the cleverest child in the school. He was active in all aspects of school life, including editing the newspaper and playing the saxophone in the marching band – a skill he shared with Greenspan. From the beginning it was obvious that he was very bright academically. His mother Edna once revealed in an interview: 'He demanded that I read to him all the time. And, all of a sudden, he would say: "Mom, I can read this story".' Bernanke was asked in later years to explain this bookishness. 'We lived in a small town that didn't have a movie theater!' he replied. On one celebrated occasion his skills nearly gained a national platform. At the age of 11 he had become the spelling bee champion of his state and failed to make it on to the televised finals by only one mark because he forgot that the word 'edelweiss' has only one i.

Overcoming this setback, in 1975 he went on to graduate, with the highest honours, in economics from Harvard and later gained a PhD from MIT after doing research into the Great Depression, one of his two obsessions and a hugely useful discipline for someone who was going to have to steer America through the credit crunch and its aftermath. His second passion was for the Boston Red Sox baseball team. 'I missed a lot of classes in my first term at MIT because of the Boston–Cincinnati World Series,' he said in an interview with Matthew Benjamin in the US *News & World Report*. 'I've been trying to wean myself from them since 1986 after their heartbreaking defeat to the Mets.' More recently, as a Washingtonian, he is believed to have switched his baseball allegiance to the Nationals team.

The boy prodigy was now well on the road that would lead, ultimately, to Washington and to becoming head of the most powerful central bank in the world. Along the way, and with a succession of impressive teaching appointments under his belt, he gained a strong reputation that would stand him in good stead for the tough world of international finance and politics. He would joke that, at Princeton the only tough decision was deciding whether to serve bagels or doughnuts at the department coffee break! Despite his academic background, he had a knack of capturing headlines. In a speech in

2002 he referred to the state avoiding deflation by printing more money. More colourfully he referred to Milton Friedman's idea of a 'helicopter drop' of money into the economy. From then on, Bernanke became known in the media as 'Helicopter Ben'.

When Greenspan announced his retirement just before his 80th birthday, there were genuine concerns in some quarters about whether there was anybody who could possibly step into his shoes. After all, Greenspan had become something of a Colossus bestriding the international scene and was widely regarded as the key architect of US economic policy. During his tenure he had steadied markets during financial crises, endorsed budget and tax reforms and led the fight against inflation. Greenspan was so highly regarded on global financial markets that traders would spread rumours of his demise – causing the markets to collapse – as a means of extricating themselves from a short position.

The hunt to find a successor for Greenspan did not prove easy. In the summer of 2005 the *New York Times* reported an official in the Bush administration as saying: 'We've got at least three good choices, but we're not in love with any of them.' Clearly, Bernanke was one of those three, and when he finally grabbed the prize, some commentators saw it as an out of the ordinary choice. Four years before he had been virtually unknown outside academia. Yet he emerged as a front-runner, leaping ahead of veteran Republicans who had advised Bush for years and helped engineer his huge tax cuts of 2001 and 2003. It was a remarkable ascent to the most powerful economic post in the nation, given Bush's tendency to promote people from a small circle of colleagues and advisers he had known for years and trusted implicitly.

In settling on Bernanke, Bush opted for a candidate with intellectual standing who would satisfy others – investors on Wall Street, lawmakers in Congress – more than himself or his Republican base. Even though he is regarded as an instinctive, yet quiet, Republican, the straight-talking, Ivy League-trained economist with stellar credentials, who possessed a reputation for eschewing political ideology, is thought to be capable of working just as easily with a Democrat administration. There were dissenting voices, though. 'Of all the Fed governors Bernanke is the one I would be most fearful of,' said Michael Metz, chief investment strategist at Oppenheimer Holdings. 'He is too fast with the trigger and his take on inflation and deflation has been proven wrong.'

Bernanke was certainly not the first choice of ardent supporters of supply-side economics, who favour deep tax cuts and tight monetary policy as the best medicine to strengthen the economy. They wanted R. Glenn Hubbard, one of the architects of Bush's sweeping tax cuts and one of the leading candidates. Others in the White House leaned towards Martin S. Feldstein, a Harvard economist who served as Ronald Reagan's chief economic adviser. Neither was Bernanke favoured by the outgoing Fed chairman, who had quietly pushed for Donald L. Kohn, a governor of the Fed and political independent who had previously been his chief of staff. Greenspan was none too enthusiastic about Bernanke's public espousal of the cause of 'inflation targeting', the method of controlling inflation used by the Bank of England. He had also suspected that the former academic might not be a Republican, though this had been disproved when Bush elevated Bernanke to the White House post of chairman of his Council of Economic Advisers. This was a job held by Greenspan under Gerald Ford. Greenspan describes it in his memoir *The Age of Turbulence* as 'a small consulting firm with a single client: the president of the United States'.

But Bernanke quickly made an impression at the Fed, speaking out on a wide array of economic topics as well as about the central bank's need to become more open and to peg policy to publicly stated inflation targets. When it came down to it, he had what many outsiders wanted: a world-class reputation among economists, credibility on Wall Street and a confidence and an air of political independence that seemed free from hints of cronyism. 'He was the safe choice, somebody with unquestioned qualifications,' said Bruce Bartlett, a conservative economic analyst who worked under

Presidents Reagan and George Bush Snr: 'We needed somebody that everybody, including the financial markets, would react to positively.'

Bernanke had also said all the right things in the past. In the world of economic policy-making, he had espoused targeting inflation and stressed the importance of communication and transparency within the Fed and argued that the final say on debt and deficits lay with Congress and the President. In fact, Bernanke effectively wrote his own job spec when he co-authored an article in the *Wall Street Journal* saying: 'The Fed needs an approach that consolidates the gains of the Greenspan years and ensures that those successful policies will continue – even if future Fed chairmen are less skilful or less committed to price stability than Mr Greenspan has been.'

Once Bernanke's appointment was announced, Greenspan was moved to say of his successor: 'The President has made a distinguished appointment in Ben Bernanke. Ben comes with superb academic credentials and important insights into the ways our economy functions. I have no doubt that he will be a credit to the nation as chairman of the Federal Reserve Board.'

As he began to settle in, Bernanke joked that the hardest part of moving to the Fed was wearing a suit: 'My proposal that Fed governors should signal their commitment to public service by wearing Hawaiian shirts and Bermuda shorts has so far gone unheeded.' Unfortunately, he was soon to discover how hard the job could be. Replacing Greenspan, sometimes called the most successful central banker ever, was never going to be easy, but the timing was particularly unkind, and Bernanke, perhaps in the spirit of an open approach, got off to an accident-prone start that sent the markets tumbling.

An advocate of more transparent Fed policy, he had to back away from his initial idea of stating clearer inflation goals, because such statements tended drastically to affect the stock market. He committed a real gaffe when he became the victim of a breach of confidence by journalist Maria Bartiromo, famed on Wall Street as 'the money honey', who disclosed on CNBC television a private conversation on Fed policy. It was a mistake Greenspan would never have made. Bernanke was attacked for naïvely making public statements directly to the media about the Fed's direction.

The job was proving a steep learning curve for this family man with two children, and the critics were soon speaking out. Some in Wall Street and the City of London were already asking whether he was up to the job. 'He's a very nice guy. He's thoughtful and pragmatic,' said Gerard Lyons, chief economist at Standard Chartered. 'The difficulty is: he's on a hiding to nothing.' He had learned that you couldn't establish transparency via a journalist's ear at a party, and so had decided that the best way would be to set up an easily understandable process. This was not something, however, that would have met with the approval of Greenspan, who offered more opaque musings on the economy. As for Bernanke's declared aim of targeting inflation, adopted in Britain and across the world, this, too, was opposed by Greenspan, who believed central banks needed to keep markets guessing about how tough they would be on inflation.

Like Greenspan, however, Bernanke is a data man, a habit acquired perhaps from devouring baseball statistics as a boy. Mervyn King, a former colleague at MIT in the 1980s, once advised him: 'Think deeply and don't get carried away with the latest statistics.' Nonetheless, Bernanke likes forecasting and has argued that central bankers should rely less on guesswork and as much as possible on the enormous amounts of economic data available to them. He concedes, though, that systems don't tell you everything, and that sound judgement is essential, too. Unfortunately for him, the first real test of his capacity for sound judgement was not far off.

When 9 August dawned and the sub-prime crisis finally registered with the markets, it was not immediately clear whether Bernanke would punish or bail out capitalism. Greenspan had been loved by Wall Street because every time the market ran into trouble, from the 1987 Wall Street Crash onwards, he had ridden to the rescue with dramatic cuts in interest rates. There were those, however, who argued that it was precisely this approach that had helped create a monster housing bubble. Mark Weisbrot of the Center for Economic and Policy Research in Washington, for example, observed of Bernanke: 'My main take on him is that he is getting a bad rap because Greenspan left him with a mess. Bernanke is getting the blame for what Greenspan did.' At first, the message from the Fed appeared to be that Bernanke would not follow the traditional Greenspan course of action. Nevertheless, while King sat on his hands on 9 August and let the European Central Bank take the strain, Bernanke showed no hesitation in calming the markets by offering exceptional funds to banks that were hurting. He did not at first, however, accompany this with decisive action on interest rates.

It soon became clear to the Fed that simply pumping short-term cash into the markets was not enough. The message from the big investment houses, via the New York Federal Reserve Bank, was that they were hurting badly. Many of the big investment houses had loaded up their balance sheets with securities based on sub-prime and their value was dropping like a stone. Investment house Bear Stearns had been among the first to be hit, revealing that sub-prime based investments in two funds it had launched could be worth as little as eight cents in the dollar. As in Europe, confidence was plunging and banks were refusing to lend to each other as they sought to hang on to cash and feared for the health of their competitors.

On the evening of 17 August Timothy Geithner, the chairman of the New York Fed, the operational arm of the central bank, and Don Kohn, the vice-chair of the Federal Reserve Board, held a conference call with Wall Street's business elite, including Citigroup, J.P. Morgan Chase and Goldman Sachs. Kohn encouraged banks to borrow from the discount window, arguing no opprobrium would attach to this and that it was a 'a sign of strength'. Then, the following day, Bernanke gave in to market pressure, and in a dramatic act, seen by his critics as a policy switch, cut the 'discount rate' (at which banks can borrow directly from the Fed) by half a point to 5.75 per cent. It was the first time since 9/11 that the American central bank had acted to cut either of its key interest rates between meetings. And it was instructive that while the Bank of England's King insisted on charging overnight borrowers, such as Barclays, a penalty rate of interest – effectively punishing them – the Fed was moving in the opposite direction and offering hard-pressed banks cheaper overnight money if they needed it. At the same time, there were heavy hints that a cut in the key Federal Funds rate would be forthcoming. Bernanke was taking the first step along the Greenspan road, bulldozing fears about 'moral hazard' to one side and putting the financial system first.

With the markets steadying, it seemed that the Fed boss had come through his first tough test over sub-prime. The pressure was off for the time being, but, of course, Bernanke still faces the challenge of trying to steer the US economy away from a full-blown recession, and how he balances inflation targets and the level of interest rates will remain critical. His response to the unfolding crisis since 18 August 2007 has been to make a series of decisive interest rate cuts, acting sometimes between meetings, seeking to ease the housing crisis and the pressure on the banking system and to keep America's consumers, the key to global expansion, spending.

Bernanke's finest hour in the credit crisis came over the weekend of 14–16 March 2008 when the historic investment house of Bear Stearns ran into difficulties. On Friday, 14 March Bernanke held an early-morning conference call with his colleagues Timothy Geithner of the New York Federal Reserve, and the US Treasury Secretary, Hank Paulson, a former chief executive of investment bank Goldman Sachs. Bernanke, the expert on the Great Depression, now came into his own. Even though Bear Stearns was not technically a bank, he proposed that regulations put in place in the 1930s allowing the Fed to provide assistance to non-banks like Bear Stearns should be used.

The Fed offered Bear Stearns a 28-day line of credit, to be activated through the large commercial and investment bank J.P. Morgan Chase. At the same time, in an effort to shore up confidence, it authorised Bill Dudley, the head of open market operations at the New York Fed and a former senior economist at Goldman Sachs, to open the discount window to all investment banks, a policy previously resisted.

Frantic negotiations took place over the weekend, and by Monday morning the Fed was in a position to announce that Bear Stearns was to be taken over by J.P. Morgan at a price of $2 a share (increased five-fold a week later) and that $30 billion of Fed funds would be made available. On 19 March Bernanke forced through a three-quarter point interest rate cut to 2.25 per cent, despite the dissent of two members of the interest rate setting Open Markets Committee. In Washington Bernanke's decisive action won him great plaudits. Chris Dodd, the chair of the Senate Banking Committee, declared: 'To allow this [Bear Stearns] to go into bankruptcy, I think, would have created some systemic problems which would have been massive.' Bernanke had found his feet at last.

Bernanke might not have got off to the quickest of starts, but he appeared to have made a reasonable fist of handling the sub-prime crisis. Wall Street nevertheless was far from satisfied, arguing that he had been 'behind the curve' in cutting interest rates in August and September 2007 when the crisis first flared up. Jean-Claude Trichet, president of the European Central Bank, by contrast, seems to have won almost universal plaudits – so much so that the *Financial Times* named him 'Person of the Year' for his performance. France has a history of producing solid central bankers and has dominated the leadership at the International Monetary Fund in Washington, producing three out of the last four managing directors, Michel Camdessus, Jacques de Larosière and the current incumbent, Dominique Strauss Kahn. Trichet himself is an experienced banker and financial policy-maker with a sureness of touch. He is also a central banker with a difference. Most are usually stolid, calm and 'details' people, such as Greenspan and King, who give as little as possible away in interviews. In contrast, Trichet cuts a far more glamorous and dashing figure, with his love of poetry, his nights at the opera and his yacht racing.

He certainly enjoys his private life and enhanced his growing reputation as a central banker-with-a-difference during a speech in the Netherlands in 2004 during which he said: 'European-ness means being unable to understand my own country's literature and poetry – Montaigne, Chateaubriand, Baudelaire and Mallarmé – without understanding Dante … Shakespeare … and Goethe.' As well as his cultural interests – what Olivier Garnier calls his 'secret garden' – Trichet likes to spend time with his wife Aline, a former head of translation services at the French Foreign Ministry, and he enjoys visiting exhibitions across Germany, where he now finds himself based. Like most Frenchmen his native capital city is his first love. 'Paris is, of course, wonderful. But I have to say that the Rhine-Main area really was a very pleasant discovery. Within 30–45 minutes of my house you have the opera houses and theatres of Frankfurt, Wiesbaden, Mainz and Darmstadt. Where else can you find so many in such a small area?'

His background is an impressive one. Born in Lyons in 1942, he comes from an academic family – his father and grandfather were language professors. He is a graduate in economics and engineering and leavened these years of intellectual rigour with hard experience working in the mines and a student dalliance with left-wing politics. He then became a civil servant, and between 1971 and 1978 held various posts in the finance ministry, followed by government advisory posts. From 1981 he spent nine years working at the French Treasury, rising to its summit. In 1987 he joined the general council of the Banque de France and represented France at the IMF and World Bank. Five years later he became governor of the Banque de France where he both forged close relations with Germany's Bundesbank and found himself under attack by French President Jacques Chirac for his defence of currency stability.

Central bankers know they are doing a good job when they are criticised by politicians.

There is one hiccup in Trichet's career, and that is the Crédit Lyonnais affair, which held up and almost scuppered his otherwise effortless progress towards the top job in Frankfurt. In 2002 he was one of nine defendants on trial over irregularities at the state-owned bank, one of France's biggest. During the 1980s Crédit Lyonnais lent money exuberantly, plunged into the red when many loans turned bad and then cooked the books to disguise its losses. Cleaning up the bank, which involved transferring much of the bad debt into another entity, was estimated to have cost the French taxpayer £19 billion. Its lending record, and the process by which it had been restructured, consequently came under investigation, and Trichet, a top Treasury official at the time, was accused of complicity in producing misleading accounts. He was found not guilty and was then free to resume his career, and it could be argued that the episode turned out in hindsight to be of benefit to him: it gave him practical experience of a full-scale banking failure and so gave him an edge over his fellow central bankers, King and Bernanke, who lacked a first-hand understanding of navigating a financial system through the rapids and minimising contagion.

In 2004 he was named as successor to Wim Duisenberg as president at the European Central Bank. In fact, he is the man many believed should have had the top job at the ECB when it was created in 1998. His failure to clinch the job first time around was put down to a political stitch-up. Germany got cold feet over the idea of having a Frenchman at Europe's economic helm and insisted on the politically neutral Dutchman, Duisenberg. An agreement was then reached that Duisenberg would step down halfway through his term to make way for Trichet and so keep the Franco-German EU axis on an even keel. After some foot-dragging, the ineffectual and shambling Duisenberg, who presided over a disastrous slide in the euro, eventually agreed to step aside.

Once in place, Trichet, who has puritanical views on monetary policy, was seen as one of the few men capable of leading much-needed and long-delayed reform at the ECB. The French had made no secret of their plans for reforming the bank: the government had commissioned two in-depth reports that argued in favour of adopting the Bank of England as a model. This, in turn, would involve slimmer administration, more transparent workings and a more realistic inflation target. So, Trichet's first few years in office were largely taken up with getting to grips with the organisation, dealing with day-to-day matters and planning for the future. Surprisingly, perhaps, for such an accomplished central banker, Trichet at times appeared irritated, confused and disingenuous in his dealings with the media. I remember encountering him at the International Monetary Fund in Washington at a time when the pressure was on his colleague Antonio Fazio to resign at the Bank of Italy. Trichet ducked and weaved and left all of those present wondering whether, despite his reputation, he was really up to the job.

Yet when the credit markets froze over in the summer of 2007 he came into his own. By chance he was spending 9 August at his French home in St Malo. Confronted with the fact that BNP Paribas had suspended some mortgage-backed securities funds, creating even more market uncertainty, he did not hesitate to agree to intervene in the markets, pumping liquidity to the tune of 95 billion euros overnight. Trichet explained why he acted so swiftly: 'The tsunami that came across the Atlantic had a dimension, when it came to our borders, which was not the same as it had at the beginning,' he said. He was also highly critical of the poor banking practice that led to the sub-prime crisis: 'The "originate and distribute" model of banking – where loans are repackaged and sold on to investors – was not without its defects,' he said with typical understatement. He believed that things needed shaking up.

His quick thinking and quick action probably came as no surprise to those who know him. A former Treasury aide, Olivier Garnier, said of him: 'One of his strengths is his ability to manage a crisis – he enjoys that.' Trichet himself liked to quote a motto attributed to Napoleon: 'Un bon croquis vaut mieux qu'un long discours (A good sketch is better than a long speech).' True, his swift intervention in the markets did initially cause shock in financial circles, but this quickly gave way to admiration for the steady hand he had shown. The ECB appeared to be setting the pace among the central banks, with Trichet now firmly seen as the senior prefect and most experienced central bank policy-maker around. The *Financial Times* noted of his performance: 'Trichet is one of the few to emerge from the turmoil with his reputation enhanced.'

He is also on record as far back as January 2007 as predicting a market correction. At the Davos economic summit that year he warned investors that they should prepare for a 're-pricing' of assets. A year later the very same bankers who had failed to heed his warning were the pariahs at Davos, the walking wounded, wondering if their jobs would still be there when they descended from the mountain top. But what really helped him was the structure of the ECB. When the euro was launched the ECB had to weave together the practices of banks from all over Europe. This gave it a far broader range of tools than its counterparts in Washington and London. Most critically, it allowed it to accept a broader range of assets, including mortgages and other credit-based assets, as collateral for short-term lending, an avenue initially closed to the other central banks.

Under his stewardship the ECB has become a very different place, and the euro, once the sick unit of the currency world, has staged an astonishing renaissance. Trichet is very much a man at the top of his game for whom August 2007 was a seminal moment. The *Financial Times* noted: 'Trichet's strength has been to give the ECB a powerful, unified voice. Using political skills honed in Paris, he has imposed discipline over ECB communication, a task not simplified by interacting in 21 languages. Governing members have learned not to stray far from the line he sets at his monthly press conferences, which remain an exception among central bankers.' He very much sees it as part of his job to give the right image as ECB president. In a magazine interview in early 2007 he was asked about central bank presidents taking great care over what they say in public. To which he replied: 'We central bankers know that we are watched very closely indeed and that any sign can be over-interpreted. But I do not think that we are very different in that respect from other people with important responsibilities in the public eye.'

The whole sub-prime disaster certainly painfully exposed weaknesses at the major central banks. The Bank of England was found wanting, having allowed its financial stability wing to diminish in stature. It was not until crisis struck in August that Mervyn King began seriously to address the issues, and his immediate response of sounding the 'moral hazard' warning struck the wrong note and led the critics in Whitehall to question his financial as well as his political judgement.

Similarly, Bernanke at the Fed did not seem immediately up to the task. It was only after some heavy pressure from the New York Fed – which is in daily contact with Wall Street bankers – that he came round to the view that determined action to rescue the financial system was needed. This was curious, given Bernanke's reputation as one of the world's leading experts on the events leading to the Great Depression. After all, he had a deep understanding of the collapse of the Austrian bank Creditanstalt in 1931, an event that was widely regarded as one of the triggering factors of the global recession that followed. If nothing else, that event had underlined a connection between financial implosion and the real economy of growth and jobs.

The central bankers had warned that financial risks were being under-priced, but no one had predicted how shocking the mis-pricing would be, had seen how foolish and greedy the private-sector bankers had been or had any real notion of the seriousness of the liquidity squeeze when it arrived so quickly. They were also far too optimistic as to how quickly it would dissipate. What followed

9 August was the explosion of a series of financial cluster bombs in every corner of the world, from New York to Hong Kong, from Newcastle to Paris. As the crisis unfolded there was a steep learning curve, particularly for King and Bernanke, relative novices when it came to financial shocks of the kind administered by sub-prime lending.

One of the lessons is that credit booms need to be headed off at the pass. Simply warning of the danger in speeches and in documents such as the Bank of England's financial stability reports is not enough. If necessary, the central bankers need to follow through on those warnings by confronting the banks fuelling the fires of future trouble. Better mechanisms are also needed for dealing with banking crises, an area where Britain has lagged far behind its competitors. The credit crunch found both the central bankers and the tools they deploy wanting, and reforms will inevitably follow. The sheer suddenness in which the markets froze was something beyond past experience, but that can be considered no excuse for the less than robust response from most central banks with the notable exception of the much derided ECB.

CHAPTER 8

Crunch Time

Slamming on the brakes

During the debt-fuelled boom of the Blair–Brown years, the UK became a magnet for overseas capital and enterprise. The country's sophisticated deregulated markets and its favourable location in the time zone between North America and the Pacific Basin made it the ideal place from which to conduct global business. As a financial centre, the City of London challenged New York for hegemony by attracting to the Square Mile and Canary Wharf the world's largest investment banks. Goldman Sachs moved its global executives to London and employed almost as many bankers at its London HQ in Fleet Street as in lower Manhattan. Similarly, Deutsche Bank was as much a presence in London as in Frankfurt. It was a golden era, in which foreign exchange and futures trading in London outstripped levels in New York, and the London Stock Exchange became the most important global centre for initial public offerings and the flotation of new companies from around the world. Soon, the City was being colonised not just by investment banks but by the international legal firms, global consultants and the private equity and hedge fund investors who had become the new demigods of the financial markets.

This was a world in which the oxygen of expansion was credit. Across the globe, from the US to Britain and Europe, banks, financiers and intermediaries were on a lending spree, and there was no shortage of clients. The more that was borrowed, the less equity or hard-earned cash was needed for a deal, so the greater the returns.

In much the same way as ordinary families and borrowers have, over the ages, been able to build up equity in their homes by leveraging through mortgages, so the private equity magnates were able to buy up huge corporations using cheap borrowings, then extract value and sell them on.

The key was the availability of free and easy credit at a relatively low cost of capital. The bubble of the early 21st century was fuelled by slicing and dicing traditional financial instruments, such as mortgages and credit card debt, and turning them into new-fangled financial instruments packaged up as securities. As the economist John Kenneth Galbraith remarked in his 1994 book *A Short History of Financial Euphoria*, all financial innovations are 'essentially variations on the theme of leverage'.

The freeze in the financial markets, which began on 9 August and was still haunting the global financial system in the spring of 2008, brought commerce to an emergency stop. Uncertainty is the great enemy of financial stability, and in the fevered atmosphere banks were gripped by fears about the extent to which their rivals' bad debts were hidden and refused to lend to each other. Nervousness soon spread from the inter-bank market to other financial markets. Shares, not just those of the banks, fell sharply too. This was scarcely surprising: as sub-prime loans were often amalgamated into mortgage-backed securities, which were then sold to financial institutions across the world, they found their way into many of the FTSE-100 companies that were likely to feature heavily in portfolios. In this way the contagion from the sub-prime inspired credit crunch spread quickly to the stock market, and shares fell sharply for the rest of 2007. Property funds were among the worst hit segment of the market, mostly because the credit crunch had affected the flow of deals in the commercial property sector. Needless to say, investment funds with heavy concentrations in banks and other financials were also hit.

At the same time, the bonanza in company takeovers was halted in its tracks, and the banks and stockbrokers that dominate the

Square Mile started to shed jobs as financial firms came to terms with the fact that they would never operate in quite the same way again. One sector particularly hard hit was that of the private equity firms and hedge funds. These live by leverage and were now finding that the cash to do the big deals was no longer there. Worse still, some of the money they had borrowed and planned to turn into securitised debt was no longer attractive to investors. Even the avenue of returning firms to the stock market was closed as a result of turbulence. Firms such as Spanish infrastructure company Grupo Ferrovial, which borrowed £9 billion in June 2006 to buy the British Airports Authority (BAA), found that they could no longer refinance the deal in the way they had hoped. Soon the flow of mergers and corporate takeovers was dwindling to a trickle.

High-profile Blackstone, founded by Stephen Schwarzmann and former US Commerce Secretary Peter Peterson, offers a case history in the problems private equity now faced. It had been among the first of America's private equity powerhouses to sell shares on the public markets, the release of its prospectus creating an outcry by revealing the huge returns reaped by the company's founders. Among its European businesses were such well-known companies and brands as United Biscuits, Orangina, Madame Tussauds and the Café Rouge chain. In America it had pulled off a record $39 billion deal to buy the commercial landlord Equity Office Properties.

By the summer of 2007, though, Blackstone was predicting a slow-down in multibillion dollar 'mega-deals'. In its first financial results since its flotation in June 2007, the company revealed that it had more than tripled its quarterly profits from $224 million to $774 million (£383 million). But Blackstone, a driving force behind many corporate takeovers, saw more difficult times ahead. While it believed that the UK economic fundamentals remained strong, new deals were proving hard to establish in the volatile climate of the credit crunch. Hamilton James, the firm's chief operating officer, predicted: 'I think there will be fewer mega-deals until the debt markets come back a bit.' In March 2008 the firm was revealing that it had turned an after-tax profit of $1.18 billion in the previous year into a loss of $118 million – a humiliating reversal of fortunes.

There was trouble, too, for another major private equity firm, Kohlberg Kravis Roberts & Co., better known as KKR. Founded in 1967, the New York-based KKR had been involved in some spectacular leveraged buy-outs in the US and the UK, including R.J.R. Nabisco (the subject of the book and film *Barbarians at the Gate*) and the Hospital Corporation of America. In March 2007 it was part of the £10 billion buy-out of Britain's Alliance Boots chain, but its fortunes dipped as the markets turmoil began to take its toll. To begin with, on 28 May KKR announced that it had withdrawn, along with CVC, from the consortium bidding for Australian retailer Coles Group. Then in October it postponed its $1.25 billion (£627 million) initial public offering after wary investors showed no appetite for its shares. KKR planned to list on the New York Stock Exchange, but the firm put the float on hold in the wake of investor jitters.

However, the biggest setback for the private equity kingpins came with the Carlyle Group, the secretive private equity firm established by the smart Washington lawyer David Rubinstein, who had once served in President Jimmy Carter's administration. Rubinstein had a knack of sucking high-powered advisers into the firm, including the former US President, George Bush Snr, and the former British Prime Minister, John Major. In the summer of 2007 Rubinstein hit on the bright idea of launching a highly leveraged, publicly quoted fund, known as Carlyle Capital Corporation, to buy up distressed mortgage assets. But instead of the value of the assets recovering, as had been expected, they went into freefall.

The fund's bankers called in the loans and, embarrassingly, Carlyle was forced to place the mortgage fund into receivership in March 2008. The ramifications were enormous. Among the lenders to the fund had been Bear Stearns, America's fifth largest investment house, and one of the biggest victims of the sub-prime meltdown. The latest loss was too much to cope with, and the company's chairman and largest shareholder, John Cayne, had to go to the Federal Reserve for assistance – in effect, it was bust. The investment bank had reached the end of the road and was sold to J.P. Morgan Chase at a bargain basement price. Its long and proud history was now of no consequence.

Banks were soon slamming on the brakes. The response of the central banks to the crisis initially had been to inject billions of pounds, dollars and euros into the world's financial markets in August and September 2007, but banks and other institutions were reluctant to lend money to each other and to customers. Conditions appeared to improve towards the end of the year, and policy-makers became more hopeful that an economic meltdown could be avoided. But as the year drew to a close and ever more banks disclosed sub-prime related losses nervousness increased again.

In an unprecedented coordinated action on 12 December the Bank of England, the European Central Bank, the US Federal Reserve, the Bank of Japan and the Swiss National Bank announced that they were prepared to pour billions more of assistance into the money markets to ensure smooth operations over the holiday period, when banks traditionally seek to square their books for year-end accounting purposes. Central banks had acted together in the past to calm foreign exchange markets, but this round of cooperation was different. It was intended to oil the wheels of business and keep the global economy healthy through a tricky period, but it appeared to bring only short-term relief, and the central banks found themselves repeating the exercise in March 2008.

Confidence in the banking system was shot, losses were still mounting on the balance sheets, and distrust was widespread. Globalisation meant that no longer could a banking crisis be contained in any one market. From Los Angeles to London banks turned away business, cut lending limits and put up interest rates. In Britain big players, such as Barclays, the Royal Bank of Scotland and HSBC, were writing off huge sums due to their exposure to sub-prime loans, and Mervyn King, Governor of the Bank of

England, was among those warning against 'reckless lending'. The Chancellor of the Exchequer, Alistair Darling, told me in a Downing Street interview on 18 December 2007: 'We need more openness so that people understand the risk to which we might be exposed. Banks need to take a long hard look at what it is they are taking on to their books.' By this stage, however, the policy-makers were preaching to the converted.

The effect on mortgage lending was particularly apparent. Almost overnight it became much harder to get a mortgage, and, where they were available, they proved far more expensive than they had been only a few weeks or months before. Many lenders reshuffled their portfolios and re-priced across the board straight away, with variable rates and tracker rates in particular suffering. In October 2007 the Britain's biggest lender, Halifax Bank of Scotland, revealed that homeowners would have to pay more for their home loans, and it then upped the ante on 20 of its tracker deals. The Abbey's tracker deals leapt from 5.69 per cent to 5.99 per cent. Much of this activity was due to the rise in the three-month London Inter-Bank Offered Rate (Libor) – the interest banks pay when they borrow from each other. At one point in September this rate hit 6.9 per cent, up from 6.2 per cent the month before. The Bank of England offered more assistance to the markets by increasing the cash available at its regular auctions, and for a time this helped to normalise Libor. But right through to the spring of 2008 Libor was consistently way above the official bank rate.

Special deals and favourable offers now became a thing of the past. The 120 per cent mortgages, the speciality of Northern Rock – popular at the peak of the credit explosion in 2006 and early 2007 – vanished as quickly as they had arrived. Buy-to-let specialist Paragon, wholly dependent on the wholesale markets, put up the shutters and turned to the equity market for new capital simply to stay afloat. Mortgage bank Bradford & Bingley raised new finance by selling off its housing association loans. Alliance & Leicester found its competitiveness undermined as it refinanced part of its loan book in a private deal with other banks at a much higher interest rate than it had been paying in the wholesale markets. Investment banker Lehman Brothers closed down its British sub-prime lending operations, the London Mortgage Company and Southern Pacific Commercial Loans. Experts estimated that the belt-tightening by mortgage originators could remove as much as £50 billion of liquidity from the home loans market.

The long period of rapid house price inflation and historically low interest rates had led to a surge in consumer debt over the decade 1997–2007. In the free-and-easy atmosphere with money readily available there was a jump in self-certification and sub-prime mortgages, which at £16 billion accounted for 8 per cent of the market. Even at this lower end of the market, firms specialising in mortgages for those with a patchy credit history and the self-employed made dramatic changes – in some cases, raising their standard variable rate by 2.5 per cent. This meant that some lenders had pushed up loan rates to an astonishing 11.5 per cent, double the Bank of England base rate. Others dropped these mortgages altogether. Leading ratings agency Standard & Poor's warned that borrowers with poor credit ratings could face mortgage rate increases of up to 60 per cent.

Finance industry experts were also warning that even those with an existing mortgage were now at risk. Any mortgage holder who had missed the odd payment on a credit card or even a catalogue purchase could see their renewal application affected. The crunch came when 300,000 fixed-rate mortgages ended in December 2007. Refinancing was no longer a case of simply turning up at the mortgage broker and finding the best deal. Discounted loans and cheap fixes were no longer easy to come by and could be withdrawn virtually without warning.

The squeeze made banks and building societies wise after the event. Stricter lending conditions were imposed, and increasing numbers of mortgage applications were rejected. A survey by the website MoneyExpert.com found that 738,000 mortgage applications had been turned down in the six months since April 2007, up 60 per cent on the previous half year. The firm's chief executive Sean Gardener commented:

> The financial environment is far more stringent than in the summer of last year and people need to be prepared for rejection. Lenders, quite reasonably, do not want to take risks when there are pressures on how much people can afford, so it's up to the applicant to convince their bank they can cope with the repayments.

Those looking for mortgages in 2008 were experiencing market conditions unknown to industry professionals for decades, if ever. Broker Chris Mayor at Simple Mortgage Solutions had never known such times. 'Would-be buyers were being hit hard in a number of ways,' he explained.

> First, they are finding it really hard to get a loan at all – the amount being offered by lenders has dropped dramatically, and most now require a sizeable deposit. Second, many lenders are not passing on the Bank of England rate decreases, so interest rate levels remain high. Third, borrowers are finding loan products are being withdrawn without notice even when provisional borrowing has been agreed.
>
> But the most serious situation could be brewing for later this year when a large number of five-year fixed rate deals finish. When those mortgages were taken out in the summer of 2003, the Bank lending rate was 3.6 per cent. In that time, many couples have got used to a certain level of budgeting and possibly started families. Now in the summer of 2008 they face remortgaging at 6 per cent plus, which is a rise of one-third in their monthly mortgage payments. This will make some homes, previously affordable, highly unaffordable and could lead to a real crisis.

Other areas of the housing market were feeling the effects, too. In November 2007 estate agents reported that the top end was being hit, exacerbating worries of a sharp slowdown in the wider property market. House prices in Britain had more than doubled between 2002 and 2007, and the London market led the way as a booming financial services sector encouraged bankers to shell out huge sums for properties in the capital's most desirable areas as well as invest in buy-to-let homes across the country. Now the air was coming out of the balloon. According to Britain's biggest estate agents Savills, in 2006 City bankers and dealers had invested £5.5 billion out of a bonus pool of some £8.8 billion in the property market, but with many financial services professionals fearing for their jobs in 2008 and bonuses in decline, demand fell back over the autumn.

The prevailing gloom was reflected in the mood of the building trade. In October a survey showed that confidence among UK house builders was at an all-time low. One of Britain's shrewdest and most respected property developers, Gerald Ronson of Heron, told me in April 2008 that outside London new home sales were down an astonishing 40–45 per cent since the start of the year. In particular there was a serious problem in the market for new-build flats. In London itself Ronson estimated that prices were 20–25 per cent down. The housebuilders were in deep trouble, too. The nation's largest, Persimmon, placed its diggers in mothballs and halted building in the spring of 2008, a sure indicator of the poor condition of residential construction. A slump in the housing market presaged serious economic consequences. Construction plays a big part in the UK economy, and people moving house are more likely to buy other goods and services, such as furniture, DIY and electrical products. Concern about the cost of mortgages in the domestic budget could also affect sales of bigger ticket items, such as cars. In his first Budget on 12 March 2008 Alistair Darling cautioned that with 'credit conditions expected to remain restrictive through 2008 prospects for household consumption have moderated'.

Inevitably, the market for all forms of credit was badly affected by the crunch. For years, consumers in the UK had enjoyed a borrowing boom with ever increasing limits on their credit cards to go with the nation's ever increasing personal debt mountain. The value of secured and unsecured credit stood at a mammoth £1,363 billion towards the close of 2007, a sum equal to Britain's gross domestic product, the output of the whole economy. But the trend in dishing out loans and credit cards to almost anyone came to an abrupt halt: banks were finding it harder to secure cash, and international rules on the amount of capital and liquidity were being tightened by regulators. Now borrowers, personal and business, were being forced to pay for the excesses of the banks in the boom years.

Lenders applied far more stringent regulations when it came to approving applications for loans, and those with damaged credit histories found it much harder now to access credit. In addition, the number of lenders offering unsecured personal loans fell, with some lenders taking their unsecured personal loan ranges off the market altogether. One industry professional remarked: 'Such a large reduction in just the last month is worrying. With no signs of rate rises slowing, it's a rather unsettled market. The credit crunch is showing its strength in the personal loan market.'

Credit cards were among the hardest hit sectors. The level of credit card application rejections climbed significantly after August as card providers began to put increasingly stringent lending criteria in place to reduce the risk of bad debt. Other measures saw some companies reducing the credit limits on their cards, while there were a large number of rate and charge increases from providers. This made it increasingly difficult for many consumers to get credit cards, and reduced the amount of credit extended to many existing customers.

Lucy Farndon reported in the *Daily Mail* that Barclaycard – among the biggest card providers – was turning down around half of applicants for its credit card in the autumn of 2007 and had cut the credit limit for 500,000 'at risk' customers. Indeed, the rules were becoming so strict that those who were behind with, say, their mobile phone bill found that they were effectively on a loans blacklist. Barclays revealed that bad debt on Barclaycard had reached £1.5 billion in the past year. The group said the strategy of turning away customers and cutting credit limits was designed to cut the level of bad debt, and Barclaycard revealed that it was looking at customers on a case-by-case basis and was using information available to it from other lenders under industry data-sharing initiatives. In some instances it left customers' credit limits unchanged while reducing the level of cash advances they could obtain with their card. The bank did this because there was evidence to show that those using their card to get cash – which attracts punishing interest rates – were more likely to be struggling with debt. HSBC contacted customers with overdraft facilities and credit cards they do not use to see if they still wanted them. As for the electronic bank Egg controlled by the mighty Citigroup, it withdrew tens of thousands of credit cards without warning.

Overall, nearly 2 million people had their credit card application turned down in the UK and, with experts predicting that the effects of the credit crunch will be around for some time, that number can only go up. Even if the Bank of England were to lower interest rates dramatically in 2008 the chances are that consumer credit will remain far more difficult to obtain. Consumers who have never had any issue with their personal credit will be paying for the misdeeds of those borrowers who have over-extended themselves. The net result of all this will be that fewer people will be granted credit cards, and those who already have one will find that they have lower credit limits and are paying more in monthly charges for the privilege.

But the effects of the credit crunch don't end in the personal borrowing sector. One leading credit card provider, Nottingham-based Capital One, announced that jobs would go, while across the city consumer credit ratings agency Experian, which employed 4,000 people, also revealed significant job losses due to adverse trading in the final quarter of 2007.

With the financial services industry under the cosh and already shedding jobs, the prospects for business in general were almost as bad. Consultants Oxford Economics warned on 17 September 2007, in the midst of the run on the Rock, that significant losses at financial institutions could lead to a general contraction in lending. For companies that interact directly with the credit markets, it looked like being a hard slog. Whitbread, which owns restaurant chains throughout the UK, announced at the end of August 2007 that it had decided to delay a possible £1 billion bond issue. Christopher Roger, the company's finance director, commented soon after: 'The propensity to lend to anyone but a sovereign government is very low at the moment.' There was also an almost immediate drop in the asset-backed commercial paper market used by banks and large companies to help them fund short-term working capital needs.

The Bank of England was lowering the bank rate and had reduced it by three-quarters of a point to 5 per cent by May 2008. But the drop in official rates was not being reflected in borrowing costs. The bottlenecks in the credit markets meant that banks were paying almost a full point above the bank rate to raise funds. Paradoxically, housebuyers, consumers and businesses were having to pay more for loans in a period when official rates were being cut on a regular basis. The credit crunch, combined with interest rate rises, was bound to tip struggling firms over the edge. By the end of 2007 the number of companies issuing warnings about future profits rose to their highest level since 2001. Research by accountants Ernst & Young found that the number of warnings issued in 2007 was up 10 per cent on the year before.

Retailing was particularly badly hit, with a record 47 profit warnings by the end of 2007 – inevitably so, given that consumers' disposable income was being squeezed by higher taxes, rising mortgages and credit costs, and household inflation caused by soaring fuel and food prices, pushed up by ever increasing demand from Asia. Among the early casualties of the squeeze was one of the stalwarts of the high street, the Dolcis shoe chain, which went into administration in the middle of January 2008. By the spring of 2008 some of the most famous names on the high street, including Marks & Spencer and John Lewis, were experiencing harder times. Mid-season sales were to become the norm. Elsewhere, the leisure trade – covering bars, hotels and travel – also felt the pinch. Even the grocers, including mighty Tesco, saw some in-store sales growth pared back. Official figures released in May 2007 showed that insolvencies and the number of companies placed in administration were soaring.

With businesses struggling to cope with the squeeze on credit, retailers turned on their suppliers, asking for tighter payment conditions and discounts. Letters sent from the headquarters of Marks & Spencer and the chemist Alliance Boots to suppliers demanding tighter terms ended up at the *Daily Mail*. As a result interconnecting vicious circles were set up. Businesses put the squeeze on their suppliers, but they also sought to pass on rising costs to customers in the form of higher prices. With problems of their own, now that a buoyant housing market and easy credit were things of the past, British consumers were being forced to cut back. Matters looked dire in December 2007, and by the spring of 2008 warnings were coming in from everywhere.

In another move brought about by the credit crunch, banks requested that major customers should not draw on agreed lending facilities in order to preserve their own balance sheets. This enabled banks to ease the pressure on themselves as they approached the financial year-end. Citigroup was among those most affected, and it asked some clients not to use standby facilities, part of the normal banking arrangements made between banks and companies. Standby financing typically is agreed for 364 days, and when it's not drawn has no impact on capital. When it is drawn, however, the risk weighting soars, making a big difference to the balance sheet.

The crunch also squeezed innovation investment and enterprise. Andy Berrow, senior business adviser for Business Link, noted: 'An increase in interest rates earlier in the year [2007], combined with a tightening of borrowing criteria, has had an effect on the ability of small to medium-sized businesses to borrow new money.'

Companies on the edge of a major corporate finance deal were being advised to check their traditional financing source. Banks were not extending the multiples of credit they had been offering before the summer break, and, where they did lend, they were looking for more security. One of the results of the credit crunch was that asset-backed lending came back to the fore. Any financial directors who contacted their banks about renewing their overdraft, for example, probably found themselves talking to those in charge about new ways of strengthening collateral through factoring or invoice discounting.

Firms grappling to fill holes in their pension funds suffered, too. Before the sub-prime crisis the gloom over pension deficits and the cost to the company purse of repairing the funds had begun to lift. Repairs carried out in the years of healthy growth had seen the pension funds of many FTSE-100 companies return to surplus. A strong performance on the stock market had lifted asset valuations, and there was a feeling that the worst of the pension storm had passed. The companies best placed to cope were those that were not in the middle of a corporate finance deal, those that hadn't borrowed large amounts that were due to be refinanced soon, and those with a pension fund that hadn't overdone any risky investments. Companies with a healthy balance sheet would not find funding a problem. But the stock market turmoil, particularly among hard-hit financial stocks, quickly saw the large deficits re-emerging.

If 2007 seemed bad, the opening of 2008 saw an increase in the number of warnings of·a severe global economic slowdown or even a worldwide recession. By now Alan Greenspan was cautioning that the odds favoured a US recession and that there were the first real signs of the pounding to come. Monday, 21 January marked a new low. Ironically, it was a public holiday in America, but the rest of the global markets were crashing on what the media hailed as another 'Black Monday'. Fears of an American slump were intensifying and propagated in a *Wall Street Journal* headline. 'US Warning Signs Point Toward a Deep Recession', America's financial bible declared.

In London alone some £77 billion was being wiped off the value of the FTSE-100 Index, which fell 5.5 per cent, the biggest one-day reverse since 9/11. The fall in share prices rolled out of Asia, spread to Europe and ended up in South America. At one stage selling was so intense that trading had to be suspended in Bombay and New Delhi for more than an hour after the market suddenly plummeted 11 per cent. It later emerged that the intensity of the fall in Europe may have been the result of French bank Société Générale unwinding the billions of dollars of trades by rogue trader Jérôme Kerviel.

In the US the Federal Reserve was watching events with increasing concern. As soon as New York opened 24 hours later, the Fed announced that it was cutting interest rates immediately and deeply. The key federal funds rate was slashed by 0.75 points to 3.25 per cent. It was America's biggest single-day cut in official rates in 25 years, and a move that took the markets completely by surprise. It signalled Fed chairman Ben Bernanke's determination to keep consumers spending as the engine of the economy. But the sheer scale and suddenness of the cut led many commentators to conclude that it was a panic move. With markets disliking uncertainty, the cut contributed to the volatility in the days ahead.

All this, combined with the collapse of Northern Rock, Bear Stearns and other banks and financial institutions across the globe, was leading experts to describe the credit crunch of 2007 as the worst crisis in recent economic history. Some went further, and made comparisons with the world recession of the 1930s. It was certainly proving to be a turning point for the British economy. In January 2008 investment bankers Morgan Stanley warned of a slump in share prices as corporate profits tumbled.

The ongoing financial crisis will have a detrimental impact on economic growth. We would not be surprised to see earnings contract over the next 12 months. We believe house prices will fall 10 per cent next year, with the possibility of further declines into 2009. Investors should beware those stocks exposed to a sharp slowdown in housing activity.

Such grim analysis was becoming common place. Gordon Brown's government, however, was in a state of denial. Instead of recognising the reality of America's recession and the impact of financial meltdown on the City, economic forecasts were being gently adjusted downwards, rather than slashed. In March 2008 budget growth was still forecast at 2 per cent for the year, a far more optimistic projection than those being made by private sector forecasters. The government was fearful that its profligacy had been revealed. In the good years, from 2000 onwards, it had spurned the chance to discipline public spending – as urged by the International Monetary Fund – and had allowed excesses across the system. The UK budget deficit stood at nearly 3 per cent of national wealth at the top of the economic cycle, and the national debt was heading towards 40 per cent of gross domestic product, the total output of the economy. This meant there was little room to manoeuvre when tax revenues from the City and the consumer fell away as tougher credit conditions began to bite. Household spending had reached an astonishing 97 per cent of disposable income – a level last seen at the height of the 1988 credit boom. That had ended with a Draconian downturn with large-scale business collapses and people losing their homes as they found themselves in negative equity (that is, when the size of the mortgage far exceeds the underlying value of the property).

Whatever the ultimate outcome of the crunch, it has certainly revealed major shortcomings in the operation of the global economy. The *Economist*, for example, has argued that the 2007–8 crisis has demonstrated major limitations of central banks in the three areas of monetary policy, economic modelling and bank supervision. It pointed out that loose monetary policy in the years that saw rash lending, securitisation and globalisation was partly responsible for the mess in which the central banks found themselves in August 2007.

It can also be argued that central banks kept interest rates too low for too long – particularly the Fed, which slashed rates between 2001 and 2003, cutting them to 1 per cent at one stage. In so doing they focused too narrowly on the short-term influences on inflation despite suggestions from the influential Bank for International Settlements that they ought to be looking at asset prices, too. The supply of money and credit that fuelled the asset price bubble in property, mortgage-based assets and shares had been largely ignored. Central bankers preferred to wait for bubbles to burst and then to mop up afterwards with rate cuts. When the sub-prime bubble finally burst it sparked a chain reaction that led to the freeze on the credit markets, failing banks in Europe and the US and delivering a crushing blow to confidence. Banks stand at the centre of the major Western economies, and the more damaged they become the greater the threat to consumer and business lending and the more vulnerable the world becomes to a financially induced recession.

Sadly, bankers never learn from the past. In each boom they invent new ways of boosting their income and profits and are applauded for it by rising stock markets. At times like this, the more cautious the bank, the more it is punished by the markets. But during the credit crunch the exotic products they created to maximise profit – products such as credit derivatives, which exploited the 'light-touch' regulatory environment – were shown to be a chimera. Instead of protecting investors and consumers, they formed part of an explosive chain that allowed the risk taken on in the trailer parks of America to be parcelled up and transported around the globe. When investors finally came to realise that the 'emperor had no clothes' and that the assets they held were essentially worthless, capitalism was brought to a grinding halt. It is amazing that it took so many sophisticated minds so long to recognise the extreme danger that had been created – and the regulators were nowhere to be seen. The *Economist* noted: 'Vital parts of the new finance took place in lightly supervised markets. Invention had raced ahead of intervention.'

The year 2007 witnessed the creation of a vicious downward spiral. As the credit markets went into freefall and banks hoarded their cash it became harder to obtain loans. It also became harder for consumers to pay back their loans, credit card borrowings and mortgages as they became confronted with ratcheted up bank charges. As the economy faltered, jobs were lost. The world was having to begin to adjust to life after 'easy money', something that will not be easy for a generation brought up on cheap credit and unaccustomed to severe downturns and tightened credit conditions. In the opinion of IMF chief economist Simon Johnston the world was facing the 'perfect storm' of a 1970s-style oil price shock combined with a 21st-century credit crunch. When the Fund issued its World Economic Outlook report in April 2008 it was exceptionally gloomy, lowering growth forecasts and adopting the apocalyptic language of the Great Depression. The big freeze in the credit markets was the conduit that linked a crisis that started in the financial markets to the real economy, with everyone now affected. All this added up, at best, to a severe slowdown in world growth; or, at worst, to a global recession.

Politicians like Gordon Brown had sought to convince the public that the 'boom and bust' cycle had been confined to the dustbin of history and that Britain faced a stable future. Certainly, it had weathered the 1997–8 emerging market collapse and the 2001–2 end of the dotcom fantasy better than most economies. But the crunch was different. It hit at the heart of what Britain was supposed to be best at – financial services. The bad times have arrived. We are now paying for what markets and individuals had been up to in the best of times.

CHAPTER 9

The Long and Rocky Road

In search of a way forward for Northern Rock

At 4 p.m. London time on 17 February 2008, a murky winter's afternoon with the natural light just fading, a grim-faced and determined Alistair Darling marched into the modern, light-filled atrium of HM Treasury in Whitehall. He was followed by a man with a mass of dark, crinkly hair who sat at a table beside the Chancellor's podium. To the right of the room government officials swarmed behind a giant translucent screen. In front of Darling was a hastily assembled press corps quickly decanted from their Westminster offices in their Sunday mufti of blue jeans and T-shirts and from suburban homes where the weekend meal had been barely digested. Preparations for the event, including the swish backdrop, had been rapidly put in place that morning by Darling's press secretary, Steve Field.

Framed against a white backdrop, Darling, with his white hair and distinctive black eyebrows, cut a ghostly figure, strangely disembodied from his surroundings. The Chancellor had a momentous announcement to make. After seven months of scratching around for a private-sector rescue of the badly damaged mortgage bank Northern Rock, the government had decided to nationalise the ailing lender. Reading from a carefully prepared script that was designed to cause the least panic among the public, Darling spoke with a slight quiver in his normal, flat voice. A Bill to nationalise the former building society would be rushed through Parliament over the next few days, and Ron Sandler, the Zimbabwe-born financier, who was at his side, would be moving into Northern Rock's headquarters in Newcastle. The government would be an 'arms length' shareholder, steering clear of everyday management. Darling assured the press corps and the far wider audiences tuned into live television that it would 'be business as usual for the Rock'.

When I asked Darling if the government would be offering compensation to Northern Rock's rebellious investors, the Chancellor observed that there would be compensation – to be determined by an unnamed independent assessor – but that it would be on the basis of there being no government assistance or guarantees to the Rock. It would be as if the mortgage lender was bust.

Sandler, a favourite of Gordon Brown, had won his spurs as the saviour of the Lloyd's of London insurance market in the 1990s. He was subsequently hauled into NatWest as chief executive after Derek Wanless, who went on to head Northern Rock's risk committee, was ousted following failed ventures in America and investment banking and failed takeover approaches. After NatWest was taken over by the Royal Bank of Scotland in 2000, Sandler was deployed by Gordon Brown as an adviser on the long-term savings market. Now Sandler, who is non-domiciled for UK taxes, had taken on the government's call to run the nationalised Rock. His goal, he claimed, would be to run the Rock 'on sound commercial principles' so that it could be 'returned to the commercial sector, standing on its own two feet'.

Darling's decision to nationalise had come after a frantic series of weekend meetings, culminating in a lunchtime session with Brown, his Downing Street neighbour. The government had been left with cruel choices for the future of the Rock. It could have placed the bank in administration at an estimated cost to the taxpayer of £7 billion, not to mention the very real risk of social disruption throughout the northeast. It could have sold to the last serious private-sector bidder standing, Sir Richard Branson's Virgin Group. But then Branson could have made a considerable amount of money from the deal. This has been estimated by some Treasury officials as up to £3 billion. Certainly, a final report by the govern-ment-appointed investment bankers, Goldman Sachs, had concluded that none of the bidders fully met its criteria for a private-sector rescue.

The only other option was to take the Rock into public owner-ship and reserve any gains from the bank's run-down for the taxpayers who were funding its survival. The Prime Minister had done every-thing in his power to avoid this, knowing that in the minds of the British public nationalisation was still associated with Labour's bad old days of strikes and huge losses at industrial giants like British Steel and the car producer British Leyland. It also evoked memories of 'Clause 4' of the Labour Party's constitution which had advocated public ownership and which had been very publicly abolished by New Labour. But in the end nationalisation was the course of action Brown and Darling reluctantly adopted.

Darling looked shell-shocked during the press conference. And as he patiently answered questions on that fateful Sunday afternoon, it rapidly became clear that many questions were going to remain unanswered. Darling had no idea how long public ownership would last, what business model Sandler – who would be paid £90,000 a month – would be pursuing and how many jobs would have to be axed. (A few weeks later it emerged that 2,000 jobs, one-third of the workforce, would go.) It was disclosed that local sentiment would be assuaged by a promise to fund the Northern Rock Foundation, the charity set up at demutualisation, for another three years at £15 million a year.

The realisation of the nationalisation option showed just how bad things had become. Even when the initial crisis at Northern Rock had died down, reports circulated that savers were withdrawing billions more, often via the internet and certainly far away from the TV camera, and it became apparent that the level of support Northern Rock would need would be far greater than advertised or anticipated. Indeed, in October Northern Rock customers moved £3 billion of their savings into building societies as they turned to the mutuals as a safe haven for their money. This was four times the amount for October 2006. The Building Societies Association confirmed in mid-October that £10.5 billion had been withdrawn from Northern Rock since 13 September.

But something more sinister was also happening and this was causing real apprehension at the Bank of England. There was a parallel wholesale run. As the Rock's borrowings from other banks in the inter-bank market fell due, they were not renewed. In a meeting with a high-level Bank official, I was told on 29 October 2007 that, on current trends, funding from the taxpayer could potentially reach £40 billion or £50 billion by the year end. It proved a prophetic assessment.

Gordon Brown was deeply concerned. He realised that the run on the Rock had the capacity seriously to damage him politically and potentially could erode his record for robust economic and financial management. He therefore asked a young, calm and trusted Treasury aide, John Kingman, with whom he had worked closely during his period as Chancellor, to be his eyes and ears during the Northern Rock crisis and to explore the possibilities for a private-sector rescue. The 38-year-old Kingman is a cool, thoughtful former Treasury press secretary who had once worked as analyst/writer on the highly regarded 'Lex column' of the *Financial Times*. He had risen rapidly through the Treasury hierarchy, becoming a managing director and a Second Permanent Secretary. His role at the Treasury had required him actively to network and cultivate the City. Kingman's appearances at the lunch table caused some merriment among colleagues when his entertainment schedule was published under a Freedom of Information request.

Intellectually, he was fully capable of understanding the complexity of the issues involved, in particular the need to make sure that whatever deals the government did would stand up to scrutiny not just in Parliament and the media but also in Brussels. Despite being a career civil servant, he also understood the need to protect his political masters, Brown and Darling, from straying into a trap from which they would not be able to extricate themselves. This must have remained in the back of his mind throughout the crisis. Kingman was the ideal intermediary between Brown and Darling and between government and the City, and he set about his task with enormous energy. He sounded out the big high street banks about cooperation for the Rock but found great reluctance among them to work together in the collegiate ways of the past. He also worked closely with the government's chosen financial advisers, Goldman Sachs, which were in and out of his offices on an almost daily basis.

In late October Northern Rock was relying ever more on money from the Bank of England to meet its short-term liabilities. The loan, underwritten by taxpayers and secured on Rock assets, had mushroomed to a reported rate of £400 million a day. Inevitably, the shares were taking a daily pummelling. On 20 November they were in freefall again, at one time down to 60p (a 40 per cent decline overnight), and trading in the shares on the London Stock Exchange was suspended three times in an attempt to bring some order to a volatile market by restricting dealings. By the end of the month Darling had spent £40 billion on propping up Northern Rock, a figure greater than the annual defence budget and one that would have bought eight Millennium Domes.

It was becoming clear that even if there were to be a private-sector rescue the taxpayer might be forced to guarantee at least £10 billion of Northern Rock loans until at least 2010. None of the companies that were expressing an interest in taking over the bank was able or prepared immediately to pay back more than £15 billion of the £25 billion loaned by the Bank of England. Under European Commission rules governments are only permitted to prop up failing companies for six months, a period which notionally came to an end towards the end of February. It looked as though Darling might well have to plead with the EU for permission to prop up Northern Rock well beyond the deadline. After that the British government would be required to demonstrate that the loans and subsidies would be repaid on commercial lines in a timely manner. Concern was mounting, the headlines were becoming larger, and the Rock, appropriately enough, was becoming a millstone round the government's neck.

There was also huge local concern about the Rock's survival. As John Shipley, leader of Newcastle City Council, put it: 'If Northern Rock were to fold it would cut 1.6 per cent off the northeast's gross domestic product. It would not only be a blow to the region's economy, it would also dent its confidence and its image.' Small shareholders, too, wanted a quick commercial solution, with Roger Lawson summing up their fears: 'There was clearly a risk of the company going into administration with the assets being split up and sold off. In that case, it would be very unlikely that shareholders would get anything.'

Among the potential buyers initially in the frame to buy the Rock were two private equity companies, New York-based Cerberus Capital Management and J.C. Flowers & Co. Both firms had hands-on experience of turning around financial groups in difficulty and emerging with handsome gains for investors. However, the *Economist* warned against a sale to private equity buyers who could make a bundle on the backs of the taxpayer, saying that it would 'set the seal on the most ignominious episode in recent British banking'. Darling was on the defensive and sought to assure the Commons that despite the big numbers being bandied around in the media, the public had nothing to worry about. 'I can tell the House that the Bank of England lending is secured against assets held by Northern Rock, which include high-quality mortgages with a significant margin built in and high-quality securities with the highest quality of credit rating. The Bank is the senior secured creditor,' he told MPs on 20 November 2007. Despite this, the degree of security for the taxpayers' money was often doubted in the weeks to come. On 11 December, after being battered for months, Northern Rock's shares, which had fallen from a peak of £12 in February to 85p in September, finally dropped out of the FTSE-100 Index. But speculative buying by profit-hungry hedge funds continued, despite all the indications that shareholders would not be bailed out by the government.

The sniping from the political sidelines intensified, with the Chancellor and Mervyn King both in the firing line. The *Mail on Sunday* reported on 15 December 2007 that King had been warned two years previously that Northern Rock was over-extended and in danger. Former Conservative minister, Gillian Shephard, now in the Lords and in 2005 a director of the Coventry Building Society, had told him she feared 'a day of reckoning' because Northern Rock was consistently offering cut-price loans. King apparently responded by telling her that there was nothing to worry about and that the Bank was monitoring the situation. King is said to have added: 'The vast majority of the debt is secured against property and it would only be of concern if that was not the case.' A further attack on King came from another quarter early in 2008 when Jon Wood, a Monaco-based tax exile and boss of hedge fund SRM, one of Northern Rock's biggest shareholders, accused him of being responsible for the bank's collapse. Wood said that the Bank of England's refusal to rescue Northern Rock in secret in August 2007 was disastrous, and he blamed the government and FSA, in turn, for not daring to criticise the Governor. On this occasion King received support from Tory Shadow Chancellor George Osborne, who instead blamed Labour 'dithering' for Northern Rock's problems and accused Downing Street of unnecessary delays in reappointing King to a second term as Governor.

With the Rock haemorrhaging and the political fall-out gathering, the search for a buyer remained of paramount importance throughout the autumn of 2007 and into January 2008. At first this search took place amid high hopes that normality would quickly return to the wholesale market for loans and that a respectable buyer would rapidly be able to convert the Bank's loans, which were propping up the Rock, into commercial borrowing, even if that meant paying higher interest charges than in the past. But as news emerged of mounting losses in sub-prime lending, particularly among the American and Swiss banks, conditions in the money markets became worse rather than better. And the prospects of a face-saving private-sector rescue became less likely.

A Citigroup team, headed by mergers and acquisitions specialist David Wormsley, was added to the advisory team steering the Rock's future. The hope was that the New York-based bank might also come up with funding. But as Citigroup revealed its own billions of dollars of sub-prime losses and had to raise $20 billion from new investors, it soon became clear that it was unlikely to be a fruitful source of large-scale new funding. Then, amid all the chaos, the billionaire entrepreneur Sir Richard Branson, never one to hide his light under a bushel, publicly threw his hat in the ring on 12 October and organised a high-profile press conference on the steps of the London Stock Exchange, in the shadow of St Paul's.

Here Branson paraded his colleague, Jayne-Anne Gadhia, managing director of Virgin Money, as the future chief executive of the Rock. He also gave the world a first glimpse of a rescue plan involving his tiny financial operation Virgin Money, an organisation that was a fraction of the size of the failing mortgage bank it was seeking to take over. The government was delighted to see him enter the fray, never mind the fact that in 2000 Branson, somewhat mysteriously, had been regarded as not the right person to run the National Lottery. Now it was privately made clear that the Financial Services Authority would be prepared to grant the new Virgin Bank a licence provided that Branson was just an investor and not directly involved in management.

Whatever qualms there may have been about Branson's bid, it did help stabilise the situation. Hopes of a rescue soared, and Branson, in typically brash style, placed advertisements in the national newspapers in the form of a personal letter outlining his plans for the Rock. Amazingly, people believed it. The outflow of deposits went from a torrent to a trickle in a matter of days. It seemed that the familiar Virgin name, much admired by the public, was becoming an early favourite to win the race to take it over. Indeed, Branson persevered until the nationalisation card was played right at the death. He wasn't the only suitor. The queues of unhappy savers in September were replaced in November by queues of businesses keen to buy the stricken bank. They tended, however, to vanish into the ether as quickly as they had arrived.

The government by now was in a deeply unenviable position. Not only did it need to find a buyer from a rapidly diminishing field, but it needed to do so quickly. It had covered Northern Rock's liabilities, yet the bank's assets belonged to its shareholders, which left taxpayers' money at risk. At the same time, European rules prohibiting state aid to industries, required ministers to cut the lifeline by the end of February or come up with a plausible reason not to. The Treasury was desperately casting around for buyers to take the bank and its problems off its hands, but none of the financial world's best and brightest seemed willing to assume full responsibility. All bidders – including Virgin – valued the bank well below even its current market capitalisation and all asked for public-sector credit lines or loans.

The bluff northeasterner Bryan Sanderson, parachuted into the Rock as chairman on 19 October, after a search led by head-hunter Anna Mann, wanted his own team to restructure the Rock, and he swiftly appointed private equity specialists Blackstone as the company's advisers. The Blackstone team was led by John Studzinski, a financier with an unrivalled reputation, prodigious appetite for work and an ego to match. His day would begin with a work-out soon after 4 a.m. before walking his dog and devouring the newspapers – a particularly lengthy task in the final months of 2007 when the Rock was rarely off the front pages. It was soon clear that Sanderson, who had worked closely with Studzinski at BP and valued his skills in restructuring businesses, had placed the Blackstone man in the driving seat.

The ailing Rock now had no fewer than three of the City's most colourful merger specialists advising it: the mercurial Studzinski, the terrier-like Greenburgh from Merrill Lynch and Wormsley of Citigroup. They, together with lawyers and PR experts, would run up advisory fees of £41 million. Blackstone was soon off the mark, and its masterpiece 'Project Wing', a briefing memorandum on the Rock (identified in the 13-page document as 'Blackbird'), fluttered around the City. The institution described was unrecognisable from the injured bank dissected in Parliament and the media. 'Blackbird is the UK's fastest growing mortgage company having grown residential assets by 22 per cent to £77 billion in 2006 and underlying profit before tax by 16 per cent to £588 million,' it crowed. Blackbird, it went on, had increased its share of Britain's mortgages from 2.7 per cent in 1996 to 7.6 per cent in June 2007.

The document also revealed that Blackbird's assets would be transferred to a new company, FinCo, with the objectives of achieving an orderly run-down of the balance sheet, the repayment of creditors and, 'if appropriate', the return of residual value to the Rock's shareholders. It outlined the full details of the business's planned future, including 'the funding advantage of Granite and the Covered Bond Securitisation programmes'. This, ironically, was precisely the innovative financial model that had brought the Rock to its knees when the markets froze over in August. The document further showed that the Rock had on its balance sheet £3.3 billion of unsecured 'Together' loans and a further £4.5 billion of unsecured accounts. Studzinski, famed for his network of contacts, was in his element. 'This is not going to be like Disneyland, there is going to be a deadline,' he told colleagues. Within days he had contacted some 50 institutions, including French, Spanish, Indian and Chinese banks, to widen the pool of bidders. Blackstone also approached lenders to secure credit lines totalling £25 billion, promising to improve Northern Rock's credit rating, in the bargain.

Soon, the few runners and riders in the 'takeover stakes' began to prepare for the official start. Branson's Virgin Group, whose proposal would have seen Northern Rock keep its stock market listing, had declared before the highly confidential 'Project Wing' document had been distributed. Branson believed that he had funding in place from the Royal Bank of Scotland to immediately repay £10 billion of the Rock's borrowings. It was reported that the RBS team included Citigroup, and that there was an intention to provide a loan of up to £20 billion. Virgin strengthened its offer with the choice as executive chairman of former chief of Lloyds TSB, Sir Brian Pitman.

Two other bidders were in the frame by the official 20 November deadline. One was US private equity firm J.C. Flowers. It had a track record of turning around failing banks, and planned to run the business as it stood and to invest £1 billion to refinance the bank's ravaged balance sheet. The Flowers offer initially looked quite promising. It proposed an expert management team, headed by former Marks & Spencer chairman, Paul Myners, and Dick Pym, the retired chief executive of Alliance & Leicester and a serious mortgage banker. Myners had been an adviser to the Treasury on fund management and is chairman of the Guardian Media Group.

The other bidder was Olivant, a private company funded by wealthy families and led by confident former Abbey boss, Luqman Arnold. Olivant's bid committed to repaying the Bank loan 'promptly' using external market funding. Arnold also planned to put in his own management team and take control of the company. Luqman's backers intended to buy 10–20 per cent of the company at a price similar to where the shares stood in late November. This was believed to be well in excess of the price offered by rival bids.

A possible fourth suitor, the private equity firm Cerberus, pulled out because of the fear of protracted negotiations and because it was itself feeling the effects of the credit crunch. The government announced at this point that it was allowing Northern Rock's directors some breathing space to consider the options.

None of the potential bidders was ideal. The Flowers team sought to impose an impossible condition on any deal: the right to sell on the Rock to another party, if a suitable offer came along, even if the taxpayer loans had not been repaid. Kingman recognised that it was not an offer he could recommend to Brown or Darling. The Olivant offer looked unattractive because Arnold could not commit to repay the Bank of England by 2011, believing that it could take up to five years to do this.

The Virgin offer posed its own set of problems. On the one hand, it did win the Rock board's support, a week after the 20 November deadline, giving it 'preferred bidder' status. It also won some support at the Treasury which liked Virgin's commitment to an immediate repayment of £11 billion of the Bank's loan, with the rest paid over three years. With the Rock needing to be propped up more each day – following a rush of withdrawals, at its peak running at £200 million a day – this had a strong appeal, especially as such a deal also avoided the prospect of having to put the bank into administration. On the other hand, the official attitude to Branson himself seems to have been ambivalent. Although he was a member of Gordon Brown's prestigious Business Council, Branson was never fully trusted in Whitehall. And if the government was somewhat wary of Branson, his bid was certainly unpopular in other quarters.

Critics saw the bid as a way for Branson to get the company on the cheap, a view that Darling eventually came to share. Virgin would have had to bid £5 billion earlier in 2007 to acquire Northern Rock; by November it stood to pick it up for just over £1 billion. In so doing, it would find a place in the high street from where it could challenge the Big Five banks. Branson would also acquire 2 million customers, a massive mortgage book and a prestigious headquarters, and the Virgin Money brand would be seen around the nation's shopping centres.

In an attempt to answer public criticism, Sir Brian Pitman, who stood to run the bought-out Northern Rock in a Virgin takeover, suggested that the bid be stress-tested. He said that Branson and his colleague Stephen Murphy, chief executive of the Virgin Group, might have been too optimistic with their figures. 'You have got to assume an extremely rough time in the UK,' he told them bluntly, 'a recession to be precise.' The 76-year-old Pitman, as shrewd as ever, readied himself for a final challenge. 'I have seen banks go bust and it is extremely negative.' Having lived through the secondary banking crisis of the 1970s, when the Bank of England had launched a lifeboat, he believed that a commercial rescue would be preferable to public ownership. 'When you nationalise something, it normally takes a long time to return it to the market,' he told me.

The launch of the Bank of England's lifeboat in 1973–4 had allowed a relatively orderly reorganisation of the fringe banks that were rescued. Rotten institutions, such as London & County Securities, were simply wound up, but larger groups, such as the First National Finance Corporation, were propped up, new management was brought in, and they survived and prospered. Only in the special case of merchant bankers Slater Walker Securities did the Bank feel the need to take full responsibility for its future. It eventually took Slater Walker loans on to its own books and finally sold off the last assets in 1990, demonstrating why public-sector ownership can be a long-term proposition.

Leading the charge against Branson from another direction were the Northern Rock shareholders, both large and small. In December a meeting of small shareholders in Newcastle put the knife in by issuing a statement saying: 'Branson's management team has never run a public company, let alone one in crisis. We would rather it went into receivership than give it to him on his terms.' The biggest shareholders, hedge funds RAB Capital and SRM Global, which accounted for 13 per cent of the bank's equity, called for the auction of the stricken bank to be abandoned. RAB's boss Philip Richards took to the airwaves to make the case against the Virgin offer, but he didn't win many friends in Whitehall or the City when he launched an unfortunate fusillade against those responsible for handling the crisis.

The hedge funds argued that the company should not be sold or broken up – an explosive demand that potentially threatened to derail the sale process. The rebel shareholders came out in support of the Olivant bid, largely because it offered them 85 per cent of the business and bigger incentives in terms of share price value. Unfortunately for the backers of the Olivant bid, it did not appeal to chairman Bryan Sanderson, who insisted that Olivant had to be part of the auction process and that there could not be a buy-in process led by its boss Luqman Arnold. Sanderson's rejection of Olivant's approach and his insistence that Olivant join the bidding process left Arnold seething.

The rebels successfully petitioned for an emergency meeting of Rock investors to block any Virgin deal. Sanderson and his reconstructed board agreed, and the extraordinary general meeting was fixed for January 2008. The more the shareholders – which included 180,000 small investors – took apart the Virgin offer, the less they liked it. Under Branson, they were being asked to take what they saw as a huge hit and own only 45 per cent of the new business. On top of which they understood that buried in the small print of his proposals Branson wanted royalties for the use of the Virgin brand and a £5 million fee to cover takeover costs.

Shareholders also voiced concerns that too much bureaucracy, with all its associated costs, and too little business acumen surrounded the takeover process. At one point, as many as 30 Whitehall civil servants were working on the Northern Rock crisis. 'Too much was going on around the company and not enough inside it,' was how one shareholder put it. Mainstream institutional investors, sensing drift, were disillusioned with the bank's management, with one commenting: 'The most frustrating thing about Northern Rock now is that there seems to be absolutely no one at the company who is acting on behalf of shareholders. I have never witnessed such a shambles.'

Matters were not helped by the report that the business minister, Baroness Shriti Vadera, who had played a key role in the Railtrack administration in 2001 as a special adviser at the Treasury, was involved in the background, providing informal advice to the Prime Minister from her berth at the Department of Business, Enterprise and Regulatory Reform. Her presence on the government team would have been a red rag to a bull for shareholders. Vadera, a shrewd former investment banker, had reportedly shown contempt for private investors in Railtrack, indicating that the government should not worry about 'grannies losing their blouses'. She would later state that these were not her words but had been copied and pasted from an email drawn up by someone else. Nevertheless, she had earned a reputation for being insensitive to the interests of small shareholders. The *Financial Times* tried to get to the bottom of what was going on via a Freedom of Information request but what came back revealed nothing.

The constant glare of publicity, including bidders dropping in and out of the process, was certainly not calming the situation. The negotiating team under Kingman was acutely aware of the direct correlation between negative stories about the Rock's future domination of the headlines and an outflow of deposits from the injured bank. Despite offering some of the more generous interest rates in the market and the presence of a government guarantee – making it among the safest places for the public to keep its money – a second silent run on the bank took place in early November. Kingman and the government's worries increased. Daily reports received from Newcastle told them that £200 million was vanishing by the day. At this rate there would be no cash left in the Rock by the end of the year. The bank was down to its last £11 billion as people removed their money via the internet. The much trumpeted electronic systems could barely cope, and there was a new urgency in Downing Street that the situation needed to be resolved – and quickly. If the bank went in to administration, one result would be that the government itself would end up ranking below bond-holders as priority creditors and so would take a huge hit.

The government asked Bryan Sanderson and the management team to put in place contingency plans so that if it became necessary to close the bank and repay the depositors, it could be done swiftly and with the least pain, and without causing panic on the streets as had been the case in September. Remarkably, no one at Northern Rock had ever considered such a possibility and no such scheme existed. Indeed, as had been seen in September, the small branch offices with their limited numbers of cashiers, were unfit for purpose when it came to a rush of withdrawals. When the contingency plans were leaked to the *Daily Mail* in January 2008, there was a fear that they could trigger a third run to follow those of September and November. Andy Kuipers, the new Dutch-born chief executive who had replaced Adam Applegarth, told me: 'We believe that this poses a real risk of scaring our customers now that we are in a much stabler period. Another run could be a possibility here again.' Kuipers personally begged me, as City editor of the *Daily Mail*, not to run the story. Alistair Darling followed up Kuipers's call with a personal plea to desist, fearing a further run that could destroy the bank. As a result, the paper decided against publication.

The situation as the end of 2007 approached was distinctly unpromising. There was real concern that, with Northern Rock borrowings from the Bank piling up, none of the bidders could afford to raise enough money to pay this off and recapitalise the business. Moreover, the ubiquitous Goldman Sachs, whom Darling had brought in as advisers, had reported on 19 November that all the initial bids received had been 'below current market value'.

Against this background public ownership – perhaps along the lines of the Johnson Matthey Bank rescue in 1984 – was increasingly being seen by some officials at the Bank of England, if not necessarily the government, as possibly the best solution. In public at least, though, the Bank's Sir John Gieve was hastily pointing out that a commercial deal was still preferred and that nationalisation was very much 'Plan B'.

The taxpayer now faced the real prospect of propping up the Rock for months to come. The *Sunday Telegraph* reported that advisers to the Chancellor were working on plans that would allow all or part of the £25 billion lifeline already extended to Northern

Rock to continue indefinitely. Although EU rules blocked the bank from receiving state aid beyond February, lawyers were drafting documents that could change the status of the funding to 'restructuring aid'. This would allow the Bank to continue to provide funding and aid any takeover of the bank. In fact, Northern Rock was considering a European option itself. Because of its Irish branch, the bank qualified for European Central Banking emergency funding, and it looked into the possibility of applying for a loan.

Meanwhile, as Virgin and Olivant squabbled in public over which was better qualified to the run the bank, an anxious Newcastle City Council wrote to the bidders spelling out its concerns: 'We want to highlight the importance of maintaining the company as a going concern, keeping its headquarters within the city and core functions within the region.' In the midst of such uncertainty, it was no surprise that Bryan Sanderson's seasonal message amounted to a warning that there would be no decision on the bank's fate until well into the New Year. The borrowings just grew and grew, topping £55 billion on 18 December, including the indemnity to depositors. The Treasury had extended financial guarantees to Northern Rock at the bank's request. This now meant that taxpayers were now theoretically exposed to the tune of £2,000 each.

The holidays brought a welcome break from the relentless round of headlines and speculation surrounding the company. One way or another, Northern Rock had never appeared to be out of the news since September. For two weeks, at least, there was a brief spell to come up for air and take stock of what had happened in just four months. But by 5 January normal service was resumed as Alistair Darling announced plans for fresh powers to prevent a repeat of the banking crisis and gave a very strong hint that the government was coming round to the view that Northern Rock might have to be taken into public ownership. In essence, his reforms would allow watchdogs to seize and protect customers' cash if another bank got into difficulties, and there would be a pre-funded insurance scheme for depositors plus a financial emergency response unit, based on the government's Cobra committee, which handles terror attacks or other civil crises.

In the middle of the month, and as the clock ticked down, the government was considering four options. First and foremost was a sale to the private sector. Northern Rock's management had now recruited Paul Thompson, the former chief executive of 'zombie' insurers Resolution. It specialised in buying up 'closed' or dead life funds sold off by insurers. Thompson joined the hunt by tabling a bid that would see the company's asset base halved and significant job cuts. The diminutive Thompson, who had left Resolution a rich man, began an intense personal PR campaign designed to win the support of the media. Neither Thompson nor Sanderson appeared to be aware of the potential conflicts of interest involved by an 'insider' bid from the very people who had been recruited to move Northern Rock on to its next stage. Thompson's group would also refine its offer later on to commit to repaying all government loans within three years.

The second option was public ownership. The government had begun careful contingency planning, including the recruitment of Ron Sandler as the potential executive chairman of the nationalised group. His name had been leaked to the BBC by Whitehall officials, who sought to show that there were options other than Branson's proposal and private-sector bids. The third option was a run-off that would admit defeat and just let the business slowly wind down. But it would have meant a long-term commitment for the government. Finally, there was administration, but this was seen as very much the worst-case scenario because of the enormous cost – estimated at up to £7 billion by officials close to Darling – job losses and disruption.

Tuesday, 15 January dawned as a drizzly morning on the Tyne. Northern Rock staged its extraordinary general meeting of shareholders at the behest of hedge funds RAB Capital and SRM and with the support of smaller shareholders groups fearful for their holdings. With more than 180,000 small shareholders, many of them living in and around the North East, Bryan Sanderson had expected a football crowd and hired the Metro, a great bunker of a location with seating for 11,000. At one stage it looked as if the media, camped outside from dawn, would outnumber the shareholders, but in the event around 1,000 investors turned up.

Outside the arena workers from the Unite union, wearing T-shirts bearing the ironic slogan 'Rock Solid', had gathered, adding to the gaiety of the occasion. Sanderson described the business as 'sound', called for shareholders to be 'responsible' and underlined the importance of a solution that kept Northern Rock as an 'important northeast company'. He drew a laugh from the audience when he described his job as chairman as 'the second toughest job in Newcastle', a reference to the travails of Newcastle United – sponsored by the Rock.

As expected, much of the noise came from the hedge funds – the latecomers to the Rock's share register – which were looking for a quick killing. They now feared that the bank would disappear in a Virgin takeover or, worse still, nationalisation. The boss of RAB, Philip Richards, portrayed himself as the hero of the small man, although his own multi-million pound investment must also have loomed large in his mind. He bashed the Bank of England – not a terribly sensible tack when the audience is the City of London – and then claimed to be driven by Christian beliefs that 'righteousness and justice are important', a somewhat bizarre claim for a man who made his money from Hedge Funds. Richards was followed by SRM's Jon Wood, fresh from his haven in Monaco, who attacked Mervyn King for failing to mount a covert operation to save the Rock. All in all, the meeting provided an opportunity for investors to vent their spleen, but in the end, resolutions seeking to tie the management's hands were roundly defeated.

With so little consensus on the way forward, the idea of nationalising Northern Rock was slowly taking root. My own inclinations, I have to say, were not in favour of allowing Northern Rock to fall under the hand of public ownership, and in a *Daily Mail* leader page article on 16 January I wrote:

> The dramatic step of nationalisation would be the day when Labour's hard-won reputation for economic competence is finally lost. Mervyn King and Alistair Darling should call Britain's leading banks to the Bank of England and demand, for the sake of the City of London's reputation, that they each inject billions of pounds of capital and deposits into Northern Rock in exchange for new shares. The British taxpayer – which is sacrificing so much – deserves no less.

Oddly enough, in the days that followed, the likelihood of nationalisation receded as the government decided to offer much greater financial support to any private-sector rescuer. In a clear boost to a possible commercial deal, the Prime Minister had backed a plan from bankers Goldman Sachs, advising on Northern Rock's future, to convert the Bank of England's loans into bonds, which could then be sold off to wealthy investors in the Middle East and Asia. There was an irony in the Goldman Sachs proposal in that it followed a similar path to the aggressive securitisation of Northern Rock mortgages by Adam Applegarth that had led to the Rock's problems in the first place.

This time, however, they would have the government's imprimatur, giving them almost gilt-edged status. This was not a totally revolutionary proposal. The American government used a similar device in the late 1980s to bail out US banks in danger of failing because of their over-exposure to Latin American debt. The loans were parcelled up, given a US government guarantee and sold in the markets, taking on the title of Brady Bonds in tribute to the then US Treasury Secretary Nicholas Brady, who dreamed up the scheme.

Goldman Sachs's bond proposal, unveiled on 21 January, would stay on the public-sector balance sheet until conditions improved in the financial markets. They would then be sold to investors in small parcels every few months. And, as if to beef up the significance of this approach, the Chancellor told MPs a few days later that if Northern Rock was nationalised, shareholders would receive little or nothing, because the value of shares would be based on what the business would be worth in the absence of any government support. Shareholders were being scared into accepting the bonds idea.

Reactions to the proposal were mixed. Some experts argued that by issuing millions of government bonds to pay off Northern Rock's debts, the bank would then simply be made ripe for a private bidder. In other words, the taxpayer could end up supporting Northern Rock for years, simply to enable a takeover by Branson or others. The scale of the support promised by Darling – at least £25 billion – was without precedent. My colleague Anthony Hilton took a more positive view. In his London *Evening Standard* column, he saw the bonds guarantee as an ingenious plan that might attract more prestigious bidders, such as Lloyds TSB, to the table. As it turned out, this would not prove true.

Despite intermittent upbeat talk, the gloom surrounding Northern Rock's prospects was never far away. Holes were being picked in the government's rescue plan almost daily, and by the end of January reports were suggesting that hidden penalties of £1 billion would sink it. At the same time, Sandy Chen at stockbroker Panmure Gordon warned that Northern Rock's business model was unravelling fast, and in his forecast he valued the firm's shares as worth nothing. Shortly before the 4 February deadline for bids, there was the first bit of good news surrounding Northern Rock for several months. By selling off a chunk of its loan book to J.P. Morgan, it had been able to pay off £2.5 billion of its Bank of England loan.

Meanwhile, the bid process was proving as confusing as ever, with the public relations spinners working overtime to gain positive publicity. Virgin, Olivant and the management team from

Northern Rock, now headed by insurance whiz Paul Thompson, looked to be in a fight to the finish for a dubious prize. Northern Rock's management team had been quietly encouraged by Kingman to come up with its own bid as part of his efforts to ensure that there was more than one offer on the table when the deadline was reached. The government was gradually tightening the screw on the bidders, fearing that the failure to do so could provoke an onslaught from the opposition benches. The Liberal Democrats continued to push the case for nationalisation, while the Tories, having vacillated for months, favoured a Bank of England-led rescue. The Treasury's response was to demand a 'performance warrant', which would allow the government to share 10 per cent in any financial recovery by the bank.

Whether this affected the issue materially among the bidders is hard to say. But, on the eve of deadline day, it was revealed that Olivant had dropped out of the running. Luqman Arnold had found it all but impossible to deal with what he saw as a dysfunctional Northern Rock board and could not meet the government's conditions. It had planned to raise up to £650 million by issuing new shares, after which it would have paid £150 million in return for a minority stake in the business. It would have repaid between £10 billion and £15 billion of the Bank loan immediately, with the rest settled in 2009. Northern Rock's board, however, felt that this offer fell short by at least £300 million.

The government was now left with Virgin, a management buyout or nationalisation. In this situation, Virgin clearly felt that it was in the driving seat. Sir Brian Pitman went on a PR drive, seeking to reinforce the Virgin case in the press. Branson, though, did himself few favours by using a trade mission by Gordon Brown to China and India to suggest to the travelling media that he had the inside track. Leading critics of his business methods, including biographer Tom Bower and *Private Eye*, went on the rampage, determined to stop him getting Northern Rock. Bower managed to place Branson-bashing columns in the *Mail*, the *Evening Standard* and the *Guardian*.

Branson, the master of publicity, was, it seemed, starting to lose the PR war. Kingman and the government, however, were not repelled by the anti-Branson rhetoric, having carried out research that suggested that the Virgin brand would be mildly helpful.

By deadline day, the Virgin offer amounted to putting £1.3 billion into Northern Rock in return for a 55 per cent stake. Some £11 billion of the loan would be repaid immediately, with the balance cleared over three years. Virgin's Jayne-Anne Gadhia also warned of cuts – so going back on a previous pledge. The Northern Rock bid, beefed up by the arrival of Paul Thompson, had managed to find favour with major shareholder RAB Capital and Monaco-based SRM. Significantly, the buy-out bidders also warned that up to 1,000 jobs were under threat.

As the runners approached the finishing line, and in the face of shareholder opposition, it looked as if Virgin was still out in front. After all, it had something that Northern Rock desperately needed – a fresh and trusted brand. And that, at one level, appeared to be that. But the government had not been bluffing when it had tightened the terms. A final report from Goldman Sachs had concluded that neither the Thompson-led internal bid nor the Virgin offer was up to snuff. It conceded that if a choice had to be made between the two, the Virgin proposal would probably offer the taxpayer the better chance of recovery, but there was a risk that Branson, already in receipt of government largesse for his rail franchise, would be gifted billions of pounds, and, in the process, create a huge embarrassment for the government.

Sunday, 17 February started like any other. There was not even a hint in the Sunday papers that the government had finally made its decision on the fate of the Rock. But that lunchtime the Chancellor and Prime Minister sat down and made the critical decision to nationalise the Rock. The payback period proposed by the private-sector buyers was considered too long, and the risk to the taxpayer was too high. Alistair Darling broke the news to Branson in an 'acrimonious' phone call: Northern Rock was 'being taken into temporary public ownership'. Ron Sandler, the man handed the task of turning the company around, revealed that this could take several years.

Sandler, now the biggest player on the Northern Rock stage, lost no time in travelling to Newcastle to talk to staff and the local media. He was taking over the reins at a bank that had been on the floor – its trading was severely depleted and it was kept going only through public money. It had been a highly unusual situation for New Labour, sensitive to any suggestion of a return to the 1970s and state aid for ailing companies. Sandler's task had to be to turn Northern Rock around and get it ready for a sale to the private sector. It might take upwards of two to three years and involve heavy cuts in the 6,500-strong workforce and the branch network.

To assist with his task, Sandler recruited Ann Godbehere, formerly of Swiss Re, as his chief financial officer. It was quickly established that she, like Sandler, was a non-dom – granted special tax status for the super-rich – even though she would be put in charge of billions of UK taxpayers' money. With her severe, blond hair, she was teased in the *Evening Standard*'s gossip column as a look-alike for Pat Butcher, the fearsome character from the BBC1 soap *EastEnders*.

Other new recruits included Stephen Lester, as non-executive deputy chairman, who brought to the job his experience at turning around the Abbey. As chief executive of British Land, he also had expertise in property. His company embarrassingly had just written down the value of its property portfolio by £1.4 billion, largely as a result of the credit crunch. Simon Dingemans, who had provided the government with advice throughout the crisis, was brought in from Goldman Sachs. Bryan Sanderson and Sir Ian Gibson – seen in Whitehall as one of the few heroes of the whole saga – quietly vacated their desks. At the end of February Northern Rock's deputy chief executive David Baker completed the passing of the 'old guard' by taking early retirement.

Deciding to nationalise Northern Rock had not been easy. For months Darling, who, ironically, is a Northern Rock borrower, had sat in his Treasury office wrestling with the bank's future. But the decision was never his alone. The Prime Minister had insisted on being intimately involved throughout and was in constant contact with Kingman. If the Chancellor had found a private-sector buyer with a firm promise to repay taxpayers quickly, it would have been the tidiest solution. The problem was that no such private-sector buyer seemed to exist in credit markets where lenders had no confidence in each other. Everybody was relying on Darling to underwrite the deal for a considerable period. Such a subsidised sale would give the bank's new owners most of the upside, should gains emerge, while leaving the taxpayer with most of the risk, if losses ensued instead. A second option would have been to force Northern Rock into bankruptcy. Aside from proving the government's toughness and its unwillingness to take on 'moral hazard', this held few attractions. Deposits would most likely have been frozen for weeks or even months, and news of savers struggling to get their money back might have sparked runs on other banks – the contagion that Darling and the other members of the Tripartite system most feared. In the resulting fire sale, Northern Rock's assets would probably fetch much less than they were worth.

That left nationalisation, which increasingly came to be viewed as the least worst option from the taxpayers' point of view. Public ownership would let the state retain any future gains by going slowly – even entering into a private-sector partnership – in the somewhat unlikely event that credit markets, house prices and Northern Rock's reputation recovered quickly. Nationalisation would be politically awkward – there would be claims of unfair market competition and shareholders might sue – but the lesson from other crises, such as those in France, Mexico, Sweden and Japan, was that emergency state ownership should be brief and at arm's length. The government knew that it had to maintain the stability of the financial system. It also had to get the taxpayer off the hook as fast and as thoroughly as possible.

Following Darling's announcement, legislation was rushed through the House of Commons, and by Friday, 22 February the Bill was passed and the government was free to issue the orders that formally saw Northern Rock pass into public hands. But nearly seven months after the crisis first broke, that was not the end of the matter. The political storm had passed, but Darling was still facing challenges.

The government's failure to include Granite, Northern Rock's Jersey-based securitisation arm, in the nationalisation, would prove to be an irritant. Granite had been set up in 1999, and it allowed the Rock to borrow funds at an extremely competitive rate. By the end of 2007 some £49 billion of Northern Rock mortgages had been shunted into the vehicle. These mortgages, according to some experts, included the lender's better quality loans. The beneficiary of Granite, when the trust winds up, would be a Down's Syndrome charity located in the northeast. Owing to an alleged oversight at Northern Rock, the charity had never been informed of its status, and nor had it ever received a penny of donations from the Rock or its charitable arm, the Northern Rock Foundation, for the use of its name.

The real concern of politicians is that should something go wrong at Granite the liability will fall back on the taxpayer, raising the eventual cost of the rescue. As worrying for the government will be prolonged litigation from shareholders looking for compensation. The two biggest investors, SRM and RAB, facing combined losses of £170 million through nationalisation, have revealed that they plan to sue the government. The move is backed by the company's small shareholders, who are considering legal action of their own. For the second time since it came to power – the first occasion being the Railtrack affair – the government appears to be headed for court, even though it believes that it has indemnified itself against having to pay out huge sums in compensation by exhausting the private-sector rescues before taking the bank into public ownership.

One of the City's most respected investors, Legal & General, which holds 5 per cent of the stock, disagreed. It argued that the crucial factor in the Rock's failure was the Bank of England's decision not to act in the money markets when the whirlwind hit on 9 August. Had it done so, the Rock could have obtained the required cash in the money markets, without stigma, and the lender of last resort bail-out in September would not have been necessary. L&G, which has a history of litigation against the authorities, pointed to the European Central Bank's extraordinary actions after the credit freeze as the correct blueprint.

So far as Ron Sandler was concerned, his first task was to plot a new course for Northern Rock. He carried out what is known in the City as a 'kitchen sink' job by clearing out all the junk left by his predecessors. And there was plenty of it. Northern Rock had, after all, managed to accumulate losses of £410 million on American sub-prime mortgages, and Sandler felt it necessary to put aside £240 million to cover future losses on its mortgages and unsecured loans. It also needed £41 million to pay City fees, including those of the government's advisers Goldman Sachs. As a result, the bank, which had made profits of £443 million in 2007, plunged into losses of £199 million, becoming the first British bank to go into the red as a result of the credit crunch.

The advisory fees were bad enough, but what really caused a public outcry was the disclosure that the man most responsible for the Rock's demise, Adam Applegarth, would suffer virtually no financial hardship at all. Rock employees would pay with their jobs, but Applegarth received his full £760,000 salary for 2007, plus a further £25,000 in the shape of non-cash benefits. As if this were not enough the Sanderson board at the Rock had also agreed a top-up of £346,246 to his pension fund, bringing it up to £2.62 million. The scale of the largesse, including a preferential rate on Applegarth's £75,000 mortgage, was described as 'outrageous' by the LibDem Treasury spokesman Vince Cable. 'This is straightforward reward for failure.'

Applegarth was not the only one to survive largely unscathed. The 2007 Northern Rock report and accounts show that former chairman Matt Ridley received a director's fee of £223,000 for that year. Even Paul Thompson, who was at the bank for less than five weeks and spent some of that time promoting his own bid, collected £100,000. The government, the proud owners of the Rock, were strangely quiet on the payoffs, and there was clearly an unwillingness to challenge the contracts and have the sordid affairs of the bank exposed in the courts.

As for Sandler's promise of 'business as usual' on the day the Rock was taken into public ownership, it proved to be far from that. Sandler revealed on 31 March 2008 that his real plan was to axe one-third of the bank's staff, shed 60 per cent of the company's mortgage customers and to repay all but £1 billion of the government's £24 billion of loans by the end of 2009. Not surprisingly perhaps, the first jobs to go would be among the mortgage sales team who, through their aggressive approach, had grabbed 20 per cent of the market in the first half of 2007, setting the Newcastle bank on its course to disaster.

Instead of promoting Northern Rock's competitively priced mortgages, the bank would be advising customers to refinance with other lenders. In the days following his appointment Sandler had aggressively advertised for retail deposits, much to the annoyance of rivals who did not enjoy a government guarantee. That policy was now to be reversed in the face of the need to satisfy the European Commission and keep the complaints of rivals at bay.

The year 2007 had seemed to offer untold promise for Northern Rock. It was flying high, having transformed itself in less than a decade from a provincial also-ran into Britain's fifth largest mortgage lender. In the first six months of 2007 alone it had captured a huge chunk of all new mortgages sold in Britain. By the end of the year it was on its knees. A share price of over £12 in January had crashed to under £1 in December. A valuation of £6 billion had turned into one of around £100 million, and the company that was once a darling of the City was down and out. Northern Rock had become Northern Wreck. It had passed into government ownership and was being shrunk in dramatic style by its new owners, despite the promise of business as usual.

There was bitterness and public anger at the failure of the new board and government to control the fabulous payouts to the former directors and the City. Far from representing the virtues of thrift, once so valued by the building societies, Northern Rock was just another rapacious bank, caught up in the greed and get-rich culture of the early 21st century. Its failure and nationalisation are testimony to New Labour's tolerance of a credit-fuelled economy and its unwillingness to tackle the very worst of financial behaviour.

CHAPTER 10

Fall Guys

How the bankers lost their shirts

James Cayne, the hard-bitten boss of investment house Bear Stearns, has earned a reputation for insouciance. When the credit crunch first struck in the summer of 2007, pushing two of the group's hedge funds into the sea, Cayne, who was one of the house's biggest shareholders, was spending part of his time honing his golf strokes on the fairways and greens close to his New Jersey home. At other times he was pursuing his passion for bridge. Yet only eight months after the crunch started to bite, Bear Stearns, a securities house that can trace its history back to 1923 and that had survived the Great Depression, came tumbling down.

No doubt 74-year-old Cayne believes, as many Americans do, that bridge is good exercise for the brain, which needs to be razor sharp in the rough and tumble world of Wall Street trading. But for the thousands of shareholders in Bear Stearns stock and the investors in the collapsed funds that were so heavily exposed to sub-prime mortgages Cayne's occassional absences in the middle of what former Federal Reserve chairman Alan Greenspan calls the worst financial crisis since the Second World War looked like arrogance.

On Tuesday, 11 March 2008 the financial markets, roiled by the length and depth of the credit crunch, turned against Bear Stearns. It was feared that, in addition to the problems in its own investment funds, it might be heavily exposed by the collapse of the publicly quoted Carlyle Capital Corporation, an offshoot of the secretive private equity firm Carlyle Capital. In highly nervous markets fears about the safety of Bear Stearns – never the most collegiate of Wall Street firms – grew to a crescendo. On Friday, 14 March it was revealed not only that the house was so damaged that it had to turn to the Federal Reserve and the blue-blooded bank J.P. Morgan Chase for a rescue but also that some $30 billion of assistance had been provided with a guarantee from the American taxpayer.

Cayne may have been in self-denial about events at the securities house he headed, but he only had to look across the landscape of Wall Street to understand how shattering the credit crunch had proved. On the wider stage the six months since the sub-prime melt-down had seen a series of deadly blows to the British and global banking systems. Goldman Sachs forecast losses for the entire financial sector of around £200 billion on Valentine's Day 2008. This was double the figure the trusted investment bank had forecast a few months earlier when it had sent share prices skidding on both sides of the Atlantic. In hearings before the Treasury Select Committee in early December, the heads of Citigroup, Goldman Sachs, UBS and Deutsche Bank – all of which had reported huge losses – said they could not have foreseen the credit crunch.

The markets were not impressed, however, and bank shares continued to tumble. The world's top 531 banks saw their value slide by £85 billion in just four trading days in early December, and about £15 billion was wiped off British banks alone. Mervyn King detected a 'palpable sense of fear' gripping the financial system and threatening to send the global economy into a tailspin. He thought things would not return to normal until banks felt more confident about lending to one another.

It was among America's investment bankers that the seismic shocks were first felt. Thanks to the sub-prime crisis, running a Wall Street bank was not much fun any more, and many of the leading names in American finance lost their jobs as major investment houses buckled under huge losses. The biggest beasts in the jungle left as firms suffered astronomical losses, leading to the reshaping of global banking. There was no more doleful sight than the once all-powerful

Wall Street moguls, who had enjoyed pay in the hundreds of millions of dollars, traipsing out to the Gulf statelets, Singapore, Beijing and Shanghai in search of new capital because US markets were no longer willing to finance their excesses. The top bosses had presided over a situation in which the prospective profits on the bundled-up sub-prime loans were so great that nobody had looked too closely at what was going on. When it all went wrong, the market for such toxic investments didn't simply slump, it vanished altogether, along with reputations and faith in banking probity. The hubris of the failed bankers was something to behold.

The bankers had behaved in a morally and socially irresponsible way, and someone had to carry the can. From heroes to zeroes in a matter of months, greedy bankers were getting their comeuppance. The procession of departures had actually begun in February 2007, when Britain's HSBC announced that it had fired its head of North American operations, Bobby Mehta, after its bad debt, much of it from sub-prime 'piggyback' loans, rose to $6.8 billion. Soon afterwards New Century Financial, the second biggest sub-prime lender in America, came crashing down, carrying $23 billion in debt.

In July 2007 one of the first really big-hitters to get the chop, Peter Wuffli, chief executive at Swiss bank UBS (Union Bank of Switzerland), was ousted in a boardroom coup. UBS, one the largest losers in the sub-prime disaster, shattered the illusion that no matter how dodgy other banks turned out to be, the Swiss banking giants, with their survival through world wars and revolutions, could always be relied upon. Ironically, even as UBS was reporting some of the biggest losses of all on its sub-prime investments – more than $10 billion in all, pushing the whole bank into deficit – it was still taking advertisements on national television and in glossy magazines across the globe that boasted of its wisdom as the world's largest manager of private wealth.

Until the credit crunch came along the McKinsey & Co. alumnus and trained banker looked like one of the financial world's untouchables. After he took over UBS, with its $971 billion balance sheet and $1.8 trillion of invested assets, the bank's performance improved dramatically and it gobbled up market share in its two key businesses of wealth management and investment banking. Unknown to shareholders, however, much of its newfound growth and profitability was built on the weak foundation of sub-prime. UBS was in the red to a meaty $4 billion in 2007 after a total write-down of a jaw-dropping $18.4 billion. In February 2008 UBS was sued by HSH Nordbank, one of Germany's largest financial institutions, which claimed that it was mis-sold hundreds of millions of pounds worth of sub-prime securities. This legal move was seen as the first of such actions that could stretch into the next decade. Once, the plan had been for Wuffli to take the post of chairman on the board of directors, then held by Marcel Ospel, but the board had had enough and ruthlessly replaced him with his deputy Marcel Rohner.

But the troubles were not over for UBS. In April 2008 it shocked the markets again. A huge clean-up operation had been going on behind closed doors, and remarkably the Swiss bank had found another $11.9 billion of sub-prime related losses. This time it was the chairman himself, the seemingly indestructible Marcel Ospel, who had forged the merger of the UBS with the Swiss Banking Corporation a decade earlier, who was forced out.

UBS was not alone. Next door in Germany the crisis had spread from IKB, which was rescued three times in 2007–8, to the Deutsche Bank, the nation's mightiest lender, which was headed by Josef Ackermann, one of the banking world's greatest survivors. With markets still deteriorating, Deutsche Bank decided it had to reveal $3.9 billion of losses, largely involving securities based on home mortgages. It was to claim that these were not sub-prime, but of a higher quality. This was hardly very comforting given that it suggested the crisis was spreading to different types of security that other banks – including Britain's Barclays – had claimed were sound.

Among the most emblematic of the casualties of the sub-prime earthquake was Stan O'Neal, who headed America's largest brokerage house Merrill Lynch, the 'rampaging bull', a firm with branches in every major US city and a huge presence in London. After days of speculation, Merrill announced in October 2007 that 56-year-old O'Neal would be retiring, having agreed with the board that a change in leadership would 'best enable Merrill Lynch to move forward'. He had lost the confidence of the board after the bank's sub-prime exposure resulted in the worst quarterly loss in its 93-year history and in overall losses of $7.9 billion. 'Losing a lot of money for share-holders is the surest way to end a career on Wall Street,' the Bloomberg wire remarked. He was also attacked for failing to reveal the extent of the problem and for making a behind-the-scenes merger approach to a rival commercial bank, Wachovia, without informing his board.

O'Neal hired a top New York remuneration lawyer to negotiate his severance terms and left with $160 million in shares and options built up over his years at the top. O'Neal announced: 'The company has provided me with opportunities that I never could have ima-gined growing up, culminating with my leadership of the company over the past five years.' He was a ruthless operator who clawed his way up from an impoverished childhood in a rural Alabama commu-nity to become not only the first black chief executive of a Wall Street bank, but also head of the largest brokerage in the world. In delivering record profits during his five-year tenure, his tough, 'take-no-prisoners' drive saw him sack 26,000 staff, though he was fond of saying 'ruthless isn't always that bad'. When I met O'Neal in London, in the incongruous setting of an elaborate Merrill Lynch marquee at the Chelsea Flower Show, I found him a courtly figure, friendly but reluctant to engage. A loner, who preferred to play his rounds of golf unaccompanied, he was a victim of some poor decision-making and suffered from having made few friends as a result of his severe cost pruning.

Next to go, in early November, was Chuck Prince at Citigroup, which had an astounding $55 billion of exposure to sub-prime loans. Prince had inherited the top job at Citigroup in 2003 from the entrepreneurial Sandy Weill, the rampant deal-maker who had trans-formed Citigroup into the world's largest commercial bank. As a lawyer who blended into the boardroom, Prince was seen as a safe pair of hands who would steer Citigroup through the regulatory minefield. He certainly managed to deal successfully with the aftermath of Citigroup's involvement with the failed corporate giants Enron and WorldCom and in keeping senior executives free of trouble. He also pushed Citigroup into fast-growing emerging markets and invested heavily in branches and technology to bring a new look to its anaemic American retail operations.

But when it came to attempting to steer the company into becoming an international financial supermarket, his touch failed him. Prince had been under intense pressure before the sub-prime crisis overwhelmed him, and the bank had already had to swallow $1.4 billion of losses stemming from over-exuberance in leveraged buy-outs. These headaches, combined with $26 billion-worth of acquisitions over the past year, had deflated the bank's capital cushion. With revenues frustratingly flat and a cost base stubbornly bloated, Prince quickly drew up a drastic cost-cutting plan. In August, as the first wave of sub-prime woe came crashing over the markets, he nevertheless blithely claimed that customers flocked to Citigroup in such trying times because 'we are a pillar of strength'. Events did not bear out this optimistic view.

Soon troubles crowded in. Prince came under huge pressure over a sagging share price and Citigroup's slip-ups in mortgage-related businesses. The bank later reported a sharp drop in profits thanks to write-downs of $3.6 billion. The mood darkened further after sharp-witted and glamorous Wall Street analyst Meredith Whitney questioned the extent of Citigroup's capital cushion and suggested that it might have to cut its dividend. Her comments sent the share price down by more than 8 per cent in a single day, and by the end of the first week of November 2007 Citigroup's shares had plunged 33 per cent from their level at the beginning of the year and were now below where they had been when Prince took over in 2003.

The sudden ebbing of confidence was driven mainly by concern that Citigroup would have to take even bigger hits as it reassessed its giant portfolios of asset-backed securities and mortgage loans, a large chunk of which were to sub-prime borrowers. Those fears proved justified as the bank reported that it would increase write-downs by a further $8 billion to $11 billion, dragging down net income by some $7 billion. Citigroup's exposure to mortgage-backed securities came as a shock. It had kept the full truth of its exposure to sub-prime under wraps, and it was claimed – as was the case at almost every bank – that Citigroup's sub-prime was different because it was highly rated. But the prized triple-A rating had become a misnomer, an empty joke. So rapidly did sub-prime mortgage defaults rise that it was soon downgraded by the very same rating agencies that had talked it up in the first place. The credit crunch contributed to the bank's misfortune before it had time to show results, and having dubbed 2007 'the year of no excuses', Prince was left with no choice. He was forced to resign, with the chairmanship temporarily passing to Robert Rubin, a former US Treasury Secretary and one of his closest advisers. Sir Win Bischoff, veteran of the patrician London merchant bank Schroders and head of Citigroup in Europe, became interim chief executive, later stepping up to chairman.

Because of its vast scale and huge retail base, Citigroup was America's biggest bank in terms of assets and was sufficiently robust to survive the hurricane blowing through global banking. The same could not be said for Bear Stearns. Its disappearance from Wall Street after more than 80 years of independence was a body blow. On Monday, 17 March, the company was sold lock, stock and barrel, including its $1.2 billion flashy Manhattan headquarters, to J.P. Morgan Chase for just $2 a share or $240 million, a figure eventually revised upwards to $10 a share or $1.2 billion. At the start of the year the investment house had been valued at one hundred times that.

It had first been revealed in July 2007 that squalls had hit two of Bear Stearns' investment funds. The reverberations reached far and wide, alerting markets to the impending sub-prime disaster and helping to set up the conditions that caused the markets to freeze on 9 August. Before the sub-prime crisis Bear Stearns had been planning an international expansion, much of it in Canary Wharf in London's Docklands. But this was soon off the agenda.

Bear Stearns quickly came to be seen as the weakest of the Wall Street investment houses. Its stock suffered more than any of Wall Street's other firms, dropping 53 per cent in 2007. The fourth-quarter loss of $854 million was the first in the firm's long history. Not surprisingly, therefore, questions started to be asked about its boss. Cayne had had a good run. The architect of the securities house's modern ambition, he had grown up in New York City, the son of a lawyer. His first job was as a travelling salesman, selling copiers. He moved into the financial world when fellow bridge-player Alan Greenberg, then a relative novice, hired him as a stockbroker at Bear Stearns, where he became president in 1985 and CEO. Rated among the 400 richest Americans in 2005, Cayne is a world-class bridge player, having won more than a dozen national championships and having represented the US in international tournaments.

He was, however, not the most bankable figure among Wall Street's Masters of the Universe, and when the Fed was organising a 'private-sector' rescue of the super hedge fund Long Term Capital Management in 1998, Bear Stearns – although it did business with LTCM – was the only major financial institution to refuse the central bank's call for help. In a way it was somewhat amazing that he had managed to hang on at Bear Stearns at all after it was first savaged by the first sub-prime tornado in July 2007.

The *Wall Street Journal* claimed that in July 2007 Cayne would take a break from office routine to play golf or bridge. He himself later strenuously defended his conduct during the crisis, stating that he had remained 'intensely focused'. Whatever the facts of the matter, throughout this critical period his company was haemorrhaging money from two hedge funds that had been caught up in the fallout. With investors clamouring for their money to be returned and lenders demanding more collateral, both funds collapsed. In January

2008 Cayne finally relinquished his job as chief executive, but, as the holder of 12.2 million shares or 8.35 per cent of all the stock in issue (a stake once worth almost $2 billion) it proved hard to remove him from his chairman's seat. Indeed, even after the group's downfall he and another multi-billion dollar investor, the British-born mogul Joe Lewis, could not accept that Bear Stearns had been sold off so cheaply. After protests from Cayne, Lewis and other large shareholders, J.P. Morgan eventually improved its original, humiliating $2 a share rescue offer by a factor of five.

In the wake of such disasters federal regulators and Wall Street started to rally around in the spring of 2008, worried that unless they did something the contagion would spread. Ben Bernanke, the Fed chairman, working with the US Treasury Secretary Hank Paulson, was speedy, sure footed and determined, and drew on special powers unused since the historic trauma of the Great Depression. Their resolve provided a stark contrast to the fumbled and legalistic handling of the Northern Rock crisis in Britain in September 2007 and the dithering over a sale or nationalisation, which had lingered on until February 2008. Even so, the shock waves from Bear Stearns sparked a new round of questions about US financial houses, and Lehman Brothers, just one step ahead of Bear Stearns, became the subject of concern. This was followed by a malicious whispering campaign against Halifax Bank of Scotland (HBOS) in Britain, which was considered bad enough for the Financial Services Authority and Bank of England to issue statements complaining of market abuse.

The trio of high-powered American banking bosses – O'Neal, Prince and Cayne – led the way in the 'Big Losers' stakes, although it was only Cayne who saw his equity all but wiped out. Their institutions – Merrill Lynch, Citigroup and Bear Stearns – had not shown the prudence expected of bankers and had become carried away with the lure of leverage, Bear Stearns ending up reduced to rubble and absorbed by rival James Dimon at J.P. Morgan Chase. But they were not the only ones in this position. Many banks and insurers on both sides of the Atlantic posted mega-losses through sub-prime exposure, even if few were as badly hit. Some that, at first, had boasted clean hands, like Lehman Brothers, Goldman Sachs and Credit Suisse, eventually unveiled big write-downs in the days after Bear Stearns failed in spring 2008. Among the second-line losers was the insurer Swiss Re, which initially revealed a £524 million loss from sub-prime in November 2007 after two of its credit default swaps, complex hedges taken out to protect against sub-prime losses, were hit by the credit crunch. The company marked down the value of some of its asset-backed securities to zero, and its sub-prime securities were written down to 62 per cent of their original value. In the aftermath, Swiss Re suspended the head of the unit responsible.

In Britain, after the embarrassment of Northern Rock – seen around the world as the unfortunate blueprint for what could happen when the fortunes of banks take a turn for the worse – there was intense focus on the performance of the nation's other financial institutions. The UK, in keeping with the City's role as a world financial centre, has among the most sophisticated business press anywhere in the world, applying a forensic scrutiny to the behaviour of banks, financial groups and their bosses. After the Rock and the funding problems for Barclays in the summer of 2007 – when the Bank of England was still keeping a tight grip on the purse strings – it was inevitable that all the British banks would come under the microscope.

Minor sub-prime exposures were uncovered at some British insurers, including Prudential, but they were more than offset by growth elsewhere in the world. Bank trading and profits figures revealed the institutions' exposure to sub-prime debts, but in comparison with what was happening across the Atlantic – and for that matter in Switzerland – the British exposures were surprisingly modest. Yet the shock of Northern Rock meant that nerves were jangling. The inter-bank market remained as constipated as ever, and bear raiders were active, frequently selling bank shares short in search of quick profits. The former building societies, such as Alliance & Leicester (A&L) and Bradford & Bingley (B&B), were seen as particularly vulnerable because of what was perceived as their over-reliance on the wholesale markets to fund their mortgage lending.

In late November 2007 B&B denied that it had been forced into disposing of assets to build its liquidity. It admitted, however, that it would make a book loss of between £15 million and £40 million on the sale of its housing association book to a specialist lender, Dexia, for £2.2 billion and its commercial property mortgage book to GE Real Estate for £2 billion. The £4.4 billion of funding would be enough to see it safely through to early 2009. Its chief executive Steven Crawshaw claimed that the sales were part of a 'strategic review' and had been in train for some months. It was quite possible that they were, but after the difficulties of Northern Rock it was working closely with the regulator, the FSA, which was anxious to make sure adequate funding was in place.

In 2007 B&B's pre-tax profit almost halved to £126 million from £246.7 million the year before, after the bank wrote down assets, including those tied to US mortgages. B&B said that if it had not been for 'unusual and extreme external events' its underlying profits would have been up. But bad debt charges on its residential mortgages had trebled to £22.5 million in 2007 as borrowers came under pressure. It lost £58 million when it sold a portfolio of commercial property and was dented by problems relating to housing association loans. B&B sought to reassure the market by noting that customer deposits funded 60 per cent of lending, but it was a less than comforting report. The cost of raising money had increased, so B&B's future profits margins were shrinking. The number of mortgage borrowers in arrears on their payments by three months or more had gone up by 42 per cent. In May 2008 it would disappoint the market again when it unveiled a shock £300 million rescue rights issue. The troubles continued and on 30 September 2008 B&B was nationalised.

The picture was not much brighter at A&L. It revealed it would take a £185 million hit from losses on complex financial instruments, more than three times its previous estimate of £55 million. The sceptics doubted that even this higher number conveyed the full impact of some of the detritus that A&L had taken on to its balance sheet.

The bank also said that it had organised enough cash to replace those medium-term loans that would come up for renewal in the money markets in 2008. The shares had fallen to half over the previous 52 weeks as investors voted with their feet. Some assurance about the immediate future was provided in November when it announced that it had agreed a £4 billion, two-year financing facility through Credit Suisse. A&L said that the crisis in credit markets cost it an extra £150 million a year in securing funds for new business, which could make growing the bank more difficult. Profits dropped sharply to £170 million, down from £399 million in 2006.

The reality, as I commented in the *Daily Mail* on 21 February, was that A&L was a bank going nowhere:

Alliance & Leicester's progress as a fully independent bank ... has been brought to a juddering halt. The group's write-downs of £185 million of toxic assets comes as no surprise, as A&L has been careful to keep the market informed. It is the future of the business model which is more in doubt ... The best hope for A&L's future would be as part of a larger financial group.

Mortgage banks need a ready supply of new retail cash deposits or funding from the wholesale markets to grow. A&L had secured the funding but at a relatively high cost, which would damage its margins and make it more difficult for it to grow its mortgage book and profits. As part of a larger bank – with a better credit rating – it would have a brighter future. In July 2007 A&L was sold to Santander of Spain, owner of the Abbey, for £1.3 billion.

Another struggler was the niche lender Paragon, Britain's third-largest buy-to-let mortgage lender. Towards the end of 2007 it was finding it hard to raise enough money to keep going, and its share price tumbled by 30 per cent. Paragon had lost 82 per cent of its value in 2007 and by late November in that year was worth just £141 million. Its problems were echoes of its troubles in 1991, when the company, then known as National Home Loans, came close to insolvency. But the lender was determined not to give up the ghost. It arranged to refinance by means of a £280 million rights issue to existing shareholders, underwritten by UBS, which was a brave decision amid the market turmoil. Remarkably, the issue, at a huge discount to the quoted share price worked, and the company and its determined chief executive Nigel Terrington had bought themselves more time.

Throughout much of the autumn of 2007 the finger of market suspicion was pointed at two of Britain's biggest banks, Barclays and the Royal Bank of Scotland (RBS). Earlier in the year the two banks had found themselves in opposite corners of the ring in the takeover battle for the Dutch bank ABN Amro, a battle eventually won by RBS in the autumn of 2007. But before the ink was even dry on the deal, the markets had turned their guns on the UK banks. In August Barclays twice hit the headlines when it was required to borrow from the Bank of England's emergency window, paying a penalty rate of interest of one point above base rate. The second loan of £1.6 billion, made on 31 August, was attributed to a fault in the 'clearing system', and Barclays was so fearful of stigmatisation by other banks that it felt it necessary to issue a statement assuring the markets that it was 'flush with liquidity'.

Because of the role of its investment bank arm, Barclays Capital (BarCap), in the securitisation trade right at the heart of the subprime crisis, Barclays looked an easy target to the bear raiders who were stalking the market. BarCap's American president, Bob Diamond, is the highest paid banker in Britain – he earned £21 million in 2007 – and was regarded as a financial genius for the way in which he had transformed a second-rate investment banking business into a world leader. But its prominence in the mysterious world of off-balance sheet vehicles and complex securitisation made it an easy target for critics.

Similarly, the finger of suspicion was pointed at RBS. The purchase of ABN Amro, in the middle of the worst financial crisis since the Second World War, began to look over-ambitious, even though large parts of the business had been pre-sold to other European banks. Its ownership of a large banking network in the US, home of the sub-prime problem, also caused disquiet. With the value of bank shares dropping on both sides of the Atlantic, it was noted that for the price that RBS had paid for ABN Amro it could have bought itself three of America's top investment banks, including Merrill Lynch.

The reputation of both banks took a hammering. Yet when, early in 2008, Sir Fred Goodwin at RBS and John Varley at Barclays revealed details of their exposure to the sub-prime crisis and the broader global credit crunch, the damage turned out to be less than expected. Barclays revealed write-downs of £1.7 billion. RBS rolled in with £2.9 billion of write-downs, swelled by problems found in the balance sheet of ABN Amro. HSBC, which had kicked off the whole saga, revealed that its credit losses were £8.5 billion and that it was not yet out of the woods in America, where loans losses had spread from mortgages to credit cards and car loans.

Britain's largest mortgage bank, Halifax Bank of Scotland (HBOS), has also had its detractors. There was concern that with 40 per cent or so of its lending dependent on the wholesale markets, it could be the weakest of Britain's biggest five banks. There was also worry that the group's brilliant young chief executive, the 40-year-old Andy Hornby, who had arrived at HBOS via a career in retailing at Asda, lacked the hard market experience required of a banker in the heat of the worst financial convulsion for decades. HBOS found itself the subject of a bear raid in the tense days following the collapse and rescue of Bear Stearns.

Dealers' suspicions of a problem were aroused when HBOS went to the markets in mid-March 2008 and issued a ten-year £750 million bond at the extraordinary interest rate of 9.5 per cent. The new money was intended to strengthen the bank's capital base, but there was no escaping the fact that it was paying 3.5 points above the charge it was making to its mortgage customers. Small wonder that the stock, with its handsome yield, was two times oversubscribed.

Yet it also provided an opportunity for mischief-making. Early on the morning of 19 March rumours circulated on the trading floor of the City that one of their number had caught sight of an email suggesting that HBOS had run short of ready cash and, like Northern Rock, had had to turn to the Bank of England for lender of last resort funding. This provided an excuse for a bear raid on the company's stock. In a few frantic minutes the share price plummeted 17 per cent. If the rumours were not killed, the risk was that the speculation would become self-fulfilling and that the share price drop would turn HBOS into a pariah in the global markets. Urgent action was called for.

The group's thoughtful but excitable chairman Lord (Dennis) Stevenson went directly to the Chancellor with his fears, and Hornby had no choice but to contact Hector Sants at the FSA. In a rare public intervention, which flashed across the City screens, the regulator dismissed the rumours of difficulty and promised to track down those responsible for 'market abuse'. The Bank of England weighed in too, describing reports of staff leave being cancelled at the Bank over the Easter weekend to deal with an impending crisis as 'pure fantasy'. All of this was highly unusual, since regulators dislike responding to market rumours. It exposes them to the risk that when they fail to say anything – which is most of the time – the market will misinterpret the silence as a sign of assent. On this occasion, however, the authorities were worried enough to telephone City editors to reassure them that there was no truth in any of the vicious and inaccurate rumours or emails allegedly circulating. The FSA revealed that it would launch an immediate investigation, and that it would focus on sell orders thought to have originated in the Asian markets, where such wild raids are far more common. There also was the possibility that ruthless hedge funds were seeking to make a profit by selling HBOS shares short on a false rumour that they had circulated.

Nevertheless, the incident – which had been without foundation – was a shock to Hornby. When we spoke on the day he reassured me about the security of HBOS's wholesale funding and accused unnamed conspirators of being 'scaremongers'. As had been the case with Barclays some months earlier, a major British commercial bank was having to remind the public that it had adequate funding – a highly unusual event. The media took a responsible line, and the following day's headlines concentrated on the denials rather than on the share price fall and its causes. The reporting had moved a huge distance from September 2007, when the BBC's excitable reporting of Northern Rock's troubles may have contributed to the vehemence of the run on the bank. The last time that regulators and a bank has felt it necessary to take on the rumour mongers was three decades earlier, when National Westminster (now part of RBS) had to issue similar assurances amid the financial chaos of the 1973–4 secondary banking crisis.

But few analysts were convinced that this was the end of the story. It seemed extraordinary that, despite their strong presence in the American marketplace, the losses of the big UK banks were so much more modest than their American and Continental European counterparts. The heavy falls in the shares of British banks told their own story: no one believed that the full extent of their losses had yet been recorded. There was a conviction in the City that before the crisis was over Barclays, RBS and the other UK banks would need to increase the level of write-downs, rather than simply hope that eventually the value of the toxic assets on their balance sheets would recover. The Bank of England, meanwhile, made no secret of its belief that the capital of the British banks needed to be reinforced and that before the crisis was over the banks would be looking for additional strategic shareholders or tapping their existing investors for new equity.

The Royal Bank of Scotland's stormy annual general meeting at the Edinburgh International Conference Centre on 22 April 2008 certainly seems to bear out the suspicion that there is more to come. What it revealed was that RBS's takeover of ABN Amro, in the middle of the credit crunch, was a huge error, and that the bank's high-risk strategy of running its affairs with the minimum of capital and liquidity has proved disastrous. Chairman Sir Tom McKillop, brought into RBS from the pharmaceutical industry, and chief executive Sir Fred Goodwin found themselves forced to eat humble pie when they revealed that the losses from sub-prime and other foolish investment had been mounting and that the bank would have to write down a further £5.9 billion.

Not only did the bank admit dreadful mistakes, it also asked shareholders to pick up the tab. It wanted them to back the biggest issue of shares to existing investors in Britain's history: a whopping rights issue of £12 billion as the company sought to strengthen its capital. It would also begin a fire sale of businesses, disposing of its interest in insurers Direct Line and Churchill in an effort to raise up to £8 billion more. In effect RBS was raising £20 billion of new funds, a shocking admission of failure. Private shareholder John Steen summed up the mood of frustration when he told the meeting: 'You guys are paid as though you are superhuman and it's very clear that you're not.' His comments were met with loud applause.

Goodwin explained to investors that 'the world had changed'. Not surprisingly, they were not impressed. McKillop sought to defend his chief executive, arguing that 'no single individual was responsible for the events'. He, too, came under fire. He was criticised for failing to restrain an ambitious executive. McKillop's lack of banking background and the 'Scottish' nature of the board – where nationality could seem as important as banking experience – also rankled among major investors.

In the event, McKillop and Goodwin survived the immediate crisis at RBS and the company's British-dominated share register was less inclined to pull the trigger than at the bank's American counterparts. But there was little doubt that once the humiliating fund raising operation was completed that the search would be on for replacements. 'Fred the Shred', as he was known in the City for his cost cutting prowess, would this time be shredded himself.

RBS was not alone. On Tuesday, 29 April 2008, after weeks of speculation, Halifax Bank of Scotland held its annual general meeting in Glasgow where chairman Lord Stevenson revealed to shocked investors, including its army of 2.1 million small shareholders, that it would be asking them for £4 billion of new capital through a rights issue. Chief executive Andy Hornby admitted that HBOS's gung-ho days of expansion were over and that it would be adopting more cautious targets for future growth. Hornby, like Goodwin, would face a struggle to hang on to his job over the medium term.

The recent experiences of RBS and HBOS demonstrate very clearly how every bank in the world has been touched in some way by the credit crunch, and how some are still in denial. In Britain RBS and Barclays had given the greatest concern, because of their size and the nature of their investment banking operations. According to research notes from institutions such as Citigroup and Morgan Stanley, their balance sheets had been under more strain than those of any of their European peers. The City was also sure that Barclays was one of the many European banks that took advantage of the liquidity facilities made available by the European Central Bank and that several billion euros had been drawn from Frankfurt. Nevertheless, even given the Bank of England's miserly approach to liquidity, in the early days of the crisis the British banks – while losers – had emerged relatively unscathed when matched against their American and Swiss counterparts.

The big beasts in Britain's banking jungle will recover from the shocks of the credit crunch, but there would be no going back for Northern Rock, its executives, shareholders and staff. Northern Rock shareholders in particular found themselves on a steep learning curve. When the former building societies converted into banks and came to the stock market, private investors regarded the shares they were awarded as a gift from heaven. Many sat back with satisfaction, watching with amazement as they rode the bear market up and doubling and even tripling the value of the free issue. What they perhaps failed to grasp is that when a company runs into trouble the shareholders are the cannon fodder. They carry most of the risk and, in the case of liquidation, are normally wiped out.

Big investors, such as hedge funds SRM Global and RAB Capital, which joined the share register only in the autumn of 2007 in the hope of making a quick killing, knew the odds. By buying shares at around £1 they expected to make money when Northern Rock was passed on to a private-sector rescuer and eventually turned around, at which point its share price would zoom up again. But they miscalculated. With public ownership came the unwelcome (for them) news that the bank's shares were to be valued by an independent assessor on the basis of no government assistance – the value of their investment had been all but wiped out. The hedge funds had taken a punt in the market and came unstuck. They squealed loudly, but few mourned their plight.

A more sympathetic case could be made for Northern Rock's 180,000 small shareholders, some of whom were staff taking shares instead of cash as part of the company's reward package. Another large section of the small shareholders were the savers who had been with Northern Rock when it was a building society and had been given shares when it demutualised. 'Shares should come with a government health warning,' argued the Northern Rock Small Shareholders Group. When the bank's fate was finally announced in mid-February the shareholders, large and small, with the insurer Legal & General (L&G) in the forefront of the complaints, threatened to take legal action against the government. L&G was convinced that if the Bank of England had offered more assistance to the money markets in August 2007, when the European Central Bank had stepped in, there would have been no crisis at the Rock, so the government should compensate them. But it is highly questionable whether taxpayers should be required to buy out greedy hedge fund investors – late to the party – or naïve small shareholders who seemed oblivious to warnings that shares can go down as well as up.

Arguably, the biggest loser from the Northern Rock debacle will be the UK taxpayer. The Office of National Statistics put the cost to the public purse of the whole operation at £100 billion. Gordon

Brown and Alistair Darling dressed up the decision to nationalise the bank as being in the interests of the taxpayer, arguing that the private-sector deals would not be as beneficial to taxpayers as state ownership. Even though nationalisation would result in UK taxpayers bearing the cost of a £25 billion loan to Northern Rock plus £30 billion in guarantees plus the untold millions spent during the bidding and advisory process and of costs going forward, this, they argued, having spent six months guaranteeing deposits with no assets secured, would mean that taxpayers would get their money back, with interest, when market conditions allowed for the sale of the bank back to the private sector. This could be at least three years away, so, like it or not, the government was now in the mortgage business.

Across the Atlantic the focus was on fixing the system rather than apportioning blame. Clearly, bank managements – which paid with their jobs – were huge losers. The departures were swifter and more brutal than anything seen in Britain, despite the billions of losses run up in sub-prime here. Some commentators seemed intent on blaming former Federal Reserve chairman Alan Greenspan for the sub-prime debacle because of his decision to hold American interest rates so low for so long in the early years of the decade. His reputation appeared to have been damaged.

But much of this was displacement activity. The reality is that it was over-ambitious, imprudent and foolish bankers who caused the sub-prime debacle and who created the monstrous debt instruments that led the world to the brink. They have banked their personal profits and bonuses, but although their behaviour had been socially reprehensible, they were surely not without some conscience about the damage they had caused. They would have to live with their mistakes for the rest of their lives.

CHAPTER 11

Painful Lessons

Private greed, public neglect

When the credit crunch first came to public notice in the summer of 2007 no one could have imagined how long the crisis would last, how deep and damaging it would be, and how much of an impact it would have on so many lives across the Western world. Far from being a one-off, the credit crisis would drag on relentlessly, producing ever more and bigger shocks to the global financial system. In Britain, which experienced its first mass run on a bank for over a century, it was to be a defining event that would fundamentally alter the fault lines of British politics.

New Labour spent its first ten years in power distancing itself from its past as the party of over-centralisation and economic mismanagement. It built on the Conservative economic legacy of free and open capital and labour markets and, in the process, established a reputation for economic competence, presiding over a decade of uninterrupted wealth creation. Admittedly, this was achieved against a global background that initially saw the prices of most finished goods fall dramatically. Yet there was no escaping the fact that the systems put in place largely by Gordon Brown as Chancellor of the Exchequer – an independent Bank of England and rules designed to keep fiscal policy on track – proved astonishingly successful. The UK economy was remarkably resilient, despite the shocks of the emerging crisis in 1997–8, the terror attacks of 9/11 and the bursting of the dotcom bubble. It was the period in which Labour learned to live with business and in which the City attracted to London the best and the brightest from around the world to work in the Square Mile's well-developed financial markets and the towers that sprouted like a rainforest in Canary Wharf.

Unfortunately, the politicians, the policy-makers and the bankers began to believe their own myths. Brown, who became Prime Minister in June 2007, and his key allies in setting economic policy lost their sharp focus on prudence. In New Labour's first years in office Brown and Blair had been obsessed with establishing the credibility of the new party. Public borrowing had been ratcheted down and Gordon Brown earned the title 'Iron Chancellor'. I clearly remember attending a briefing at the Treasury in the late 1990s on public finance, conducted by Gus O'Donnell (who went on to become Cabinet Secretary under Blair and Brown), at which the main purpose was to explain to the gathered economic scribblers how cutting borrowing and the national debt was having the effect of lowering long-term interest rates and providing a dramatic boost to the public finances. Prudence was good, and the whole country was benefiting.

But because the government defied the odds so many times and managed to ride out global instability, they came to believe that they had abolished the economic cycle – the boom and bust so characteristic of Britain's post-Second World War history. As a result, in the latter years of Brown's stewardship, the economy was allowed to start building its own unsustainable bubble. The volume of credit pumped into the British economy soared to in excess of £1,300 billion, a sum greater than the total gross domestic product. Frugality was gradually jettisoned, and the public finances, while still meeting Labour's self-imposed fiscal rules, were allowed to roam much more freely. The so-called 'golden rule' – which allowed government borrowing for 'investment' in public services over the economic cycle – was stretched forwards and backwards so that it would not be seen to be breached. And the sustainable investment rule, which required the Treasury to hold the national debt below 40 per cent of the nation's total output, was also fiddled. Large amounts of public spending, through the private finance initiative and public–private partnerships, were put off balance sheet and not fully accounted for. Only a small part of the liability was recognised in the annual budget documents. It required painstaking analysis of the complex 'Consolidated Fund Bill', presented to parliament annually, to determine the underlying cost of public private partnerships. Unfunded public-sector pension liabilities were also ignored.

As the government loosened its rules and annual public borrowing headed towards the £40 billion mark, the government chose to ignore the entreaties of the International Monetary Fund in Washington and the OECD in Paris. Both these august organisations had urged the British government to use the years of above-trend growth for 'fiscal consolidation' (IMF-speak for strengthening the public finances). This would have provided the cushion needed to boost the economy if it became necessary when it hit the iceberg of the credit crunch. Eventually the government had to accept a breach, albeit of a temporary nature, of its 'golden rule' when Northern Rock was taken into public ownership. The Office of National Statistics ruled that the £100 billion of liabilities would have to be added to the national debt until such time as the bank shrank in size or was sold on. The result was that for the first time since New Labour had assumed power it was in breach of its own self-imposed sustainable investment rule.

If it was governments and monetary authorities that, by failing adequately to control debt creation, created the circumstances under which the credit bubble was born, it was the bankers and financiers who exploited their weakness. They had every incentive to do so. The more profits the banks made, the more their companies would be lauded by an investment community primarily interested in short-term gains, and the higher the shares of their companies would surge – and the richer the bankers would become. Incentive arrangements throughout the financial system were based on short-term gains, and the longer term consequences were easily ignored. Consequently old rules that governed lending against homes were abandoned and replaced by sophisticated new scoring systems that allowed advances beyond the dreams of avarice to be made. Among the excesses were 125 per cent mortgages, zero-interest credit cards distributed like confetti to all and sundry and 40-year and interest-only mortgages, which provided an illusion of 'no pain'.

Although the credit crisis has been a global event that has affected almost every Western nation, it fell particularly hard on the United States and Britain: countries that have open economies, lighter touch regulation and heavy dependence on financial services. The low savings rates on both sides of the Atlantic made American and British banks far more reliant on the wholesale markets for their funding than was sensible. They came to believe that in a world flush with liquidity the markets could always be tapped for more cash. It was an attitude that permeated a financial system in which almost everyone believed that they could benefit from leverage, the huge value accretion that comes from using borrowed money rather than equity to invest. Indeed, Northern Rock in Britain and Bear Stearns in the United States – two of the most prominent victims of the credit crunch – were both in their very different marketplaces wedded to the same concept. The belief trickled down to many ordinary Britons, who, for instance, had obtained buy-to-let mortgages from companies like Bradford & Bingley and Paragon in the belief that property values were ordained to continue to rise as they had done from the mid-1990s.

It has to be said, though, that while both bankers and the general public were hit almost simultaneously by the credit crunch, individual bankers have tended not to be the big losers. In years when profits dipped or dreadful mistakes were made bonuses might be scrapped – John Mack, the ruthless boss of Morgan Stanley, took no bonus in 2007, for example – but there was no mechanism whereby organisations could claw back the bonuses already made on the dubious deals that had fuelled the sub-prime bubble and the securitisation bonanza in previous years. As for sacked heads of American banks and Adam Applegarth of Northern Rock, they walked away from the credit crunch very wealthy men.

It has been estimated that some 40,000 City bankers and traders will lose their jobs in 2008, as the full impact of the crisis is felt across the City. When they clear their desks, though, many have the comfort of knowing that the Porsche will remain in the underground garage of their high-tech, minimalist apartment overlooking the Thames. There is no threat to the beach house in St Mawes or the country pile in the Cotswolds. The incentive arrangements are in place to satisfy their voracious hunger for ever more riches. If the growth in income was to the benefit of clients, shareholders and other stake-holders so be it. But the fundamental be all and end all of financial enterprises is the bonus and personal gain, and if that means selling investors debts that are known to be rotten or overvalued, so what? The financiers who created the new sliced and diced debt vehicles behaved like the second-hand car dealers of old. The body-work looked shiny, but underneath the bonnet the vehicles were broken.

Inevitably, Northern Rock, as the biggest British victim of the credit crunch, is the institution that has received most public attention and opprobrium. To some extent it has also been regarded as something of a unique case, an 'outlier' in the British financial system in that it was so heavily dependent on wholesale financial markets, where it obtained 70 per cent of its funding. It was certainly unusual for a mortgage bank, but it has to be said that it was not that exceptional. Paragon, among other financial groups, was wholly dependent on wholesale markets. Halifax Bank of Scotland, despite being one of the largest savings concerns in the nation, depends on wholesale finance for 40 per cent of its funding. The whole business of Barclays Capital, the investment banking arm of Barclays, is based around taking wholesale debt, packaging it up and passing it on to others in the marketplace.

Where Northern Rock was unique, though, was in its over-dependence on wholesale funding. There was a mismatch between its borrowings – which could, and did, vanish overnight – and the lack of understanding in the marketplace, among regulators and even on its own board about what its chief executive, Adam Applegarth, was up to. It has to be said, too, that there was no more dysfunctional board in the financial sector than that of Northern Rock. The attempt to create a northeastern private-sector champion, in a region so dependent on public-sector subventions, was admirable. But in choosing Matt Ridley as chairman, the bank's directors showed they were living in a past age when adorning the boardroom with the local toff was considered the normal thing to do. Northern Rock's boardroom was filled with dignitaries, and an upstairs and downstairs attitude prevailed. Nowhere was this more evident than at the Newcastle United football ground, where the bank had extensive facilities. Ridley and his friends occupied a box where they enjoyed starched white tablecloths, cut glasses and silver service; the executives, meanwhile, were downstairs in the main dining room – with other guests – awaiting the summons from above. The one non-executive director with the knowledge and experience that should have kept trouble at bay was the chairman of the risk committee, Sir Derek Wanless. But, just as he had failed at NatWest, so he failed again at the Rock. The Northern Rock board, with its cadre of weak non-executives, was ideal for Applegarth. It allowed him to run riot, without checks and balances.

Here yet again, though, a fair measure of blame has to attach to the authorities. The fact is that they made it easy for Applegarth to work without proper supervision. Ironically, Gordon Brown had regarded the Tripartite system of regulation, involving the Treasury, the Bank of England and the Financial Services Authority, as a model for the world. But his personal removal of a generation of civil servants from the Treasury left it woefully short of experienced officials who would have been capable of managing the government's way through the crisis when it arrived, and in the event things went far from smoothly. As I wrote in my *Daily Mail* column on 19 February 2008:

The tragedy is that the run on the Rock was a British problem based around the failure of our own institutional arrangements. The Tripartite system put in place by Gordon Brown as Chancellor in 1997 let the taxpayer down badly. The FSA and the Treasury Select Committee made clear that this system failed to supervise the Rock properly. The team assigned to supervise was underweight and inexperienced and took no steps to ensure that the highly unusual securitised system of borrowing had been properly risk tested. The Bank of England stuck to the script of the Tripartite system so carefully that the Governor, Mervyn King, declined to step on the toes of the FSA. This meant that in the most serious banking crisis for three decades, it never became fully engaged.

I wasn't the only one to be critical. Surveying the British regulatory scene early in 2008, the *Wall Street Journal*, under the heading 'Darling's follies', highlighted the Chancellor's inept handling of Northern Rock. It criticised his misplaced reforms which aimed to grant new powers to the Financial Services Authority despite its poor performance in supervising Northern Rock. It also questioned the credibility of the nation's financial regulation. As I noted at the time, this must have discomforted many in the higher echelons of the Treasury, and there was also some pretty unpleasant reading in the first report into Northern Rock by the Treasury Select Committee. The 180-page report made it quite clear that not only had the way Northern Rock been set up and run its business proved disastrous, but also that the Tripartite arrangement was not up to the task of preventing the first mass run on a bank for over 100 years.

The committee placed the main blame for regulatory failures at the door of the FSA. Chairman, Labour MP John McFall, said: 'The FSA appears to have systematically failed in its duties, and this failure contributed significantly to the difficulties.' It was an excoriating report, which made for uncomfortable reading in Downing Street. Paradoxically, its findings were tame compared with the internal audit commissioned by the FSA itself, which uncovered a catalogue of errors that would have been almost comical had they not been so serious. The Rock had been inspected by insurance regulators rather than by banking experts. Meetings with management had been infrequent, and record-keeping was virtually non-existent. No one seemed to have noticed the bank's exponential growth in a period when its peers had begun to tighten up on their lending. It was not until February 2007, long after the first cracks in the sub-prime mortgage markets had emerged, that the FSA recategorised Northern Rock as a 'high-impact' firm to be assessed against its peers in the banking sector and deserving of special attention. And even then it was largely ignored.

In the months that followed the Northern Rock fiasco the FSA's chief executive, Hector Sants, squeezed out all those involved in supervising the bank. The last to go was the managing director of its retail business unit, Clive Briault, who left by mutual consent in April 2008. Briault had headed the team responsible for supervising Northern Rock. The sadness of his departure may have been softened by a pay-off of £380,000, an extraordinary sum for someone in the public sector who clearly had been less than successful in his job.

Yet although individuals were to take the rap, it was the FSA itself that had been poorly designed. It had never been able to establish itself as a respected regulator or to attract the best people – like the City takeover referee, the Panel on Takeovers and Mergers. It had been stretched and pulled in all directions by its masters at the Treasury. Over the decade of its existence more and more functions had been dumped on it, from supervising the back street trade of insurance brokers to financial education. It had become a direction-less bureaucracy, never able to develop the can-do attitude expected of a focused regulator. The prized regulatory culture that makes the Securities and Exchange Commission in the US so effective was lacking, and the FSA attracted City rejects rather than anyone from the top drawer. Instead of being the voice of the Square Mile – as Gordon Brown's then Economic Secretary Ed Balls told me he had envisaged – under Sir Callum McCarthy it was barely visible. His speeches rarely troubled the scorer. In brief, far from being the brilliant creation Brown had imagined, the FSA was ineffectual. Worse, when the credit crisis blew up the weakness of the legalistic Tripartite agreement was immediately exposed, and no one was capable of seizing leadership.

The Bank of England, too, fell short. Under Mervyn King the Bank became so wedded to its role of controlling inflation that ensuring financial stability assumed a secondary function, inadequately staffed and without real decision-making powers. The Court of the Bank of England, although filled with people with good reputations, was consulted too late in the process, was too large to be an effective monitor of Bank behaviour and too politically correct in its appointments. As it also turned out, the Bank's relations with the banking community and the City had been allowed to silt up. When the Governor needed most to use the informal power of his office, his performance was compared unfavourably with that of Jean-Claude Trichet of the ECB and Ben Bernanke of the Fed, both of whom were prepared to go the extra mile.

The fact was that in the broader credit crunch it was the central banks with the fewest constraints that were most decisive. The ECB had inherited a wide mandate, encompassing the rules from central banks right across Europe. This meant that it was able to take almost any collateral on to its balance sheet, improving the liquidity of endangered banks. In the USA as the difficulties emerged Ben Bernanke's team in Washington and Timothy Geithner in New York quickly discovered the inadequacies of the Fed's apparatus for providing liquidity to the markets and improvised to find ways of making sure there was adequate cash available.

The closeness of the central banks to the market, combined with the respect and fear that commercial bankers have for central banks, made them the ideal institutions for crisis resolution. Indeed, when in the spring of 2008 it looked as if one of Britain's big five clearing banks, HBOS, could be damaged by bear raids, the Bank of England assumed its historic role of dealing directly with the needs of the banks. It was the first time throughout the crisis that Mervyn King and the big five had sat down together, and the event demonstrated the power of the office of Governor when properly exercised.

Not suprisingly, given the events of autumn 2007, the Treasury Select Committee recommended restoring the powers of the Bank of England over banking supervision. It called for the appointment of a new Deputy Governor with specific responsibility for managing financial crises. The Chancellor of the Exchequer had promised to await the Treasury Select Committee's finding before introducing his own reforms. He waited but wasn't really paying attention. Just days later, the Chancellor proposed reforms that would actually strengthen the hand of the FSA. In future, the FSA would have tougher powers to examine banks' books, would be able continuously to check their liquidity and would be able to step in rapidly if there was trouble. Despite reservations in the City about the enhanced role for the FSA, Darling was determined to stick to his guns and grant it new powers to intervene in future banking crises.

This was a serious misjudgement and reflected the Treasury's obsession with keeping the Bank of England's independence of action as narrowly constrained as possible. It is scarcely surprising, therefore, that tensions between the Treasury and the Governor surfaced during the Northern Rock crisis. King, for example, had recognised from almost the moment that the Rock had sought lender of last resort assistance that Britain's system of deposit insurance was wholly inadequate. With the insurance limit set at £35,000 and only 90 per cent covered above the first £2,000, no one in their right mind would want to risk their savings. But there is a dispute between King and the Treasury as to when he recommended that the Bank of England's lender of last resort loans to the Rock be accompanied by an announcement that the government would guarantee all deposits. There are also signs of strained relations between King and Darling in November 2007. Darling was said to be 'more than a little irritated' when King gave an interview to the BBC's business editor Robert Peston, a man Darling regarded as *persona non grata* because of his role in disclosing the lender of last resort loan that had precipitated the run on the Rock. Even worse, during the interview King implied that the Chancellor had ignored his advice that deposits at the Rock should be guaranteed. At the time of the interview King was at his lowest ebb. The constant unanswered drumbeat of criticism from the banks, which had, in fact, brought their troubles on themselves, was regularly regurgitated in the media, and it affected his temper. His normally playful manner was subdued, and he was suffering from acute back pain caused by a tennis injury. There was no shouting when the two men spoke, because Darling does not raise his voice. However, in the midst of the crisis – a time when cooperation was essential – Britain's two most powerful economic leaders had become deeply suspicious of each other.

For his part, Darling has inevitably attracted his share of criticism. With his near white hair, dark eyebrows and quiet demeanour, the Chancellor looks every bit the Edinburgh advocate, and his years in Blair's government, when he occupied almost every major domestic role, from Social Security to Transport, have made him a man for all seasons. Before Blair left Number 10, Darling was seen as a Brownite trouble-shooter and a 'safe pair of hands'. Once Chancellor, though, he found that the Treasury was constantly being second-guessed by No. 10 and Treasury exiles dotted throughout Brown's administration. The extent of Brown's input became public when, after nationalisation, the two men appeared jointly to face the slings and arrows at the Prime Minister's monthly Downing Street press conference. Darling did not give the impression of being a man in charge of events.

When he presented his first Budget in March 2008, he certainly gave no public clues as to any unease about Britain's future prosperity in the wake of the credit crisis. Britain was a victim of international conditions, he said, not the risks taken with its own economic and financial management. Privately, Darling came to recognise that the economic forecasts that he had given in the Budget, in which he reduced the 2008 growth rate by just a quarter point to 2 per cent, were less than robust and that the economy was sliding fast. He and the Tripartite regime had also learned to respond more quickly to potential crises. When rumours swirled around the far larger HBOS in March 2008, sending its shares down 20 per cent in a few minutes, the authorities quickly rallied. Over the stormy Easter weekend that followed deputies from the Tripartite members secretly gathered in Whitehall to put in place contingency plans should an organisation far bigger and more critical to the economy than the Rock hit trouble. Never again did the government want to be caught short on preparations, as it had after 9 August 2007.

The fallout from the Rock will be with us for a long time to come. Some results have been positive. Darling and the Treasury, for example, recognised in the wake of the initial panic at the Rock that a deposit guarantee was essential and proposed to raise the insurance limit to as much as £100,000 in a pre-funded scheme. The banks may have resisted the idea, questioning its expense through the trade organisation the British Bankers' Association, but to my mind it is only right that the banks – which are so quick to seek assistance when their own foolishness and excesses place strains on their balance sheets – should be prepared to offer their customers immediate protection.

Other effects are less easy to pinpoint precisely as yet. There is no doubt that credit has become harder to come by in Britain, that the cost of mortgage finance has soared (despite several cuts in the bank rate), that the choice of mortgages on offer has dropped dramatically, and that the availability and cost of all credit has been affected. On the other hand, manufacturers and exporters have been helped by the declining value of the pound on the foreign exchange markets, and will continue to be provided that the slowdown does not prove to be global. That said, the rundown in Britain's manufacturing base in favour of an economy building on the nation's skills in financial services, make it peculiarly sensitive to global financial events such as the credit crunch.

So far as the City is concerned, there has been much talk in the Square Mile about damage to London's standing as a financial centre in the aftermath of the Rock crisis. After all, the reputation of Britain's markets and regulators has been vital in attracting new businesses to London and the light-touch regime of the FSA has been seen as an important competitive advantage after the collapses of Enron and WorldCom and accounting frauds in the United States in 2001 led to tighter regulation there. Northern Rock and the government's handling of the affair must cast doubt in some quarters over New Labour's competence. In March 2008 a symposium at the Cass Business School sought to answer the question: 'How badly has Northern Rock damaged the reputation of the City of London?' While the participants, including the LibDem MP Vince Cable and Labour MP John McFall, agreed there had been terrible shortcomings in the regulatory response, no one believed there had been lasting damage to reputations. Despite all the turmoil over the Rock and the row over non-domiciled tax privileges being curtailed, new financial business was still attracted to London. In the midst of the Rock affair GE Capital, the financial arm of the world's largest corporation, announced that it was moving its global headquarters to London.

Moreover, as the turmoil in banking deepened across the globe, it became increasingly evident that what had happened in Britain was not unique to this country. The speedy demise of Bear Stearns and the failure of US regulators to spot its weaknesses pointed to a systemic issue for financial markets rather than one confined to Britain. So the fears that the City's reputation had been damaged became less pronounced, with the blame instead being ascribed to government itself. That, of course, could eventually be repaired by regime change if the electors were eventually to decide that New Labour had outlived its purpose.

Alistair Darling was partly right when he blamed international conditions for the problems in Britain and the global credit markets, and there is no escaping the fact that even though Britain, with its free and easy credit regime and lax attitude towards debt and saving, was part of the problem, the crunch had come out of the United States. What was most morally reprehensible in the whole affair was that the American financial system encouraged a system whereby those people least able to pay were actively encouraged to take on mortgages at the highest interest rates. As Alan Greenspan has made abundantly clear, the demand for these mortgages was fed by Wall Street with its insatiable desire for high interest rate yields in an era of low interest rates. The inventiveness of the financiers was extraordinary. They created asset-backed, securitised products, often stuffed with low-value mortgages but labelled as first class. Had the financiers been food manufacturers or carmakers they would have been sued under the Trade Descriptions Act.

In fact a kind of reverse morality worked in the financial markets. It was revealed by the *Wall Street Journal* that in December 2006 Goldman Sachs chief financial officer David Viniar suggested to colleagues that it was time to adopt a bearish financial position towards sub-prime. He was ahead of his time. The company recognised the risks and took out a huge hedge, an insurance policy, against losses. At the same, Goldman Sachs adopted a policy of divesting as much as possible on unsuspecting competitors and others in the marketplace. Its behaviour was later hailed as an act of genius. It may have been for the investment banks, its investors and managers. But it was not a financially responsible act.

What the sub-prime crisis has revealed is the need to be wary of banks that think they have reinvented the wheel. Securitisation, in itself, is not an evil concept. Turning high-quality assets into traded securities is a useful way of creating extra liquidity and lending capacity. What the banks did in the sub-prime crisis is indefensible, however. They packaged up rotten assets with good assets, called them collaterised debt obligations, asked the credit rating agencies to stamp them of good quality and then sold them on. This was misrepresentation on a grand scale. Even worse, they created off-balance sheet funds, filled them with this doubtful debt, and then sold it on to unsuspecting clients, thus breaching their trust with clients and customers. When these off-balance sheet vehicles went wrong, as was the case with Whistlejacket at the British bank Standard Chartered and Carlyle Capital (the offshoot of the Carlyle private equity concern), the owners simply allowed them to sort out their own difficulties. This is like pretending relations you do not like are not part of your family.

The Group of Seven richest countries (the USA, Japan, Germany, Britain, France, Italy and Canada) and supervisors on both sides of the Atlantic are already moving to close down the regulatory gaps exploited by financial groups in the credit crunch. Off-balance sheet vehicles, the structured investment vehicles and conduits, where much of the sub-prime detritus ended up, are being brought back on to the main accounts. Reforms of the credit rating agencies are also being contemplated so that they are no longer fully dependent on the debt issuers for their income – a clear conflict of interest.

The credit crunch has certainly exposed the shortcomings of the rules governing bank capital. These rules, known as Basle II, were set by a committee of banking experts and regulators who hold their meetings at the Bank for International Settlements in Basle. In the most recent set of regulations the Basle committee sought to move responsibility for policing balance sheets from regulators to the banks themselves, who were trusted to monitor and measure their own risk. It rapidly became clear in the credit crisis that Basle II was malfunctioning badly. First, the strict focus on capital meant that Northern Rock and others were deemed to have adequate capital, but no one was paying any attention to liquidity (the amount of ready cash or near cash on their balance sheets). Second, Basle II had a distorting effect. It encouraged banks and financial groups to set up separate but related vehicles, because these could be heavily leveraged without having any impact on bank capital ratios. More transparency about ownership and responsibility for such off-balance sheet vehicles would certainly have helped.

But while such technical changes are clearly important, it is the mindset of the Masters of the Universe that needs to change. The investment bank chieftains live in a world divorced from the realities of life for ordinary people. It is a world of corporate jets, chauffer-driven cars, first-class hotels, Dom Pérignon, the Hamptons and – in the case of Bear Stearns – golf and bridge contests. The idea that any of the banking chiefs would have visited the faded downtown streets of Cleveland, the black suburbs of Chicago or the trailer parks of California where their associates were selling mortgages is fanciful. They were far too busy thinking of new ways to distribute to someone else the known risks they had taken on.

The extraordinary incentives for bankers and the ways in which they are paid through share awards and bonuses – often unrelated to performance – which can be ten times or more their basic salary distort values systems. They are an invitation for traders to cut corners, for investment bankers to promote deals that distort and destroy value and for the people down the line – the mortgage and credit originators and brokers – to over-sell. It is a system in which there is no reward for good practice but every incentive to inflate profits and to cover up mistakes. Moreover, in this protected environment the risk of transactions and deals going wrong is always mitigated. Rewards and bonuses are taken upfront, so if they go wrong in subsequent years, as was the case with sub-prime lending, the Masters of the Universe have already feathered their nests. Middle America paid when the bailiffs arrived on the doorsteps. The loss for the Masters is a retreat to the yacht for a few months' sailing leave before landing the next job on Wall Street. Those sacked at the top, like Stan O'Neal of Merrill Lynch, left with rewards beyond the dreams of avarice despite the disastrous mistakes made on their watch.

The awful truth is that the investment banks and financial houses have created their own form of the arms race. People are their business, and, like the top football teams, they are so afraid that they will be poached by competitors that they have established every kind of reward to keep them happy. Long-term incentives, attached to share performance over five- or ten-year periods, simply do not come into it. Yet as one senior investment banker told me, unless investment houses take a stand against the rewards they will eventually create ever more burdens for themselves and a form of mutually assured destruction. The higher they lift the rewards, the greater the risks and the more likely they are eventually to over-reach themselves in the manner of Bear Stearns.

In the heat of the crisis the arguments about 'moral hazard' so eloquently expressed by Mervyn King when the markets first froze over had to be put to one side. Preventing contagion and keeping the financial system functioning were seen as of overriding importance. Policy-makers took the view that the crisis of 2007–8 was more analogous to the financial events that forced Japan into a decade of recession and the Great Crash of 1929 than anything seen since the Second World War, and this required governments to go the extra mile. Failure to have done so could have endangered Western prosperity and employment for years to come.

But this did not stop questions being asked about whether bankers should be bailed out. In most financial collapses the consumer is the innocent bystander, although the old maxim *caveat emptor* (let the buyer beware) holds true. If a financial institution offers returns that are too good to be true – they probably are and should be given a wide berth.

As far as the architects of the credit crunch are concerned, bail-outs of foolhardy mortgage originators, banks and managers must be regarded with deep suspicion. The rescue of some of the most privileged people in our society looks – and is – plain wrong. Once the situation has stabilised it should be the duty of governments, regulators and law enforcement agencies to investigate what went wrong and bring those culpable to justice. We know that mortgages on both sides of the Atlantic were agreed without proper fact-checking. In the US much of the documentation was invalid, and some of it was forged. Similarly, in slicing and dicing debts and selling them on to clients as something they were not, the big financial groups were also culpable of wrongdoing.

The USA has a strong tradition of prosecuting financial misdeeds, and the Securities and Exchange Commission and the FBI are already engaged in broadly based inquiries. In Britain financial justice moves much more slowly, but at the very least, when public money is placed at stake, full investigations are justified and prosecutions should be pressed if wrongdoing is uncovered. No one wants to see those responsible for damaging all our lives – the greedy financiers and the exploitive hedge fund managers – escape without penalty.

The credit crunch will be with us until all the banks come clean and all the toxic debt they are holding is out in the open, written down and accounted for. Only then will faith in the financial system be restored. The longer the cover-up continues, the more prolonged the crisis will be. The revelation, for instance, that bankers at Credit Suisse systematically sought to cover up losses is a shocking indictment of management. More than that: it is a stain on the whole financial system, which will not be cleansed until every house decides that openness is the best policy.

One worrying lesson for bankers and regulators everywhere to bear in mind is post-bubble Japan. In the 1990s its leading bankers not only hung on to their jobs, they also refused to recognise and shed bad debts, in effect keeping 'zombie' loans (those worth nothing) on their books. The result was an asset prices decline unlike anything seen in modern times, with property values being halved and people's pension funds wiped out. The resulting economic stagnation lasted for almost a decade, despite the biggest public works programme ever implemented by any government. The quicker bankers are to come clean about their losses the better, and the temptation to hold on to doubtful assets in the hope that their value will eventually recover is foolishness. It is why bank shares have been so punished by investors, who have lost trust in what financial groups are saying. The slow drip, drip of bad news has only added to the distrust in the markets, while the new 'every bank for itself' attitude has clogged normal operations.

It would be bad enough if it were the financial sector alone that was affected, but crises that begin with the financial markets have a nasty habit of transmogrifying into broad-based economic pauses or recessions. The collapse of the housing market and the tightening of consumer and business credit are threatening to stop the global economy in its tracks. At present it is being kept afloat by the industrial and economic ambitions of China and India. Over the decades, however, the real driver of the growth has been American consumers, who still account for up to 20 per cent of global demand. When they stop buying the world economy will slam to a halt. It is possible that the emerging economies might pick up the slack in future, but they are not yet ready to do so. Per capita incomes in these countries are still pathetically small, and the leaders of China are too scared to unleash consumer power for fear it will create a great inflation and, more importantly, disturb the carefully created balance between laissez faire capitalism and state control. It is amazing to think that a problem that began with a few mis-sold trailer park mortgages could have spun so far out of control that the whole world economic order has been endangered.

The best scenario for the world is that lower interest rates and the huge credit injections by central banks, most notably the Federal Reserve, will be enough to restart a stuttering economy and that, after a brief recession, the world will come bouncing back in 2009–10. But the longer the credit crisis goes on and the further it spreads into new asset classes – including prime mortgages, commercial property, private equity debt, hedge funds and consumer credit – the harder it will be to contain. Almost every day brings a new shock to the financial system, and there are only so many shocks it can take before imploding. The present crisis feels much closer to the Japanese asset meltdown of the 1990s and the Great Depression than anything we have seen since the Second World War. Fortunately, the safeguards put in place since the depression of the 1930s, including welfare for the poor and arrangements to rescue failing banks, mean that history will not be repeating itself.

Nevertheless, clearing the detritus of the credit boom of recent years and cleaning up the banks will be a long-term process. The fear must be that the real economy of growth, jobs and rising living standards could be affected well into the next decade.

Galloping Towards Slump

On the Precipice?

When I finished writing the previous chapter of this book in May 2008 I concluded that cleaning up the financial mess caused by the credit crunch would be a long and painful operation. The process of deleveraging the financial system and removing the toxic debt and excessive credit from bank balance sheets, would, I reckoned, take several years, and the consequence for the global economy would be a nasty recession. After all, liquidity – freely available cash – is the lifeblood of the international economic system. If you cut off the blood supply, even for a relatively short period of time, it is fatal for global commerce. I could see banks tightening credit conditions – for individuals and companies – throughout the early part of 2008 and so a severe downturn seemed inevitable. Britain, after a modern record-breaking run of 63 successive quarters of expanding output, must be heading for a slump. The 'nice decade', as Bank of England governor Mervyn King described it, must be coming to a sudden and bad end.

However, there did appear to be some faint glimmerings of light. The case-by-case approach to the rescue of broken financial institutions on both sides of the Atlantic, together with robust co-operation by central banks, broadly seemed to have stabilised the situation. Despite the struggles of a small group of UK financial institutions to recapitalise themselves – by raising money from existing or overseas investors – the worst of the crisis that had swept Northern Rock into nationalisation, taken Bradford & Bingley to the brink and led the Royal Bank of Scotland to raise £12 billion through a rights issue

– looked to be over by July 2008. It was possible to share a commonly held belief that much of the toxic debt, estimated by the International Monetary Fund in March at $1 trillion, was accounted for.

The summer of 2008 saw repairs being made to the financial system on both sides of the Atlantic. The atmosphere felt less tense than a year earlier when the money markets had first frozen over. But cracks were nevertheless beginning to show. Richard Holbrooke, senior director of the global insurer the American International Group (AIG) and writer of many of the insurance contracts covering sub-prime lending, securitised loan packages and credit default swaps, resigned suddenly after the group reported two successive quarters of loss. At broker Merrill Lynch the toxic debt losses continued to mount, with the group revealing a further $9.4 billion of write-downs and admitting to investors that it still had a further $50 billion of contaminated collateralised debt obligations (securitised debts), sub-prime mortgages and real estate loans on its books. Several US banks, including North Carolina-based Wachovia and Washington Mutual, located in the Pacific North West, reported tens of billions of losses. A warning that the credit crunch could actually lead to a large American bank collapsing was issued by Kenneth Rogoff, former chief economist at the IMF, on 19 August. He added for good measure that Fannie Mae and Freddie Mac – the mortgage intermediaries – would cease to exist in their present form. It turned out to be a prophetic judgement. A few days later, on 28 August, new management was installed at Fannie and Freddie – clearly the prelude to something much bigger.

The European situation was also proving far from rosy. In Germany Deutsche Bank revealed that it had made write-downs of $7.8 billion. In Britain Northern Rock, with its new management team under the chairmanship of Ron Sandler, became the first UK bank to seek recapitalisation from the British government. Alistair Darling duly agreed to swap £3 billion of loans from the Bank of England and £400 million of preference shares for £3.4 billion of shares in the Newcastle-based lender, the government offering to swap less risky loans, secured against mortgages, for new capital in the hope that when and if the Rock were returned to the private sector it would receive a share of the proceeds. Then the Royal Bank of Scotland revealed that it had made a loss of £691 million in the first half of the 2008 financial year and that its profits had been wiped out by write-offs of £5.9 billion of bad debts, mostly in the United States. The bank disclosed it was close to recruiting three new directors. One of them was Stephen Hester, chief executive of British Land. He would later be parachuted in to replace Sir Fred Goodwin, the banker who a year earlier had become involved in a bidding war for Dutch bank ABN Amro just as the credit crunch was intensifying.

In early September 2008 the American bankers returned from their yachts and the Hamptons to their desks in Manhattan. And legislators on Capitol Hill sought to come to grips with the ever-growing problems of Fannie Mae and Freddie Mac. Shares in the two mortgage lenders had been falling like a stone and there was a fear in Washington that if they were allowed to collapse they could bring much of the American banking and financial system down with them. It was also feared that their collapse would jeopardise the US housing market yet further, since the two institutions between them held an astounding 50 per cent of the $12 trillion of mortgages on American homes on their books.

Frantic negotiations took place at the US Treasury. Hank Paulson, the combative former chairman of Goldman Sachs and President Bush's able Treasury Secretary, recognised there was little choice but to take the two institutions into public ownership. Fearing the political back-lash that would come from outright nationalisation – seen as a nasty socialist practice in the USA – Paulson opted for the more polite option of 'conservatorship', although it meant much the same. His announce-ment – as with so many throughout the tumultuous months of September and October – came just before the opening of the Asian markets on Monday morning. It was a classic piece of hasty but firm decision-making that sought to avoid the prospect of panic selling and the worldwide crash that that might entail if things were left in the air.

Paulson ordered the injection of $100 billion of taxpayer cash into the troubled mortgage lenders so that they would be able to meet their obligations. To help provide liquidity the government offered to buy back the mortgage bonds backed by the companies, starting with an initial $5 billion. Over the next two years the lenders, it was planned, would be able to increase their lending – part of an effort to restart the housing market – but a cap of $850 billion was placed on their balance sheets which would have to shrink by 10 per cent a year until reduced to $250 billion. The Treasury bailouts of Fannie Mae and Freddie Mac were recognition of the confused status of these behemoths. They dated back to the Great Depression years and the efforts of Franklin D. Roosevelt to refloat the housing market in the 1930s. Over the decades, however, they had been allowed to transmogrify into something different. They had ceased to be government agencies, and were floated on the stock exchange. During the 1990s they expanded hugely, particularly during the administration of Bill Clinton when they were effectively ordered to refinance mortgages for modest- to lower- and middle-income Americans seeking access to the housing market. Ultimately, because both had the word 'Federal' in their names, the authorities felt that they had, as a matter of honour, to prop them up, even though they had been operating at arm's length from the Treasury and with minimum supervision from a poorly resourced Congressional agency.

The collapse and rescue of Fannie and Freddie was the opening scene in a drama that would challenge perceptions about the safety of banks and financial groups across the world, leading to unprecedented turbulence on financial markets. The true extent of the toxic debt in the system – in other words, the sliced and diced securitised loans – became an ever-increasing focus of concern, and the perceived value of the loans dropped accordingly, despite the high ratings conferred by the credit rating agencies. Their downward spiral was accelerated by accounting rules in the US, which demanded that the loans be 'marked to market' – that is, given a current market valuation. Since no one in the market wanted to hold them, their value declined continuously. It was not until October 2008 that accounting rules were relaxed somewhat, allowing banks or financial institutions that intended to hold the securities until maturity not to have to mark to market. This meant that they could continue to hold the loans on their balance sheet, without taking regular losses on their value and charging them against profits. This move, accepted by accounting groups on both sides of the Atlantic, was intended to provide a measure of balance sheet stability. I have to confess I was less convinced. In my columns in the *Mail* I argued that what was needed was more transparency rather than less: I could not help feeling that the true reckoning was simply being postponed.

The fix at Fannie and Freddie and the relaxed accounting standards came too late to save Lehman Brothers. Founded in Montgomery, Alabama in 1844 by three immigrant German-Jewish brothers, Lehman Brothers had been in the firing line ever since March 2008 when Bear Stearns had collapsed and then been rescued by JP Morgan Chase. Now its share price went into freefall. On 11 September Lehman's reported its worst loss ever of $3.9 billion, following $7.8 billion of credit write-downs. Its high-profile chief executive Richard Fuld sought to restructure the bank by spinning off $30 billion of property. His plan failed to restore confidence, however, and the slump in Lehman shares continued, spreading gloom across the whole of the broker-dealer sector and dragging down Merrill Lynch and even the august names of Morgan Stanley and Goldman Sachs. Over the weekend of 13–14 September dramatic efforts were made to save Lehman from disaster. Initially Bank of America was seen as the leading contender to take over Lehman, joined by the private equity firm J.C. Flowers and the China Investment Company. But as the books were scrutinised the buyers fell away, leaving Britain's Barclays Bank as the only potential buyer.

Lehman's was not the only one in trouble. Merrill Lynch, Wall Street's 'raging bull', with retail branches on main streets across the United States, was in difficulty after a 70 per cent fall in its share price. It fell gratefully into the hands of Bank of America, which duly removed itself from the Lehman rescue. Meanwhile the huge insurer AIG opened discussions with the Fed as it sought to raise up to $20 billion of capital by selling shares to private equity firms.

Lehman's future, however, hung in the balance until, at the end of a frantic weekend of talks held at the Federal Reserve Bank of New York, where until recently Fuld himself had a been a director, the US Treasury and the Federal Reserve finally decided they could not use public funds to rescue the bank. Their rationale was two-fold: they felt that because the markets had had six months (since Bear Stearns) to prepare for the worst, allowing Lehman's to fail was a reasonable option; and they felt that because the Federal Reserve had an emergency liquidity facility, Lehman's could be allowed to fail in an orderly way.

On the night of Lehman's failure I was in Wimbledon in South London doing a question and answer session on Northern Rock and the credit crunch. When I returned home later that evening there was a frantic message from my news desk alerting me to the collapse. I recognised it as a defining event: here was the first major Wall Street house since the crunch that had been allowed to collapse. But like most commentators and the policy-makers themselves I had no inkling just what an impact it was to have on the whole system of Anglo-Saxon capitalism.

In fact, as it quickly transpired, the Lehman collapse dealt a fatal blow to confidence among banks and financial institutions. Now the trickle of lending among banks froze altogether, and central banks around the world had to step into the breach, pumping in money. With disarray in the markets the Federal Reserve felt it had little alternative but to take the giant insurer AIG – which had insured many of the toxic loans held by banks – into near-public ownership. In exchange for pumping in $85 billion of emergency funds it grabbed a 79.9 per cent stake for the US taxpayer and kicked out the existing management.

In Britain the fallout came almost immediately. On 17 September, while the Chancellor Alistair Darling was delivering a breakfast speech at Bloomberg to the British–Israel Chambers of Commerce, Halifax Bank of Scotland shares fell heavily for the second day in a row. In the *Mail* that morning we reported that Lloyds TSB, Britain's most conservatively run bank, stood ready to step in and rescue HBOS should its survival as an independent bank be threatened. The BBC's Robert Peston went so far as to say that talks were at an 'advanced' stage. These were clearly desperate times that demanded desperate solutions. The government had agreed to waive competition rules that would normally have prevented a merger that ceded 30 per cent of the mortgage market and an even larger share of Britain's retail savings to one institution. The deal had the blessing of the Prime Minister who had been seen, a few days earlier, in deep conversation with Lloyds chairman Sir Victor Blank – a courtly and respected figure in the City, and a supporter of the Labour government. It was a case of the hare, in the shape of HBOS with its Asda-style marketing campaigns, devised under the stewardship of its young chief executive Andy Hornby, being overtaken by the Lloyds tortoise – the British bank which was most risk-averse.

When I met with the Chancellor for a sandwich lunch at the Treasury that day he was calm. He was also still sticking with a case-by-case approach to the financial crisis – the HBOS–Lloyds TSB tie-up being, of course, a particularly high-profile example. That said the Chancellor recognised that the decision over Lehman's had changed the landscape and that more action would be required. In particular he was fearful of the problems that were building up for the real economy of jobs and output. He felt that his observation in August to a *Guardian* interviewer that we were facing 'arguably the worst' crisis for 60 years was proving prescient.

The HBOS crisis was just one of the symptoms of the worsening situation as the process of winding down Lehman's trillions of dollars of open transactions began. In response, on 18 September, central banks around the world launched their biggest ever joint operation to prop up confidence, injecting more than $180 billion into the financial markets in an effort to ease the growing pain. On both sides of the Atlantic the practice of short-selling financial shares, in the hope that the price would fall further, was temporarily banned. It was also becoming apparent to the US Treasury that the current 'case-by-case' approach to the crisis was not sufficient to stop it in its tracks. Now only a comprehensive scheme, in which all banks could participate, looked to be the answer. Accordingly, amid huge euphoria on stock markets around the world, Hank Paulson announced that he would be going to Congress to seek authorisation for a $700 billion plan to take toxic debt off the books of the banks at a negotiated price and to hold it in a government agency.

The possibility of a bail-out fund did not take the pressure off the two remaining broker-dealers, Morgan Stanley and Goldman Sachs. To ease their plight the Federal Reserve therefore decided to change their status from investment banks to bank holding companies. This would give the Fed the right to intervene if necessary; it also meant that the two institutions could develop a retail deposit base, making them less dependent on volatile money markets and subject to stricter capital requirements that would inspire more confidence among investors and market participants. On 24 September Goldman Sachs sought to underpin confidence with the announcement that the legendary investor Warren Buffett, the Sage of Omaha, would inject $5 billion into Goldmans in the shape of preference shares, convertible into ordinary shares, with a coupon of 10 per cent. This was to prove highly significant because it was to become the benchmark for the subsequent recapitalisation of the British banks.

Meanwhile Paulson's bail-out plan for Wall Street was proving controversial. At hearings on Capitol Hill the proposals for the 'troubled asset relief plan' (TARP) unleashed a torrent of criticism from Congressmen fired up by the anger on 'Main Street USA' about the greed and appalling behaviour of the Wall Street executives now demanding government help. But as Congress deliberated the crisis deepened. The weekend saw frantic negotiations and activity on both sides of the Atlantic. On 26 September regulators seized the assets of Washington Mutual which, with $8 billion of debts, now earned the dubious distinction of becoming the biggest banking failure in American history. The pain was eased somewhat when J.P. Morgan acquired the bank's deposits, assets and mortgage portfolio from the federal government. In Britain it was the end of the road for Bradford & Bingley which, despite a £300 million capital-raising exercise led by existing shareholders and the high street banks, was unable to finance operations in the inter-bank market. The government nationalised the mortgage book and sold off B&B's deposit book of £21 billion and branch network for £600 million to Spain's Santander, owner of high street lender Abbey and Alliance & Leicester.

Despite all these very visible signs of the worsening conditions in the money markets, and despite the pleas of President George W. Bush, populist resentment of the banks in the United States led Congress to vote down Hank Paulson's $700 billion TARP scheme. The rejection provoked a crash on the stock market, with Standard & Poor's 500 Index dropping 8.8 per cent, its biggest fall since the crash of 1987. The Dow Jones tumbled 778 points, the worst ever points decline in its history. Meanwhile, the carnage among American banks deepened, with North Carolina-based Wachovia – with 4,300 branches – sold off to Citigroup for $2.2 billion. As part of the deal the Federal Deposit Insurance Corporation acquired a $12 billion stake in Citi in the shape of warrants and preference shares. The shape of future recapitalisation rescues was starting to emerge. Citi would eventually be edged aside in the battle for Wachovia by San Francisco-based Wells Fargo which would make a better $15.1 billion offer, unencumbered by government interference.

On a single day, 29 September, the Lehman aftershocks could be felt everywhere. The European Central Bank, together with central banks from Holland, Belgium and Luxembourg, agreed to nationalise the trans-national bank and insurer Fortis, pumping in 11.2 billion euros. Hypo Real Estate bank was bailed-out by the German government and other banks after a 50 billion euro crisis. And the government of Iceland, which would soon declare itself all but insolvent, nationalised Glitnir, the nation's third-largest bank. Back in the US it was the turn of Morgan Stanley to receive a $9 billion injection from the Japanese bank Mitsubishi in exchange for a 21 per cent share stake.

A day later, on 30 September, Ireland sought to underpin its financial system by guaranteeing the deposits of its whole banking system. The move led to accusations of beggar-thy-neighbour policies – similar to those which took place in the Great Depression – when unilateral actions by one state led to problems for other governments. Germany behaved similarly a few days later, on 5 October, when its government said that it would guarantee all privately held German bank accounts. These were worth some 568 billion euros.

In the US, after days of wrangling, the House of Representatives finally passed the $700 billion TARP bail-out deal on 3 October. It had been frightened to death by the falls on Wall Street and the succession of stock market and retail runs on the banking system, and felt it now had no alternative. There remained questions as to how effective the scheme would be and how long it would take to be up and running. In fact, it would substantially change the following month.

Even the TARP bail-out, however, provided little respite. Share prices around the world continued to tumble, with the Dow Jones plunging below the 10,000 mark on 7 October, the first time since 2004. During the same month the IMF was to up its forecast of contaminated debt to $3 trillion – triple its previous estimate. Clearly the piecemeal, scatter-gun approach to the funding crisis for banks was not working, even though massive funds were being injected into the money markets by central banks. A more coordinated approach was called for.

In a little-noted speech back in January 2008 the Governor of the Bank of England had floated the idea of recapitalising the banks. Now, behind closed doors, the Bank of England was developing what Mervyn King described to me as an 'economist's' approach to bailing out the banking system. Essentially, it involved recapitalising all the banks on the same day. The argument was that by stabilising all the banks at a stroke, even if this meant part-nationalisation, trust in the system would be restored. Of course, the King scheme, which was in time adopted by the Treasury and Number 10, would need to be international in its approach if it were to work properly.

Alistair Darling and his point man at the Treasury, Tom Scholar, began working on the recapitalisation plan initiated by King and the Bank in mid-September. The scheme was based on the bail-out of the Swedish banks in 1992, and on similar measures used by the Japanese government to repair its banking system in the 1990s. Details of the plan were thrashed out on 1 October in the offices of Peter Sands, chief executive of Standard Chartered. (Standard Chartered was one of the few UK banks not exposed to the credit crunch because the larger part of its operation was based in emerging markets rather than the advanced economies.) At the meeting Sands was joined by Lady Shriti Vadera, a trusted Brown aide and minister in the Department of Business; investment banker Robin Budenberg from UBS; and Michael Klein, the former vice-chairman of Citigroup. The bold scheme the group discussed involved injecting up to £50 billion of new capital into Britain's high street banks, as well as refloating the money markets through an extensive system of guarantees. Prime Minister Gordon Brown was reportedly reluctant at first but, on the advice of Vadera, eventually signed up.

On 8 October the broad outlines of the radical banking bail-out plan were unveiled. Only eight months earlier the nationalisation of Northern Rock had proved an excruciating decision for a Labour government anxious to avoid the taint of nationalisation. Now it was proposing to take several of the high street banks under state control.

The plan was essentially three-pronged.

Firstly, all the high street banks would be examined by the Financial Services Authority to see how much new capital would be necessary to make them absolutely safe. Some £50 billion of government resources would be made ready for this purpose and the funding would be by way of a combination of interest-bearing preference shares and direct share stakes.

Secondly, the government would guarantee up to £250 billion of loans made through the inter-bank market. The charge on these loans would be based on the so-called 'credit default swaps' rate – the cost above the inter-bank rate of insuring deposits.

Thirdly, the government would bolster its special liquidity scheme by £100 billion to £200 billion. Under this plan banks and building societies would be able to exchange mortgage securities for Bank of England bonds.

To make the scheme even more watertight, so that all maturities of debt would be covered, the Bank of England also proposed simplifying the process by which it made overnight funds available to banks. It would follow the American Fed model of opening a 'discount window' from which the banks could borrow without the threat of stigmatisation which arose from the previous auction arrangements.

Now the plan needed to be implemented. The following day, 9 October, Alistair Darling set out for Washington to attend meetings of the Group of Seven richest countries and the International Monetary Fund. The visit clearly provided an ideal opportunity for Darling to sell what was now known as the 'Brown plan' to the other rich nations. Before leaving for the airport he checked the Blackberry on the desk of his Principal Private Secretary, Dan Rosenfield. The market screens were showing disturbing streaks of red. There would be much work to do both at the IMF meeting and afterwards.

When Darling arrived at the British Embassy in Washington he was shown the first draft of a Group of Seven communiqué on the crisis. He was shocked. It was three pages long and, it seemed to him, went nowhere near recognising the scale of the crisis facing the Western banking system since Lehman had been allowed to fail. Hank Paulson, who looked terrible after weeks of frantic negotiations, informed Darling that he, like the Brits, intended to recapitalise the American banks the following Monday. The Europeans planned to do the same, after diplomatic pressure from Gordon Brown. President Sarkozy of France, however, was reluctant to allow

Brown to claim the political glory for the scheme. Eventually a brief communiqué was agreed in which all the countries involved pledged cooperation. So far as the markets were concerned, it didn't go far enough. There was no direct promise to recapitalise banks – even though most governments were looking at it – nor were there plans to bolster inter-bank lending through the guarantees mentioned. But behind the scenes the ideas were gaining traction. It would be another race against time, with an agreement essential by the time the financial markets reopened on the morning of 13 October.

Throughout that weekend the midnight oil was burning at the Treasury on Horseguards Parade, at the Financial Services Authority at Canary Wharf, at the Bank of England and at banking parlours across the City. All the banks had been stress-tested by the FSA for the worst possible circumstances. The two most international banks, HSBC and Standard Chartered, were felt not to need any immediate recapitalisation. Barclays, reluctant to feel the heavy hand of government on its shoulder, refused public money and turned to investors in the Gulf instead. Royal Bank of Scotland, Halifax Bank of Scotland and Lloyds TSB – its merger partner – would take the government money despite the strict conditions imposed. Some heads would roll. In the case of RBS the ruling knights Sir Tom McKillop and Sir Fred Goodwin agreed to depart without compensation. Goodwin was to be replaced by Stephen Hester, chief executive of British Land and a former investment banker. At HBOS, chairman Lord Stevenson and chief executive Andy Hornby were to be forced out. The Lloyds TSB management team of Sir Victor Blank and the quiet American Eric Daniels would be in charge. There was a wobble on Monday morning when investment bankers Matthew Greenburgh of Merrill Lynch (the banker who had a year earlier sought to broker a deal between Northern Rock and Lloyds TSB) and Simon Robey for HBOS disagreed on critical aspects of the plan, but this was eventually patched up in the corridors of the Treasury after the Prime Minister and Chancellor had been roused from their sleep to intervene.

Under the plan the government would pump in £37 billion of

new capital in the shape of preference and ordinary shares of the rescued banks. As a result it would become the majority shareholder in the Royal Bank of Scotland and would have a 40 per cent stake in the new 'big bank' made up of Lloyds TSB and HBOS. In exchange for government funds the banks would be required to promise that there would be no payment of ordinary dividend until the preference shares, priced at 12 per cent (two points above the charge made by Buffett to Goldman Sachs), had been repaid. There would be an end to fat bonuses to top executives. The recapitalised banks would have to promise to maintain mortgage lending at 2007 levels at least and ensure that the taps were not turned off to small- and medium-sized enterprises. In an interview with me later that week, in his Gresham Street offices, the dapper Daniels – dressed in his trademark white-collared, monogrammed shirt with distinctive gold cufflinks – insisted that he had an agreement with the Treasury that would eventually enable him to pay a dividend to shareholders. He also said he could pay bonuses, although in year one they would be paid in shares rather than cash.

The reshaping of British banking over the weekend of 11–12 October 2008 was one of the most momentous in the history of UK finance. The aftershocks, as banks, government and shareholders jockeyed for position, will be felt for years as the new system settles down. A new body, UK Financial Investments Ltd, chaired by Sir Philip Hampton, chairman of Sainsbury and former finance director of Lloyds TSB, was set up on 4 November with the Treasury's John Kingman as chief executive, to supervise – at arm's length – the government's relationship with its new banking clients. But it was certainly not going to be easy. As interest rates fell in the latter months of 2008 in response to an enveloping recession and growing concerns about deflation – falling shop and asset prices – the newly nationalised banks found themselves trying to improve their financial position while simultaneously under intense political pressure to pass on interest rate cuts to personal, mortgage and business borrowers.

Later on 13 October President Sarkozy of France announced his own recapitalisation scheme. Some 360 billion euros of liquidity would be provided to French banks. A new guarantee scheme of 320 billion euros would be set up. And there would be a 40 billion euro fund for those French banks in need of new capital. Similar plans were announced in Holland and Italy. And an initially reluctant Germany approved a 100 billion euro stabilisation fund, offered guarantees of 400 billion euros to money market transactions and also imposed limits on executive pay.

The biggest U-turn came in the United States where Hank Paulson put to one side the TARP plan to buy toxic debt and instead adopted the British approach. The US agreed to pump $125 billion of capital into its nine major banks, Bank of America, J.P. Morgan Chase, Citigroup, Merrill Lynch, Goldman Sachs, Morgan Stanley, Bank of New York Mellon and State Street. A further $125 billion would be used to prop up the capital of smaller banks across the United States. Under the plan there would be limits on fat cat pay for bankers – the culture of greed that had helped fuel the credit crunch was now being tackled on a global basis. None of this was enough to prevent another run on the shares of Citigroup in November 2008. Two years earlier it had been valued by the stock market at $267 billion; now it was worth a fraction of that. The bank's chief executive, Vikram Pandit, less than a year into the top job, was forced to shed 52,000 jobs worldwide and seek yet another injection of capital to shore up collapsing confidence.

All this financial turmoil had a major impact on the race for the White House. In the end US presidential campaigns are almost always settled by pocket book issues and the Republicans, rightly or wrongly, took the blame for the mess unleashed by the bankers and financiers of Wall Street. The dog days of October proved particularly disastrous for the Grand Old Party, with President Bush isolated in the White House and the Republican candidate John McCain, although considered a maverick, unable to separate himself from the Bush legacy. Former President Bill Clinton's message 'the economy, stupid' lifted Barack Obama, the Democratic candidate into the White House and cemented the Democrats' control of Congress.

The American recapitalisation of the banking system came at a relatively low cost to the financiers. The charge on the preference shares would be 5 per cent against 12 per cent in Britain. I was told by Treasury officials that the British preference shares had deliberately been priced higher so as to encourage the banks to work harder to pay off the government loans and so take them off the official books as soon as possible. The highest price of all was paid by Barclays Bank chief executive John Varley. Steadfastly determined to keep the government off his back and preserve the freedom to pay his employees as he felt fit, he raised £7.3 billion of capital from investors in Qatar and Abu Dhabi, paying 14 per cent for the privilege. The deal was arranged through a glamorous intermediary, Amanda Staveley, a former escort of Prince Andrew, whose company collected a £40 million commission.

In a phone call to me Barclays chairman Marcus Agius defended the cost of the package. He argued that because the interest charge was tax deductible the cost was virtually the same as UK government debt where there was no such tax break. Nevertheless, shareholder reaction was negative and Barclays' shares fell heavily. Under pressure from long-term British investors and the Association of British Insurers, Barclays eventually relented on bonuses. It promised that its four top-paid executives, including Bob Diamond the President of BarCap, who received a £20 million bonus in 2007, would take no such payments in 2008. The whole board would put itself up for re-election at the 2009 annual general meeting.

Barclays may have gone it alone, but all over the world, from Switzerland to Australia, the Brown government-led approach was being adopted. In essence governments had accepted the need to semi-nationalise their banking systems if they were to find a route out of the credit crunch. There was an impressive consensus that the risk of a cascading series of large bank collapses across the world was simply too appalling to contemplate.

No sooner had the bank recapitalisation push been implemented than another potentially highly destabilising problem loomed. The conventional wisdom, since the credit crunch came to the fore in August 2007, was that despite all the problems that were cropping up, the world was a much safer place than it had been during previous worldwide financial turbulence because it could rely on the vigour and the strength of emerging market economies. Even if the West were to move towards a slump, it was argued, the strength of Asia and other emerging markets vis-à-vis the advanced countries would prevent global output from plunging. In fact, this judgement turned out to be wrong. Russia experienced a stock market crash. The government of South Korea, one of the Asian tigers, had to launch a $130 billion rescue package for its banking system. Pakistan sought $10–$15 billion from the IMF. On 26 October the IMF approved a loan of $16.5 billion to Ukraine and on 28 October Hungary received a $25.1 billion IMF loan. Elsewhere in late October a series of bilateral deals were done between the US Federal Reserve and central banks in New Zealand, Brazil, Mexico and Korea in an attempt to improve the liquidity of the financial system. Growth in the mighty Chinese economy was slowing and in early November the Beijing government unveiled a massive $586 billion plan to support output.

The crisis that had begun in Cleveland's slums really had reached every corner of the globe. The credit crunch may have struck in Europe first, with Northern Rock an early casualty, but it had become a global phenomenon. Virtually no economy in the world, even the oil-rich Gulf nations which also found themselves having to support their banking systems, was immune. Worrying parallels with the Great Depression were growing. As then, commodity prices, which had been booming until early 2008, fell heavily, with the oil price more than halving. As then, there were moments when countries looked as though they were going to strike out on their own, until the Brown plan was reluctantly accepted. The concern that, as economies move towards recession, nations, including the US, will lurch towards protectionism remains a real danger.

In years of depression, as in the great Japanese crisis of the 1990s, falling goods and asset prices – deflation – become a huge problem, applying downward pressure on corporate profits, wage levels, consumption and jobs. And sure enough, at the end of 2008 deflation duly reared its head. The International Monetary Fund noted in November 2008: 'Prospects for global growth have deteriorated as financial sector deleveraging has continued and producer and consumer confidence has fallen.' Most of the world's economies, it argued, would experience recession in 2009, with Britain the hardest hit. Mervyn King warned that there might be no recovery in the UK until 2010 at the earliest. In the US the crisis was already moving from housing to other sectors of the economy. In November, for example, the chiefs of the three big US carmakers General Motors, Ford and Chrysler, all made their way to Washington, cap in hand, as the market for new cars slumped.

Paradoxically, despite Britain's huge exposure to the credit crunch, the appalling state of its public finances and the extraordinary part-nationalisation of the British banks, the reputation of the government led by Gordon Brown and Alistair Darling took a turn for the better. They had been guilty of terrible dithering when the credit crunch arrived and over the rescue of Northern Rock. But lessons had been learned. Big bold decisions were being taken to stabilise the British and the global banking and economic system. This time round the UK had been able to lead the charge, even advocating, in spite of soaring public borrowing, a big fiscal expansion in the shape of public spending and tax cuts. The question is whether all this had come too late to stave off mass unemployment and economic slump.

'Recession,' former US president Ronald Reagan, once remarked, 'is when your neighbour loses his job. Depression is when you lose yours.' Suddenly those words look horribly relevant to people in the UK and across the Western world.

Glossary

BaFin (Bundesanstalt für Finanzdienstleistungsaufsicht) Germany's central supervisory authority for financial services.

Bank holding companies Banks supervised by the Federal Reserve. Such banks are able to take in retail deposits and must adhere to strict capital ratios.

Bank of England Britain's central bank, founded in 1694, in Threadneedle Street, London, often known as the Old Lady of Threadneedle Street after a 19th-century James Gillray cartoon. The Monetary Policy Committee (MPC) was given independent responsibility for setting interest rates in 1997. The aim of the MPC is to hold inflation at the 2 per cent target set by the Chancellor. The Bank has historic powers to act as a lender of last resort to banks in distress.

Basle II An international agreement, which came into force in 2007, setting the minimum legal requirements, including capital, that should apply to both banks and investment firms.

Beggar-thy-neighbour Unilateral action by nations which harms the interest of trading parties and neighbours. The erection of 'self-ish' trade barriers during the Great Depression of the 1930s severely damaged global commerce.

Black Monday On 19 October 1987 the Dow Jones Average fell by 22.6 per cent in value (508.32 points), causing stock markets around the world to tumble.

Black Wednesday In Britain on 16 September 1992 interest rates were raised to 15 per cent in an attempt to defend the pound sterling against speculative selling. The pound was withdrawn from the ERM and allowed to 'float' against other currencies.

Black Thursday *See* Wall Street crash.

BNP Paribas The largest French bank and the largest bank in the eurozone; it has offices in both New York and London.

Broker-dealers Investment houses supervised by the Securities and Exchange Commission like Morgan Stanley and Goldman Sachs. Sometimes described as investment banks.

Bundesbank The German central bank, based in Frankfurt.

Chapter 11 A form of bankruptcy in the USA, which protects individuals and firms from their creditors, giving time for the reorganisation of the debtor's business. It is usually filed by corporations that require time to restructure their debts.

Cobra The codename for the Cabinet team, led by the Prime Minister, which is convened to deal with civil crises.

Collateralised Debt Obligation (CDO) A debt package containing junk bonds, loans or mortgages.

Commodities Futures Trading Commission (CFTC) The US regulator, created in 1974, to oversee exchange trading in futures.

Conservatorship Private corporatious brought under the purview of the US government. A halfway house which allows private sector management freedoms, under the supervision of the federal government.

Court of the Bank of England The Bank of England's board of directors, consisting of the governor and his two deputies and 16 non-executives largely drawn from the great and good of the City and business. It meets once a month to evaluate the Bank's performance.

Credit crunch Widespread restricted borrowing for banks, businesses and individuals arising out of a lack of money in the markets as banks stop lending to each other.

Credit default swap (CDS) An insurance contract used to protect investors against non-paying bonds.

Credit derivatives Sophisticated contracts taken out by financial firms to insure against market losses.

Credit reference agencies Private organisations that rate debt. They hold enormous data banks on individuals, including electoral roll status, county court judgements, and information supplied by lenders.

Demutualisation The process by which UK building societies, owned by their members, are converted into banks, owned by shareholders.

'The Desk' The Federal Reserve's Open Market Trading Desk.

Discount window This is an overnight lending facility under which banks can borrow overnight from the central bank. A longstanding feature of US banking, a similar scheme was introduced by the Bank of England in October 2006.

Dotcom bubble In the early 1990s the boom in internet-related and high-technology companies led to the Nasdaq climbing from 600 to 5,000 points. In early 2000, as optimism ebbed away, it crashed from 5,000 to 2,000, dropping to 800 in 2002. Investors lost billions of dollars.

Dow Jones Industrial Average The leading key share indicator of the New York Stock Exchange.

Due diligence The formal process by which an investor or purchaser investigates a company or business.

European Central Bank (ECB) Based in the Eurotower, Frankfurt, the ECB was established in 1998. It is the European equivalent of the Federal Reserve, and all central banks of EU member states are members. It controls the monetary policy, including setting interest rates, of the member states that use the euro. The first president was Willem Duisenberg. Jean-Claude Trichet took over in 2003.

eurozone or **euroland** Those countries of the European Union that have adopted the euro as their currency. It was established in January 2002 with 12 members.

Exchange Rate Mechanism (ERM) A system established in 1979 to control exchange rates within the European Monetary System (EMS) of the EU.

Fannie Mae The Federal National Mortgage Association, a US government-backed lending agency.

Federal Deposit Insurance Corporation (FDIC) The US agency that acts as a guarantor of funds deposited in member banks.

Federal Reserve (the Fed) The US central bank.

Financial Services Authority (FSA) The UK regulator established in May 1997. New Labour merged banking supervision and investment services regulation into the Securities and Investments Board (SIB). In October 1997 the SIB changed its name to the Financial Services Authority.

Financial Services Compensation Scheme (FSCS) The UK scheme by which depositors receive limited compensation in the event of the failure of an authorised firm.

Freddie Mac The Federal Home Mortgage Corporation, a US government-backed lending agency.

FTSE-100 The London Stock Exchange's index of the leading 100 companies.

Gross national product (GNP) A measure of a country's total economic activity in terms of goods and services.

Group of Seven The seven richest industrialised countries: the USA, Japan, Germany, Britain, France, Italy and Canada.

International Monetary Fund (IMF) An agency of the United Nations, established in December 1945. An economic forecasting authority, monitor of national economies and lender to countries in distress.

Junk bond A high-risk, low-credit-rated, non-investment grade bond.

Landesbank (LB) A regional bank in Germany.

Leverage The degree to which an investor or business uses or depends on borrowed money.

Liar loan A loan based on incorrect information and accepted by lenders in supplying sub-prime mortgages.

Libor (London Inter-Bank Offer Rate) The interest rate at which banks lend to each other.

Liquidity The ability to convert an asset into cash through buying or selling.

Long Term Capital Management (LTCM) A US hedge fund.

'Low doc' or 'no doc' loan A sub-prime mortgage involving little or no documentation for proof of income, etc.

Mark to market The accounting practice of valuing assets at the current market price on a regular basis. The dire market in securitised loans meant ever escalating losses for banks holding toxic debt.

Markets in Financial Instruments Directive (MiFID) An EU law that came into force on 1 November 2007. It aims to increase participation in the investment industry through increased transparency and competition.

Monetary Policy Committee (MPC) *See* Bank of England.

Moral hazard The term used to reflect financial authorities' concern that banks might be reckless in their dealings if they were sure central banks would step in to aid or rescue them.

Nasdaq The National Association of Securities Dealers Automated Quotations system, the world's first electronic stock market, began trading in 1971, specialising in technology and electronics.

New York Stock Exchange (NYSE) Founded in 1792 in Wall Street. Its merger in June 2006 with Euronext (the pan-European stock exchange) made the NYSE the most influential and largest stock exchange in the world.

'No doc' loan *See* 'low doc' loan.

Non-domicile tax status British citizens with foreign interests abroad can register for 'non-domicile' status, meaning that they do not pay tax in Britain on income earned abroad.

Office of the Comptroller of the Currency (OCC) A federal regulator that regulates national banks in the USA.

Office of Thrift Supervision (OTS) A US regulator, based in the Treasury, responsible for the savings and loans industry.

Organisation for Economic Cooperation and Development (OECD) An organisation to encourage world financial stability and to

world trade. It monitors the leading industrial economies
quality and quantity of aid to developing countries.

illa loan A prime mortgage offering low yields to lenders.

ce shares Fixed interest rate stock which has preferred status in the case of insolvency. This is a favoured way for governments to inject new capital into failing banks. The shares carry no voting rights.

Prime mortgage A standard mortgage offered to top-end market borrowers; this style of mortgage originated in the USA.

Recapitalisation The process under which outside investers or government plough new money, in the shape of preference or ordinary shares, into individual banks to strengthen regulatory capital ratios.

Repo (repurchase agreement) A short-term collateralised loan in which a security, in the form of assets, is exchanged for cash on the understanding that the transaction will be reversed for an agreed price on an agreed date.

Residential mortgage-backed securities (RMBS) Also known as asset-backed securities. A type of debt security based on pools of assets.

Rights Issue An issue of new shares to existing shareholders, usually at a substantial discount to the quoted market price. There is no obligation to take up the 'rights', which can be sold.

'Rust Belt' Those areas of the US with a weak manufacturing economy that have become rundown and suffer from high unemployment.

Securities and Exchange Commission (SEC) The government agency that regulates securities markets in the USA.

Securitisation The creation of asset-backed securities supported by a stream of cash flow.

Special liquidity scheme (SLS) facility which allows banks and other lenders to offer mortgage securities to the Bank of England as collateral for UK Treasury Bills with a one to three year duration.

Special purpose vehicle (SPV) A short-term fund in which investors place assets to be used as securities.

Standard & Poor's (S&P) A credit ratings agency.

Structured investment vehicle (SIV) A debt fund created out of sub-prime mortgages and sold in the bond market.

Sub-prime mortgage A mortgage offered to a borrower at the risky, bottom end of the market and often at a high interest rate.

'Teaser' rate A mortgage on a low-interest term for two years, after which the rate is reset at a much higher figure.

Treasury Select Committee The all-party committee of MPs that scrutinises Treasury policy, spending and administration.

Tripartite system (T3) The three-pronged financial regulatory structure – the Bank of England, the Financial Services Authority (FSA) and the Treasury – launched in Britain by the then Chancellor of the Exchequer, Gordon Brown, in 1997.

Wall Street crash On 24 October 1929 panic selling on the New York Stock Exchange was caused by the realisation that stocks were overvalued. By November the Dow Jones Average had fallen from 400 to 145 points. This led to the Great Depression.

Wholesale money markets The money markets where banks and large corporations lend to each other.

Zombie funds Insurance and investment funds that are closed to new business.

Zombie loans Loans which remain on a bank's books and are counted as assets when there is no possibility of them being repaid.

Select Bibliography

Atkinson, Dan and Elliott, Larry, *Fantasy Island* (London: Constable 2007)

Augar, Philip, *The Greed Merchants, How the Investment Banks Played the Free Market Game* (London: Allen Lane 2005)

Bonner, Bill and Wiggin, Addison, *Empire of Debt, The Rise of an Epic Financial Crisis* (Hoboken New Jersey: John Wiley & Sons 2006)

Bower, Tom, *Branson* (London: Fourth Estate 2000)

Chancellor, Edward, *Devil Take the Hindmost: A History of Financial Speculation* (London: Macmillan 1999)

Gapper, John and Denton, Nicholas, *All That Glitters, The Fall of Barings* (London: Hamish Hamilton 1996)

Galbraith, John Kenneth, *The Great Crash 1929* (Boston: Houghton Mifflin 1988)

Galbraith, John Kenneth, *A Short History of Financial Euphoria* (New York: Penguin Books 1990)

Gordon, Charles, *The Cedar Story, The Night the City was Saved* (London: Sinclair-Stevenson 1993)

Greenspan, Alan, *The Age of Turbulence, Adventures in a New World* (London: Allen Lane 2007)

House of Commons Treasury Committee, *The Run on the Rock, Volume 1* (London: The Stationery Office 2008)

IMF, *Global Financial Stability Report: Containing Systemic Risks and Restoring Financial Soundness* (Washington DC: International Monetary Fund 2008)

Kindleberger, Charles B., *Manias, Panics and Crashes, A History of Financial Crises* (New York: Basic Books 1978)

Langley, Monica, *Tearing Down the Walls* (New York: Simon & Schuster 2003)

Lawson, Nigel, *The View from No. 11, Memoirs of a Tory Radical* (London: Bantam Press 1992)

Mayer, Martin, *Nightmare on Wall Street* (New York: Simon & Schuster 1993)

Minsky, Hyman P., *Stabilizing an Unstable Economy* (New York: McGraw Hill 2008)

Peston, Robert, *Brown's Britain* (London: Short Books 2005)

Peston, Robert, *Who Runs Britain* (London: Hodder 2008)

Pettifor, Ann, *The Coming First World Debt Crisis* (London: Palgrave Macmillan 2006)

Rawnsley, Andrew, *Servants of the People, The Inside Story of New Labour* (London: Hamish Hamilton 2000)

Reid, Margaret, *The Secondary Banking Crisis 1973–5* (London: Hindsight Books 2003)

Rubin, Robert E., and Jacob Weisberg, *In an Uncertain World* (New York: Thomson Texere 2003)

Slater, Jim, *Return to Go, My Autobiography* (London: Weidenfeld & Nicolson 1977)

University of Iowa Center for International Finance and Development, *Credit Crisis Timeline 2003–2008* (www.uiowa.edu/ifdebook/timeline/timeline1.shtml)

Wolfe, Tom, *The Bonfire of the Vanities* (New York: Farrar, Strauss, Giroux 1987)

Woodward, Bob, *Maestro: Greenspan's Fed and the American Boom* (New York: Simon & Schuster 2000)

Index